"This empowering volume shows how to bring powerful, evidence-based methods to gender and sexual minorities (GSM): do it through the application of GSM-affirmative, scientific principles linked to evidence-based procedures. Acceptance, mindfulness, compassion, and values-based action open the door to a new and more progressive conversation with the entire field about how to best meet the wide-ranging needs of GSM populations. Comprehensive, powerful, and clearly stated, this wonderful book helps show us all a new way forward."

—**Steven C. Hayes, PhD**, Foundation Professor at the University of Nevada, and codeveloper of acceptance and commitment therapy (ACT)

"*Mindfulness and Acceptance for Gender and Sexual Minorities* is an important addition to the literature on mental health of GSM. Since the 2000's, we have seen growth in sophisticated epidemiological research leading to better understanding of patterns and causes of mental health of GSM. But guidance on treatment has lagged. We have learned a lot about minority stress but less about how to help people who experience it. This clinician's guide comes to fill this gap in our knowledge, updating the literature on treatment of GSM. The writers, experienced therapists and researchers, apply research on mindfulness- and acceptance-based therapies to treating minority stressors related to stigma and prejudice experienced by GSM. The chapters in this book bring insight to broad areas of concerns in the lived experience of GSM, from coming out, to raising families, to creating salubrious environments."

—**Ilan H. Meyer, PhD**, Williams Distinguished Senior Scholar of Public Policy at The Williams Institute UCLA School of Law, and coeditor of *The Health of Sexual Minorities*

"Skinta, Curtin, and the chapter authors respond to the need in the field to articulate ways in which mindfulness-based approaches can address many specific challenges faced by gender and sexual minority (GSM) individuals. It is increasingly important to ensure that GSM (and other minority) populations are able to access mental health treatments that are both evidenced-based and follow culturally competent, affirmative care. This book is a unique intellectually stimulating resource for clinicians to have in our tool box, both those who are familiar with mindfulness-based approaches and desire information about how to work with GSM, as well as those who work with this population and require information about mindfulness-based approaches to care."

—**Steven Safren**, clinical psychologist and professor of psychology at the University of Miami

"I finished this book feeling both humbled and at the same time empowered in my work with GSM clients. It provides a very approachable overview of the theoretical foundations central to contextual behavioral science, while at the same time being extremely practical and directly applicable for clinicians, offering numerous clinical examples and suggested exercises. This book is an essential read for any clinician working with issues of sexuality, gender and gender identity, stigma, and shame from a functional contextual perspective."

—**Jenna LeJeune, PhD**, licensed clinical psychologist, and cofounder and director of clinical services at Portland Psychotherapy Clinic, Research, and Training Center in Portland, OR

"This volume includes the latest thinking and therapeutic interventions in our field to help guide clinicians in their work with gender and sexual minorities. Each of the chapters includes the nuts and bolts involved in helping GSM clients. No stone is left unturned in the array of chapters that include such topics as coming out, same-sex parenting, shame, and being a minority in GSM communities. The book is clearly aimed at detailing therapeutic interventions for clinicians, including compassion-, acceptance-, and mindfulness-based treatments as both standalone as well as integrated with other approaches such as acceptance and commitment therapy (ACT), dialectical behavior therapy (DBT), and functional analytic psychotherapy (FAP). This volume includes specific suggestions as well as case examples that clinicians can apply in their work. It even includes a chapter to address the issues confronting straight therapists working with GSM clients. Their goals are not only to help clinicians be effective with GSM clients, but also address implications for society. I highly recommend this extremely interesting, timely, and well-written and edited book."

—**Robert J. Kohlenberg, PhD, ABPP,** professor in the department of psychology at the Center for the Science of Social Connection at the University of Washington

"Matthew Skinta and Aisling Curtin have edited the preeminent book on GSM-affirmative treatment. Writing from their core personal and professional experiences, the chapter contributors inspire readers to become not only more insightful and effective therapists, but to strive for cultural humility and societal equality. This deeply thoughtful and heart-stirring treasure trove will guide clinicians for generations to come."

—**Mavis Tsai, PhD,** coauthor of *A Guide to Functional Analytic Psychotherapy*, and research scientist and clinical faculty at the University of Washington

"*Mindfulness and Acceptance for Gender and Sexual Minorities* is an important contribution to the next wave of therapies for GSM. As we move beyond a focus on affirmative and non-pathologizing therapies, it is crucial that we begin to adapt evidence-based therapies to meet the needs of the diverse populations that we treat. Mindfulness and acceptance are approaches are especially suited for GSM clients struggling not only to accept themselves, but also to live effectively in a changing, and at times, hostile culture. This book is essential for any clinician treating GSM clients."

—**Jayme L. Peta, PhD**, coauthor of *The Gender Quest Workbook*

"There is a kind of violence that occurs when we tell people, in bold headlines and in small, quiet ways: do not express your difference, do not wonder about who you are, certainly not out loud, but really not even to yourself. Just be quiet and fit in. The palette of human sexuality is broad, and that breadth is largely unknown because we have suppressed the knowing of it, even among individuals who have a sense of these differences from the inside out. We have a choice. We can create a kinder, more curious, and more thoughtful context for our clients to come to know themselves and to help us to know them. This is an important book if you want to be part of that kinder context."

—**Kelly G. Wilson, PhD**, professor of psychology at the University of Mississippi

"This is a groundbreaking book on several levels. The expert authors bring the light of cutting-edge behavioral research to people and challenges that are often overlooked by mainstream clinical approaches. Furthermore, the book places compassion front and center in the development of new strategies. This is a must-read book."

—**Dennis Tirch PhD**, coauthor of *The ACT Practitioner's Guide to the Science of Compassion*, and founder of The Center for Compassion Focused Therapy

"The evolved human brain carries multiple possibilities for experiencing and acting in the world. Our capacity for love coexists with our capacity for hatred and cruelty; our capacity for joy lives with our capacity for depression; we are multidimensional beings. Such richness of our potential multiplicities is especially manifest in our sexualities, where many combinations of with whom and how are possible. Tragically, for complex psychocultural reasons we have sought to limit, suppress, and constrain this richness. Shaming and stigma have confined and narrowed choices, and not always in favor of the heterosexual, e.g. Sparta. We are oppressed by the repressed. This excellent book brings together a group of insightful and knowledgeable authors that address the personal and social costs of shame and stigma on sexual variations.... Sensitive, wise, and compassionate, this will be a classic in the field for many years."

—**Paul Gilbert, PhD, FBPsS, OBE**, professor of clinical psychology at the University of Derby, and author of *Human Nature and Suffering* and *The Compassionate Mind*

"This book is an indispensable resource for any evidence-minded clinician who wants to bring acceptance, compassion, and effective change to the lives of all of those they work with. This long-awaited, seminal work provides practical guidance through GSM-affirming, evidence-based treatments with care and precision. The authors and editors of this volume honor the diversity and real-world applicability of these treatment approaches with a depth and scope that is bound to be greatly appreciated by any mental health provider working with GSM clients and communities."

—**Laura Silberstein, PsyD**, director and clinical psychologist at The Center for Compassion Focused Therapy in New York City, NY, and coauthor of *The ACT Practitioner's Guide to the Science of Compassion* and *Buddhist Psychology and Cognitive-Behavioral Therapy*

"*Mindfulness and Acceptance for Gender and Sexual Minorities* is a thought-provoking journey for those who serve the lesbian, gay, bisexual, and transgender (LGBT) community. It is also a self-reflecting glimpse for those who are learning how to understand, develop, and manage the many facets of being a part of the LGBT identity, and the joys and struggles related to the process of owning your sense of self."

—**Robin McGehee**, cofounder of GetEQUAL

"I had the pleasure of attending a few ACT workshops, both daylong and brief, and found ACT's way of pinpointing, relating, and neutralizing the deeply ingrained patterns of negative self-identity as wholly refreshing. It was as if facilitator Aisling Curtin coaxed what we didn't realize we'd always known, regarding how the world can cause us to feel displaced, dysfunctional, and othered. What Curtin and coeditor Matthew Skinta have done here is apply these individuated, gentle, and psychically loosening techniques to identity groups currently in the maelstrom of public scrutiny, as they incrementally gain equal rights across the West."

—**Clara Rose Thornton**, culture journalist and radio and television broadcaster focusing on identity politics; InkBlot Complex

"Skinta and Curtin have achieved a rare feat in this volume: along with their contributors, they have delivered a book that captures the zeitgeist of today's contextual psychology with as much depth and nuance as they bring to their discussion of clinical issues and approaches with LGBT clients. The result is a text that speaks equally to experts in contextual psychology who are eager to increase their cultural competence with LGBT clients, as well as those who are keenly familiar with LGBT populations who are eager to learn and incorporate acceptance and mindfulness approaches within their work. No matter which end of the spectrum the reader comes from, they will walk away with a thorough, practical, and immediately applicable knowledge base in both arenas."

—**Mary P. Loudon, PhD**, licensed clinical psychologist and certified functional analytic psychotherapy (FAP) trainer

THE
MINDFULNESS & ACCEPTANCE
PRACTICA SERIES

As mindfulness and acceptance-based therapies gain momentum in the field of mental health, it is increasingly important for professionals to understand the full range of their applications. To keep up with the growing demand for authoritative resources on these treatments, *The Mindfulness and Acceptance Practica Series* was created. These edited books cover a range of evidence-based treatments, such as acceptance and commitment therapy (ACT), cognitive behavioral therapy (CBT), compassion-focused therapy (CFT), dialectical behavioral therapy (DBT), and mindfulness-based stress reduction (MBSR) therapy. Incorporating new research in the field of psychology, these books are powerful tools for mental health clinicians, researchers, advanced students, and anyone interested in the growth of mindfulness and acceptance strategies.

Visit www.newharbinger.com for
more books in this series.

MINDFULNESS &
ACCEPTANCE *for* GENDER
& SEXUAL MINORITIES

A Clinician's Guide to Fostering Compassion, Connection & Equality Using Contextual Strategies

Edited by

MATTHEW D. SKINTA, PhD, ABPP

AISLING CURTIN, MSc

CONTEXT PRESS

An Imprint of New Harbinger Publications, Inc.

Publisher's Note

Distributed in Canada by Raincoast Books

Copyright © 2016 by Matthew Skinta and Aisling Curtin
        Context Press
        An imprint of New Harbinger Publications, Inc.
        5674 Shattuck Avenue
        Oakland, CA 94609
        www.newharbinger.com

Cover design by Amy Shoup; Acquired by Melissa Valentine;
Edited by Jasmine Star; Indexed by James Minkin

Library of Congress Cataloging-in-Publication Data to come

18   17   16

10   9   8   7   6   5   4   3   2   1   First Printing

For Barthélémy, who constantly reminds me by his presence just how powerful a constant source of love is in mending the pains of the world.

—MDS

For Trish, the love of my life, my rock and secure base.

—AC

Contents

Part II:
Building and Rebuilding Relationships

Part III:
Life in Context: Challenges in the World

Foreword

One of the most urgent tasks facing scholars interested in the mental health of gender and sexual minorities (GSM) is the identification of treatments that can improve the well-being of this population. Given the significant mental health disparities that exist, which depend on sexual orientation and gender identity, one could argue that this task represents an ethical imperative. Evidence-minded mental health clinicians have been fully aware of this imperative for decades now. In fact, over the past few decades it has become almost habitual for authors of clinical research papers and conference presentations on stigma, minority stress, and mental health to conclude by calling for the translation of this knowledge into evidence-based practice. However, for reasons that probably have to do with stigma itself, the needed research and evidence have been slow to arrive. In the United States and elsewhere, few research funds have been devoted to developing treatments that can improve the mental health of GSM individuals.

Evidence-based treatments are typically an outgrowth of randomized controlled trials wherein the treatment under investigation is compared to a control treatment. Unfortunately, very few randomized controlled trials have examined the efficacy of psychotherapies specifically for GSM clients. And even if resources and social attitudes did allow for more such research, the sheer diversity of GSM communities would present a formidable, if not insurmountable, barrier to conducting clinical trials of treatments for each specific subgroup. So clinicians would still lack guidance on how to approach the diverse needs of diverse GSM clients. Further, psychotherapy practitioners have long bemoaned the fact that randomized controlled trials do not adequately address the needs of real-world clinical practice. Given these dilemmas, how can our field ever provide adequate guidance—with a foundation in the real world, yet also evidence based—for clinicians working across the many diverse segments of the GSM community?

The present volume offers a solution. *Mindfulness and Acceptance for Gender and Sexual Minorities* is one of the few books providing guidance on applying GSM-affirmative treatment principles to existing evidence-based mental health practices, finally answering decades of calls for such guidance. This approach solves several problems: the lack of randomized controlled trials looking specifically at GSM individuals; the huge resources that would be required to make such trials applicable to all of the diverse segments of the GSM population; and the perceived or potential lack of relevance of these trials to real-world clinical practice. By highlighting relevant GSM-affirmative principles that can infuse existing evidence-based approaches, this volume illuminates a pathway that offers a wise use of limited treatment development resources yet is also capable of reaching the full diversity of GSM populations, as well as the diversity of presenting problems. And if clinicians commit to collecting and reporting outcome data on their GSM-affirmative adaptations of evidence-based treatments, researchers and practitioners can help confirm the effectiveness of these real-world applications.

The contributors to this volume have done a commendable job of suggesting how GSM-affirmative principles can be applied to mindfulness- and acceptance-based approaches to treatment, with particular attention on fostering self-compassion, promoting awareness and acceptance of emotions, reworking early learning histories, reducing avoidant tendencies, and connecting with a supportive community. Each of these approaches addresses minority stress and how it disrupts the psychosocial underpinnings of mental health, and seeks to help clients establish a healthy footing despite the challenges posed by minority stress. Mindfulness exercises, compassionate visualizations, defusing from thoughts, values clarification and affirmation, and committed action—these are just some of the treatment strategies adapted in GSM-affirming ways in these pages. Several vivid case examples make the application of these principles concrete and very human.

In addition to furthering the evolution of mental health practice, this book offers an even greater promise. By helping clients cope with minority stress through GSM-affirmative application of evidence-based treatments, clinicians can change not just individuals, but ultimately society itself. Whether by promoting assertive self-acceptance or by instilling a mindful stance toward previously unexpressed emotions, clinicians who apply GSM-affirmative principles to their evidence-based practice can help clients become activists. Inasmuch as any social change occurs by virtue of individuals' mindful and accepting self-expression, the approaches outlined in this book promise not only a more sound approach to working with GSM clients, but also a more accepting societal approach to this sizable segment of the global population in need of effective mental health resources.

—John Pachankis
Associate professor of epidemiology,
Yale University

Acknowledgments

It takes a village to raise a book, as the saying almost goes. This process wouldn't have been possible without a great deal of cheerleading, support, and encouragement. I had no idea what I was getting myself into or what challenges editing and contributing to this book would bring. I'd like to thank Steven Hayes, who reached out to me to see if it was time for this book to appear and then subsequently walked me through the steps of bringing my vision to light. I also must thank Beth Wildman at Kent State University; though our paths haven't crossed in many years, she was the first supervisor to encourage me to read up on ACT and FAP, over a decade ago, so I could see what behaviorism made possible. Benji Schoendorff was the first person to tell me that I wrote words that moved him, and I can trace virtually all of my professional writing to an ACT and FAP matrix class he led with Valerie Kiehl. I also can't overstate the impact of my mentors in the fields of HIV and sexuality, including Allen Omoto and David Martin, who modeled what it could be like to live as authentic and out professionals in this field.

The community at the Association for Contextual Behavioral Science has helped me grow in both personal and professional ways, and their influence resounds throughout these pages. At age twenty-three, I would never have guessed that Bob Kohlenberg and Mavis Tsai, whose olive-drab FAP book was my closely held guide, would be such warm and approachable sources of encouragement. I also appreciate Aki Masuda who, after a symposium we both participated in, invited me to write my first chapter on mindfulness and acceptance. Melissa Valentine at New Harbinger Publications has been a wonderful guide through this process, and all of the contributors have earned my heartfelt thanks for their contributions and commitment to this project. A special, dear thanks to my coauthor, Aisling, for joining me on this journey.

—Matthew

I want to say a huge thank-you to all those who believed in me and supported me, first in coming out, and second in editing this book. I also acknowledge those who didn't support me during my process of coming out; these heartfelt personal experiences motivated me to contribute to this volume so I can help others find compassion and community when they experience something similar. No mud, no lotus. A very special thank-you to Trish Leonard, Tracey McDonagh, Jonathan Dowling, Christine Parsons, and Louise McHugh, who all gave invaluable editorial feedback. Thank you Benji Schoendorff and Kevin Polk, for inviting me to contribute to *The ACT Matrix*. My experience in writing that chapter gave me the desire and confidence to write more. Thank you also to Mavis Tsai and Russ Harris, my mentors, who have been huge cheerleaders.

I owe a great deal of gratitude to Jasmine Star, our copy editor. Jasmine, you have such a gentle and thorough editing style, which you communicate so sensitively. Thanks to Nicola Skidmore, senior editor at New Harbinger, for your rapid responses to questions, and to Vicraj Gill, associate editor, for helping us provide additional online resources to supplement our book. The biggest thank-you goes to my coauthor, Matthew, whose constant support and collaboration have meant the world to me. I feel blessed to have you as my collaborator and my friend. I hope we keep inspiring one another to do more in this area.

—Aisling

Introduction

Matthew D. Skinta, *Palo Alto University*; and
Aisling Curtin, *ACT Now Ireland*

The great force of history comes from the fact that we carry it within us, are unconsciously controlled by it in many ways, and history is literally *present* in all that we do.

—James Baldwin

As we write this, the first editor, located in the United States, and the second, living in Ireland, are living in countries that legally recognize marriage equality. The first has already married his husband, a French citizen, in France, while the second is beginning to plan her wedding in Ireland. This is occurring while in other regions of the globe, gender and sexual minorities (GSM) face harsh censure for living an open, authentic life. One of the greatest migrations of refugees in European history, resulting from armed conflicts in Syria and Iraq, includes a large population of GSM individuals fleeing certain death at the hands of extremists who actively hunt for and murder people who were out in their previously peaceful home countries (Porzucki, 2015; Williams & Maher, 2009). Even in the United States, trans women of color are being murdered at alarming rates (Michaels, 2015).

We are living in an era of rapid change, including in regard to gender and sexual minorities. Even in nations and cultures now largely characterized by tolerance and acceptance, the freedom to live openly without fear of job loss, familial rejection, or loss of housing or medical care has shifted within only the past few decades. Mental health disciplines have struggled to keep up with these changes, and it has fallen to legislative bodies and courts around the world to require and enforce ethical, nonstigmatizing treatment (see Duffy, 2015; Khazan, 2015). It is our hope that this volume will take the discussion a step further.

Minority Stress and Emotion Dysregulation

In 2011, the US Institute of Medicine released the report *The Health of Lesbian, Gay, Bisexual, and Transgender People*, which highlighted the unique role of minority stress in health disparities affecting GSM populations. Minority stress, which will be discussed throughout this volume, is a model of the psychological stressors and resiliencies experienced by people who occupy a marginalized and denigrated social category—in this case, GSM individuals who live in a predominantly heterosexual, cisgender world (Meyer, 1995, 2015). ("Cisgender" is a term used to denote a gender identity that conforms to an individual's sex assigned at birth.) Emotion dysregulation has been identified as a likely link between minority stress and psychological distress (Hatzenbuehler, 2009; Hatzenbuehler, McLaughlin, & Nolen-Hoeksema, 2008; Hatzenbuehler, Nolen-Hoeksema, & Dovidio, 2009), so psychologists researching therapies for GSM clients have increasingly turned to empirically supported practices that bolster emotion regulation skills (e.g., Pachankis, Hatzenbuehler, Rendina, Safren, & Parsons, 2015). Our book has been strongly shaped by this literature because we believe that contextual behavioral strategies have a powerful effect on emotion regulation skills and therefore may be particularly well suited for enhancing the lives of GSM clients and communities.

Cultural Humility

As you read this book and engage with GSM clients, we invite you to adopt a stance of cultural humility, as is necessary in any initial engagement with a different cultural group experience. Cultural humility has been conceptualized as being "respectful and considerate of the other; being genuinely interested in, open to exploring, and wanting to understand the other's perspective; not making foreordained assumptions; not acting superior; and not assuming that much is already culturally known about the other" (Hook & Watkins, 2015, p. 661). We'd like to invite you to approach this work with these thoughts in mind, even if you consider yourself part of a GSM community.

Also, while we made every effort to find, within the community of contextual behavioral scientists and therapists, a diverse group of contributors inclusive of different gender and sexual identities and ethnic and cultural backgrounds, there is the risk that we might seem to imply that the chapters included here are comprehensively representative of the variety of global GSM identities. This is not the case. In *decolonizing trans/gender 101*, b. binaohan describes promotional material for the 2013 Trans March in San Francisco that listed dozens of indigenous and globally diverse gender identities that were included under the umbrella of Trans March yet were not clearly visible in attendance. As binaohan wrote, "It had never really occurred to me, until I saw this, that the trans community was under the impression that it was including people like me. Or that I was, as far as they were concerned, part of their community" (2014, p. 4).

In this spirit, we would like to humbly note that this single volume cannot speak for every GSM client or community you may know of or encounter, and it may not reflect the GSM identity of some who will read these pages. As a brief, impartial list, this volume does not cover contemporary literature on bullying; aging and geriatric care; the presence of bias and lack of mentorship within mental health training programs; the decline of lesbian- or gay-identified neighborhoods and how this is related to the use of the Internet or smartphone apps to meet and date; or the psychological meaning of pre-exposure prophylaxis (PrEP), which has radically altered how gay and bisexual men approach sex and how those communities arrange themselves in relation to HIV status. We hope that this book will be considered a start, not a definitive statement of what contextual behavioral therapies with GSM clients might look like, and that it will encourage those working within GSM communities to publish their findings and add them to the perspectives featured here.

Overview

Each of these chapters was written or cowritten by a therapist with extensive experience working with GSM clients, and in most cases the therapists are, themselves, GSM individuals. Most of the chapters are informed by current practices or recent pilot studies.

Part 1, "Mindfulness and Acceptance for Coming Out and Shame," focuses on the roles that acceptance and commitment therapy (ACT), relational frame theory (RFT), functional analytic psychotherapy (FAP), dialectic behavioral therapy (DBT), and compassion-focused therapy (CFT) play in approaching the varied challenges of living with a hidden sense of self that might be experienced as shameful or damaged. Chapter 1, by Aisling Curtin, an expert ACT and FAP clinician, Lisa Diamond, a leading researcher on human sexuality, and Louise McHugh, a leading researcher on RFT and the formation of the self, focuses on sexual minorities, diving deeply and in an unprecedented way into how our sexual selves are constructed. In chapter 2, which specifically addresses gender minorities, Trish Leonard and Lauren Grousd outline a powerful approach to exploring gender identity using the ACT matrix. In chapter 3, Aisling Curtin, Danielle (Danny) Ryu, and Lisa Diamond describe the challenges and hurdles of coming out. Chapter 4 and 5 both focus on working with shame because it's such a challenging and pervasive experience among GSM clients. Chapter 4, by Nicola Petrocchi, Marcela Matos, Sérgio Carvalho, and Roberto Baiocco, covers recent CFT approaches, and chapter 5, by Matthew Skinta and Paul D'Alton, takes an integrated RFT- and ACT-based approach that includes a GSM hexaflex. Finally, in chapter 6, Joseph Walloch and Mary Hill discuss using ACT and DBT to help GSM clients struggling with body dysmorphia or eating disorders.

Part 2, "Building and Rebuilding Relationships," focuses on the interpersonal aspects of moving through life as a GSM person. In chapter 7, Matthew Skinta, Kimberly Balsam, and Sonia Singh consider interpersonal relationships in the context of using FAP to enhance the therapeutic relationship. Chapter 8, by Joanne Steinwachs and Thomas Szabo, extends that discussion, addressing the risk of therapists committing microaggressions in couples therapy and utilizing the FAP approach to tracking the impact of therapist behaviors on clients. Chapter 9, by Amy Murrell, Fredrik Livheim, Danielle Moyer, Melissa Connally, and Kinsie Dunham, considers what ACT looks like with same-sex parents and includes personal reflections by Fredrik Livheim on how ACT principles have shaped his own experience as a father. Part 2 ends with chapter 10, in which Finn Reygan, Aisling Curtin, and Geraldine Moane explore how GSM individuals relate to and describe their spiritual journey, which can occupy a space that exists somewhere between interpersonal relationships and the experience of GSM individuals in a transphobic and heterocentric society.

Finally, part 3, "Life in Context: Challenges in the World," expands the focus one more degree outward, considering the lives of GSM individuals in relation to society and the experiences of GSM communities. Chapter 11, by Brian Feinstein and Brian Marx, describes the challenges involved in acquiring and building resilience and offers practical suggestions on how to overcome those challenges. In chapter 12, Virginia O'Hayer, David Bennett, and Jeffrey Jacobson explore the ways that HIV continues to shape the experiences of GSM clients, despite medical advances, and discuss how ACT can help mitigate the impact of stigma. In chapter 13, by Khashayar Farhadi-Langroudi, Kayla Sargent, and Akihiko Masuda, the topic turns to the intersection of being a GSM individual and being a person of color, with an emphasis on how contextual behavioral approaches can speak to the needs of GSM refugees and asylum seekers. Chapter 14, by Frank Bond and Jo Lloyd, considers the specific challenges of GSM employees in the workplace and discusses organizational design features that can mitigate these challenges, largely by enhancing and building upon ACT processes. Finally, in chapter 15, Matthew Skinta and Kip Williams relate a recent theory on how RFT can promote social change by aiding the construction of a future-oriented vision, and then discuss how RFT and ACT might be used to support movement builders and activists.

In addition, if you're interested in further exploration of contextual behavioral strategies and integrating them into your work with GSM clients, we have prepared a variety of supplemental materials for your use. You can download these materials from the publisher's website for this book: http://www.newharbinger.com/34282. (See the back of the book for information on how to access the downloadable content.)

One final note: Throughout the book, chapter authors sometimes include client examples. In all such cases, names and other identifying characteristics have been altered to protect confidentiality.

Why Mindfulness and Acceptance for Gender and Sexual Minorities

Something interesting is happening in the field of GSM psychology. After decades of emphasis on the importance of affirmative approaches, there is a growing consensus that the field can do more than simply encourage the adoption of a nonpathologizing stance. In fact, the ethical standards of mental health organizations around the world increasingly promote this as a minimum standard for ethically competent care. What is needed now is expanded discussion and exploration of our current methods, modalities, and techniques in order to develop approaches that speak directly to the unique experiences of GSM individuals, both in terms of minority stress, and in terms of the ways that GSM cultural communities move to different rhythms, with historical milestones that may not be shared by cisgender, heterosexual communities. It is our hope that this book will be a valuable contribution to this new discussion.

References

Binaohan, B. (2014). *Decolonizing trans/gender 101*. Toronto: Biyuti Publishing.

Duffy, N. (2015, November 3). Minister calls gay cure therapy "torture"—as government rules out statutory ban. *PinkNews*. Retrieved December 14, 2015, from http://www.pinknews.co.uk/2015/11/03/government-has-no-plans-to-out law-gay-cure-therapy.

Hatzenbuehler, M. L. (2009). How does sexual minority stigma "get under the skin"? A psychological mediation framework. *Psychological Bulletin, 135*, 707–730.

Hatzenbuehler, M. L., McLaughlin, K. A., & Nolen-Hoeksema, S. (2008). Emotion regulation and internalizing symptoms in a longitudinal study of sexual minority and heterosexual adolescents. *Journal of Child Psychology and Psychiatry, 49*, 1270–1278.

Hatzenbuehler, M. L., Nolen-Hoeksema, S., & Dovidio, J. (2009). How does stigma "get under the skin"? The mediating role of emotion regulation. *Psychological Science, 20*, 1282–1289.

Hook, J. N., & Watkins, C. E. (2015). Cultural humility: The cornerstone of positive contact with culturally different individuals and groups? *American Psychologist, 70*, 661–662.

Institute of Medicine. (2011). *The health of lesbian, gay, bisexual, and transgender people: Building a foundation for better understanding.* Washington, DC: National Academies Press.

Khazan, O. (2015, June 26). The end of gay conversion therapy. *The Atlantic.* Retrieved December 14, 2015, from http://www.theatlantic.com/health /archive/2015/06/the-end-of-gay-conversion-therapy/396953.

Meyer, I. H. (1995). Minority stress and mental health in gay men. *Journal of Health and Social Behavior, 36,* 38–56.

Meyer, I. H. (2015). Resilience in the study of minority stress and health of sexual and gender minorities. *Psychology of Sexual Orientation and Gender Diversity, 2,* 209–213.

Michaels, S. (2015, November 20). More transgender people have been killed in 2015 than any other year on Record. *Mother Jones.* Retrieved December 14, 2015, from http://www.motherjones.com/mojo/2015/11/more-transgender -people-have-been-murdered-2015-any-other-year-record.

Pachankis, J. E., Hatzenbuehler, M. L., Rendina, H. J., Safren, S. A., & Parsons, J. T. (2015). LGB-affirmative cognitive-behavioral therapy for young adult gay and bisexual men: A randomized controlled trial of a transdiagnostic minority stress approach. *Journal of Consulting and Clinical Psychology, 83,* 875–889.

Porzucki, N. (2015, October 26). Some Syrians fleeing not just civil war, but LGBT persecution. *PRI.* Retrieved December 14, 2015, from http://www.pri.org /stories/2015–10–26/some-syrian-refugees-are-fleeing-more-just-civil-war.

Williams, T., & Maher, T. (2009, April 7). Iraq's newly open gays face scorn and murder. *New York Times.* Retrieved December 14, 2015, from http://www .nytimes.com/2009/04/08/world/middleeast/08gay.html.

PART I

Mindfulness and Acceptance for Coming Out and Shame

CHAPTER 1

Self and Perspective Taking for Sexual Minorities in a Heteronormative World

Aisling Curtin, *ACT Now Ireland*;
Lisa Diamond, *University of Utah*; and
Louise McHugh, *University College Dublin*

P erhaps the most important change over the past several decades in our understanding of sexual minority populations concerns their size and composition. A decade ago, a chapter such as this one probably would have referred to lesbians and gays instead of sexual minorities (SM), and it would have focused on the experiences of individuals who were exclusively attracted to the same sex and who openly claimed a lesbian or gay identity. In the past, such individuals were presumed to be the most common type of sexual minority, reflecting the widely held view that sexual orientation has only two forms: exclusive homosexuality and exclusive heterosexuality. Because of this incorrect belief, researchers studying sexual identity and orientation have historically excluded individuals claiming nonexclusive patterns of attraction, as well as those who refused to claim a gay, lesbian, or bisexual identity. This exclusion was sometimes for the sake of methodological clarity and sometimes because such individuals were suspected to be struggling with confusion, denial, or internalized homophobia (Burr, 1996; Rust, 2000; Whisman, 1993, 1996).

We now know that these assumptions were woefully inaccurate. A large number of studies using random representative samples, conducted in a range of Western countries, have demonstrated that the majority of individuals with same-sex attractions don't openly claim a lesbian or gay identity, and that there are more individuals who possess attractions to both sexes than who possess exclusive same-sex attractions (reviewed in Diamond, 2013). Additionally, we now know that, contrary to conventional wisdom, discrepancies between an individual's attractions, behavior, love relationships, and identity (e.g., desires that are never acted upon, or same-sex liaisons in the absence of lesbian, gay, or bisexual identification) are relatively common, not only during adolescence but also across the life span (Rosario & Schrimshaw, 2014). Finally, studies reliably demonstrate that some individuals undergo marked shifts over time in their patterns of attraction, behavior, and identification (reviewed in Diamond & Rosky, in press).

Yet over the years, empirical research hasn't adequately represented this diversity and has overly relied on samples comprised solely of openly identified lesbians and gays. Bisexuals in particular have faced chronic exclusion. For example, a recent search of the peer-reviewed social science literature found that from the mid-1970s to the mid-1980s, only 1 percent of journal articles that focused on sexual orientation or sexual minority individuals included the word "bisexual" in the title, and only 9 percent contained "bisexual" in the abstract. Between 1994 and 2005, these percentages increased to 14 percent and 35 percent, and during the past decade they increased to 20 percent and 55 percent. Still, this population continues to be underrepresented.

The implications of this systematic omission would not be so dire if individuals with nonexclusive patterns of sexual attraction constituted only a small subgroup of SM people. However, this is not the case, as a number of representative studies have demonstrated (Bailey, Dunne, & Martin, 2000; Garofalo, Wolf, Wissow, Woods, & Goodman, 1999; Kirk, Bailey, Dunne, & Martin, 2000; Laumann, Gagnon, Michael, & Michaels, 1994; Mosher, Chandra, & Jones, 2005; Remafedi, Resnick, Blum, & Harris, 1992; Savin-Williams & Ream, 2006). Not only do bisexuals constitute a rather large group, they are in fact the largest subset of individuals with same-sex attractions and experiences. As researchers have gradually begun to devote more attention to their experiences, a troubling finding has emerged: individuals with bisexual patterns of attraction and behavior appear to have higher mental and physical health risks than those with exclusively same-sex or other-sex attractions and behavior (Eisenberg & Wechsler, 2003; Galliher, Rostosky, & Hughes, 2004; Jorm, Korten, Rodgers, Jacomb, & Christensen, 2002; Moon, Fornili, & O'Briant, 2007; Russell, Seif, & Truong, 2001; Udry & Chantala, 2002). The mechanisms underlying these greater risks aren't clear, although one distinct possibility is that bisexually attracted individuals simply face more extreme and prolonged versions of the stressors that are common to all SM people. This may be due to bisexuals feeling stigmatized by both homosexuals and heterosexuals. (Please visit http://www.newhar binger.com/34282 for a downloadable exercise, "The Sexuality Spectrum Experiential Self-Reflection," which is suitable for both clinicians and clients.)

Most SM individuals possess an unambiguous sense of self as cis male or cis female, yet some begin to question their gender identity in the process of questioning their sexuality. "Transgender" is the descriptor typically used to denote individuals whose gender-related identification or external gender presentation conflicts in some way with their sex designated at birth, and who therefore violate conventional standards of unequivocal male or female identity and behavior. Recognition that gender is not binary (only male and female) has led to an increase in pansexual identification within the bisexual community. (See chapter 2 for more on gender identity.)

Minority Stress

"Minority stress" refers to the unique strain experienced as a result of occupying a marginalized and denigrated social category (Meyer, 2003). As comprehensively reviewed by Meyer, the chronic negative evaluations that SM people face, both with respect to widespread cultural norms and within their day-to-day interpersonal interactions, can erode their positive sense of self and cumulatively tax their mental well-being. Minority stress helps explain why population-based studies have reliably found that SM individuals, in both adolescence and adulthood, have higher rates of anxiety, depression, suicidality, self-injurious behavior, and substance use than do heterosexuals (Austin et al., 2004; Balsam, Beauchaine, Mickey, & Rothblum, 2005; Case et al., 2004; Cochran, Sullivan, & Mays, 2003; Jorm et al., 2002; Paul et al., 2002; Ziyadeh et al., 2007), and that individuals with higher levels of stigma and victimization tend to show poorer mental health outcomes (Balsam et al., 2005; Bontempo & D'Augelli, 2002; D'Augelli, Grossman, & Starks, 2005; Russell & Joyner, 2001).

Minority stress takes multiple forms. The most obvious include violence, harassment, and victimization, but minority stress also includes discrimination (both subtle and overt), social rejection, ostracism, lack of access to institutional support for identity and relationships, and persistent microaggressions (subtle experiences of neglect and substandard treatment across a variety of settings). Not only do these experiences take a cumulative toll on mental health, but they also create ongoing expectations of future rejection and denigration, leading to chronic worry, agitation, and hypervigilance.

Perhaps the most detrimental manifestation of minority stress is internalized homophobia, the phenomenon by which SM individuals gradually come to believe the demeaning and denigrating views that society holds about SM people and develop a negative sense of their own worthiness. This can create an unresolvable conflict between their same-sex sexuality and their desire for social validation and affirmation (Herek, 2004). Meyer and Dean (1998) describe internalized homophobia as the most insidious form of minority stress because it is nearly impossible to escape. Once external social judgments and rejection become internalized, they become constant companions for the SM individual, creating long-standing feelings of illegitimacy and shame that damage psychological well-being and impair day-to-day social functioning. Accordingly, internalized homophobia has been linked to mental health phenomena ranging from depression to eating disorders to suicidality (Meyer, 2003; Meyer & Dean, 1998; Remafedi, French, Story, Resnick, & Blum, 1998). Internalized homophobia also affects interpersonal functioning in both romantic relationships (Meyer & Dean, 1998) and nonromantic relationships (Otis, Rostosky, Riggle, & Hamrin, 2006). (See chapter 11 for further information on minority stress.)

Clinicians as Agents of Change

Importantly, all sexual minorities show a higher rate of mental health problems than heterosexuals, with some representative studies showing that they have twice the risk (Cochran & Mays, 2009). There are two types of skills that can increase practitioners' potency as agents of change when working with SM clients (Kohlenberg & Tsai, 1991; Plummer, 2010):

- **Intellectual knowledge:** understanding the rules and guidelines underpinning a science of behavior, which can illuminate why SM clients suffer more than their heterosexual counterparts

- **Experiential contact:** helping clients increase contact with all aspects of their experience and decrease avoidance of certain aspects of their experiences

Thus far in this chapter, we've aimed to increase your intellectual knowledge regarding who SM people are and how being in this population can affect their mental health. We included a link to the downloadable sexuality spectrum exercise to fulfill the aim of experiential contact for you, the clinician, and the SM clients you serve. We will now turn our attention to the mechanisms underlying how people construct their sense of self and perceptions of the world in general, with specific reference to SM individuals. We include a few experiential exercises (one in the text and two available for download) to fulfill both of the criteria just listed and to serve the aim of this chapter: to best equip you, the clinician, to help SM clients navigate the challenges that inevitably arise when they or the world view them as "less than."

Contextual Behavioral Science and the Self

Contextual behavioral science (CBS) is based on the premise of functional contextualism (Hayes, Strosahl, & Wilson, 1999). This is essentially a somewhat complicated way of saying that we're interested in two things:

- **Function:** What's the point of a particular action? What does it give the person or take in the long term?

- **Context:** In what settings is the person more or less likely to act in a particular way?

There is a consensus that a healthy sense of self is a prerequisite for sound mental functioning (McHugh & Stewart, 2012). As humans, we have a unique and complex way of processing and relating information (Hayes, Barnes-Holmes, & Roche, 2001). This allows us to create advanced technologies and understand how to use them. However, it also allows us to constantly compare ourselves to other people and inevitably view others as being "more than" us, particularly in areas where we fear rejection from others or society at large. The capacity to understand and evaluate ourselves can cause us to trap ourselves in descriptions that make us feel lacking in comparison to others ("Straight is better than gay"), that can hamper effective communication and relationships with others ("I must not reveal myself"), and that can result in arbitrary or random barriers to moving toward a meaningful life ("I'm not good enough").

Understanding the functional units involved in a healthy self-concept can provide vital insight into how to effectively develop interventions for SM clients. CBS provides a bottom-up account of the self, and in this section we will outline the CBS account of the self and provide some practical tips on how to put this knowledge to work in interventions.

According to CBS, the experience of self is a by-product of language. The theory of language and cognition that underpins CBS is referred to as relational frame theory (RFT; for a book-length account see Hayes et al., 2001). RFT is a theory of learning that underpins acceptance and commitment therapy (ACT; Hayes et al., 1999). It suggests that the key to language is the ability to put things into relations with each other based not on their physical or formal properties, but on cues as to which relation to apply (technically referred to as relational framing). Consider the relationship between the word "cup" and an actual cup. We treat these two things as being the same as each other, despite the fact that they are in no way physically the same. For instance, if someone asks you to give her the cup, you will hand her the actual cup. In this way, we put things into abstract relations of sameness with each other. The fact that we can relate stimuli abstractly, establishing symbolic relationships between them, is what allows us to make sounds that other people understand, rather than simply pointing and grunting at things. Furthermore, the ability to relate stimuli based on cues allows us to use symbols to refer to things that are not physically present.

We can apply many different types of relational frames, beyond that of sameness. For example, we can relate things as opposite ("Gay is the opposite of straight; being straight is good and I am gay, therefore I am bad"), different ("Boys are different from girls"), comparatively ("Jeff is more attractive than me"), causally ("If people know I'm bi, I'll be rejected"), temporally ("Rejection is already hard now; it will be worse after I come out to my parents"), and in terms of perspective ("It's harder to be gay here, in Russia, than it would be there, in Spain"). From a functional contextual vantage point, relating in abstract ways is foundational to self-development, especially during childhood and adolescence.

In addition to providing insight into how we learn about ourselves, this basic understanding of how abstract relations function for humans provides a science of behavior that allows us to change what people are learning. These patterns of relating are even more interesting in light of laboratory research (e.g., Dymond & Barnes, 1996) demonstrating that the effect something has (its function) can transform when different relational frames are applied to it. Imagine that a teenager is being bullied for being gay. He may start to relate being gay with fear. Physical functions of fear (racing heart, sweaty palms) will then occur when he hears the word "gay." If he is told that another word for a gay is "homosexual," then "gay" and "homosexual" will then be in a relation of sameness for this teenager. If someone subsequently asks, "Are you homosexual?" he will experience some of the fear he had when he was bullied for being gay. Specifically, via the relation of sameness, the functions of "gay" will transform the person's experience of the word "homosexual" or any other word in this relational network.

RFT and the Self

Language involves responding to abstract relations regarding the self and is the product of learning to put one's own behavior in relation to that of others. That statement is a bit dense, so let's unpack it. Developing a sense of self involves learning to verbally discriminate one's own behavior from others' behavior (McHugh & Stewart, 2012). This basic pattern of learning begins in early childhood. For example, if you ask a very young child what she got for Christmas, she may describe what her sister got if she doesn't yet have an understanding of the word "you" versus the word "I." She may not understand that a question about "you," demands a response about "I." As that child gets older and learns the relational frames of "you" and "I," she will be able to answer that question accurately. As a child begins to relate more and more of her own behavior ("I feel attracted to girls") and compare it with that of others ("Most other girls are attracted to boys"), she begins to develop a concept of self ("There's something wrong with me"). As children grow into adults, these repertoires of relating their own behavior to that of others become increasingly fluent.

RFT and Perspective Taking

As a sense of self develops, so too does the ability to understand that others also have desires, beliefs, and wishes. Children learn to distinguish their own behavior as different from that of others by learning three key relations of perspective, referred to as deictic frames, in RFT: "I" versus "you," "here" versus "there," and "now" versus "then." They learn to respond appropriately to questions such as "What are you doing here?" "What am I doing now?" and "What were you doing then?" As children gradually learn to respond appropriately to such questions, and as they learn that whenever they are asked about their own behavior they always answer from the point of view of "I," "here," and "now," they will learn that this perspective is consistent and different from that of other people. For example, if someone asks you about your behavior, you will always answer from the position of "I," "here," and "now" in response to the question asked by the other person from "you," "there," and "then." "I" is always from the individual's perspective, "here"—not from someone else's perspective, "there." A sense of perspective is therefore abstracted through learning to talk about one's own vantage point in relation to other perspectives.

Self-as-Content Versus Self-as-Context

CBS suggests that perspective taking, in combination with an extended relational repertoire, can broadly establish two functionally different types of self (Hayes, Strosahl, & Wilson, 2012). These are the self as the content of verbal relations (the conceptualized self) and the self as the context of verbal relations (the transcendent self).

Self-as-content consists of elaborate descriptive and evaluative relational networks that people construct about themselves and their history over time. As soon as verbal humans become self-aware, they begin to interpret, explain, evaluate, predict, and rationalize their behavior. They organize these descriptions and evaluations into a coherent and consistent "self" network that persists across time and situations.

Self-as-content problems emerge when we fuse with our content. Fusion with content—self-related or otherwise—can be thought of as buying into that content without taking perspective on what's happening. For example, if someone fuses with the thought *It's bad that I'm gay* and buys into that thought completely, she'll treat that thought and all the additional derivations to which it is related as real and true: "I'm flawed," "I'm a bad person," "I'm a reject," and so on. As a consequence of buying into these kinds of derivations, she might also experience associated painful emotions, such as regret, sadness, or shame. In addition, certain patterns of overt behavior might become more likely. For example, she might hide from others or avoid dating. In other words, when people hold what they might perceive to be a negative thought, such as *Being gay is bad*, as true, they're likely to think, feel, and act in accordance with the literal content of that thought. In the language of RFT, this is referred to as a high level of transformation of function. To examine how fusion with self-content can come to restrict behavior for SM clients, we need to consider how rule following can render people insensitive to contingencies.

In CBS, the word "rule" refers to any potentially behavior-regulating relational network, including those that don't look like stereotypical rules (Törneke, 2010). For example, a contingency such as "If I ignore my feelings of being attracted to the same sex, they'll go away" can be a rule. Although this relational network doesn't look like a stereotypical rule, it can still regulate or influence an individual's behavior. In other words, the person can pay attention to it and modify his behavior to be consistent with it, typically without even seeing that this is happening. For instance, he might act in accordance with the rule by trying to do things that will remove his feelings of attraction (and thus his sexuality), such as drinking alcohol, distracting himself, or seeking reassurance from others.

A second aspect of rules highlighted by CBS is that rules can make people's behavior insensitive to direct consequences and thereby maintain maladaptive patterns of behavior (Törneke, 2010). Continuing with the same example, this person may start doing things to remove his feelings that work in the short term, such as drinking, but that undermine or remove longer-term opportunities, perhaps by damaging his health or longevity or by negatively affecting his relationships with others or his sexuality. He listens to and follows the rule, rather than staying in contact with direct experiences that might produce a different outcome. Ultimately, his rule following leads him to avoid the direct experience of his feelings, despite the damage this does in terms of living in alignment with his values. As a remedy to these maladaptive effects of rules, CBS techniques aim to reduce the influence of rules under certain circumstances in order to bring people back into contact with their direct experience and facilitate values-based action. (Please visit http://www.newharbinger.com/34282 for a downloadable handout, "Questions to Disentangle Self-as-Content from Self-as-Context," that provides questions you can use to help clients get unhooked from unworkable rules and other difficult content.)

Self-as-Context: A Healthier Alternative

Self-as-context, or the transcendent self, is the constant factor in all self-discriminations (McHugh & Stewart, 2012). If someone answers many different questions about herself and her behavior, the only aspect of her answering that will be consistent across time is the context from which the answer is given: "I, here, and now." Since self-as-context is an abstraction from the content of verbal responding, it is content-free and thus constant and unchanging from the time when it first emerges. It is a product of verbal responding, but it is also a verbal category that applies to everything a person has ever done and therefore incorporates both the nonverbal self (as the behavioral stream resulting from direct psychological processes) and the verbal self (as both object and process of knowledge gained through relational framing). As a result, it can provide an experiential link between nonverbal and verbal self-knowledge.

All of the evaluations and judgments people make about themselves come together to create the "I" that each individual is. Therefore, any self-evaluations are subsumed into "I." Self-as-context is the CBS process used to help clients disentangle their self from their self-evaluations, allowing them to see themselves as the thinker, not their thoughts, and to be the feeler, not their feelings. And because self-as-context is a constant factor in all discriminations of perspective (e.g., "here" and "now"), it can be thought of as a transcendence of psychological content that allows acceptance of that content. The following mindfulness exercise can help SM clients connect with this perspective.

CONNECTING WITH COMMON HUMANITY FOR SM CLIENTS

To conduct this exercise, ask clients to sit in a comfortable position, close their eyes or fix their gaze at a fixed point on the floor, and tune in to their body and breath as they attend to your words:

Gently acknowledge your breath and breathing now. Simply notice the physical sensations of your breath, either at the nostrils as the air enters and leaves the body or at the chest or belly as it rises and falls with your breathing.

Once you feel settled in your breath, open yourself up to acknowledge the various thoughts you have about yourself as a sexual minority [ideally, you'd adapt the exact wording here to reflect the client's self-identification: gay, bisexual, and so on]. *Also acknowledge the thoughts and judgments you have about sexual minorities in general. Every single one of us has a constant flow of judgments, evaluations, and comparisons. It can be extremely useful to notice these from the vantage point of mindfulness, continuously coming back to the refuge of your breath and breathing.*

Now shift the spotlight of your attention to acknowledge times when you've felt invalidated or stigmatized for being a sexual minority. As best you can, allow yourself to notice the unwanted emotions that this brings up.

And now broaden your awareness to acknowledge other sexual minorities who have felt similar invalidation and stigmatization, acknowledging a thread of common humanity that runs between you. The aim of this part of the exercise is not to minimize your pain in any way, but rather to acknowledge that others also know and share the pain of your experience...

Now, broadening out once more, acknowledge the wider community of humanity across all sexual orientations. Do they know something about being invalidated and victimized? Of course, their story lines might be different than yours. The things they've been invalidated or stigmatized about may be different, yet is there something in their underlying values and vulnerabilities that you can relate to? As best you can, see if you can acknowledge a thread of common humanity that links us all, regardless of sexual orientation, gender identity, race, color, or nationality. Again, the aim is not to minimize your pain in any way. The aim is to situate you, here and now, within the context of the world at large—a place where the vast majority of people know the pain of not being accepted by others. From this context, can you acknowledge anything you need to give to yourself right now to help you heal from the wounds of rejection? Is there a way that we can integrate that into our work here?

This exercise can be an extremely powerful and effective means to go beyond the level of content that SM clients typically have about themselves, allowing them to see both themselves and others in a more expansive light. Different clients will be more or less open to this experience. It's generally best to go a bit beyond the client's comfort zone yet remain within the zone that allows for self-care. Close monitoring of nonverbal cues, such as facial expression and body language, will help you to modify the exercise to best meet clients' needs.

Conclusion

Many SM individuals have grown up in a world where they learned, directly or indirectly, that their sexual orientation is wrong, bad, "less than," or shameful. It's essential that, as clinicians, we understand the mechanisms by which SM individuals infer these kinds of unfavorable comparatives about themselves. It's equally important that we be willing to make contact with the discomfort of having difficult conversations with SM clients when doing so is in their best interests, even though it may bring up a variety of unwanted emotions, including shame, for either the client or the clinician. We need to become acutely aware of the judgments, evaluations, and comparisons that are imprisoning our SM clients and, indeed, ourselves in relation to sexuality. We need to know how our learning history impacts us so we will no longer be blinded by mental content that we assume to be true. By applying the powerful therapeutic tools of perspective taking and helping clients develop self-as-context, we can help SM clients connect with how much more vital and rich their lives are than critical cultural messages would indicate.

References

Austin, S. B., Ziyadeh, N., Kahn, J. A., Camargo, C. A. J., Colditz, G. A., & Field, A. E. (2004). Sexual orientation, weight concerns, and eating-disordered behaviors in adolescent girls and boys. *Journal of the American Academy of Child and Adolescent Psychiatry, 43,* 1115–1123.

Bailey, J. M., Dunne, M. P., & Martin, N. G. (2000). Genetic and environmental influences on sexual orientation and its correlates in an Australian twin sample. *Journal of Personality and Social Psychology, 78,* 524–536.

Balsam, K. F., Beauchaine, T. P., Mickey, R. M., & Rothblum, E. D. (2005). Mental health of lesbian, gay, bisexual, and heterosexual siblings: Effects of gender, sexual orientation, and family. *Journal of Abnormal Psychology, 114,* 471–476.

Bontempo, D. E., & D'Augelli, A. R. (2002). Effects of at-school victimization and sexual orientation on lesbian, gay, or bisexual youths' health risk behavior. *Journal of Adolescent Health, 30,* 364–374.

Burr, C. (1996). *A separate creation: The search for the biological origins of sexual orientation.* New York: Hyperion.

Case, P., Austin, S. B., Hunter, D. J., Manson, J. E., Malspeis, S., Willett, W. C., et al. (2004). Sexual orientation, health risk factors, and physical functioning in the Nurses' Health Study II. *Journal of Women's Health, 13,* 1033–1047.

Cochran, S. D., & Mays, V. M. (2009). Burden of psychiatric morbidity among lesbian, gay, and bisexual individuals in the California Quality of Life Survey. *Journal of Abnormal Psychology, 118,* 647–658.

Cochran, S. D., Sullivan, J. G., & Mays, V. M. (2003). Prevalence of mental disorders, psychological distress, and mental services use among lesbian, gay, and bisexual adults in the United States. *Journal of Consulting and Clinical Psychology, 71,* 53–61.

D'Augelli, A. R., Grossman, A. H., & Starks, M. T. (2005). Parents' awareness of lesbian, gay, and bisexual youths' sexual orientation. *Journal of Marriage and Family, 67,* 474–482.

Diamond, L. M. (2013). Gender and same-sex sexuality. In D. L. Tolman & L. M. Diamond (Eds.), *APA handbook of sexuality and psychology. Volume 1: Person-based approaches.* Washington, DC: American Psychological Association.

Diamond, L. M., & Rosky, C. J. (in press). Scrutinizing immutability: Research on sexual orientation and legal advocacy for sexual minorities. *Annual Review of Sex Research.*

Dymond, S., & Barnes, D. (1996). A transformation of self-discrimination response functions in accordance with the arbitrarily applicable relations of sameness and opposition. *Psychological Record, 46,* 271–300.

Eisenberg, M., & Wechsler, H. (2003). Substance use behaviors among college students with same-sex and opposite-sex experience: Results from a national study. *Addictive Behaviors, 28,* 899–913.

Galliher, R. V., Rostosky, S. S., & Hughes, H. K. (2004). School belonging, self-esteem, and depressive symptoms in adolescents: An examination of sex, sexual attraction status, and urbanicity. *Journal of Youth and Adolescence, 33,* 235–245.

Garofalo, R., Wolf, R. C., Wissow, L. S., Woods, E. R., & Goodman, E. (1999). Sexual orientation and risk of suicide attempts among a representative sample of youth. *Archives of Pediatrics and Adolescent Medicine, 153*, 487–493.

Hayes, S. C., Barnes-Holmes, D., & Roche, B. (Eds.). (2001). *Relational frame theory: A post-Skinnerian account of human language and cognition.* New York: Kluwer Academic.

Hayes, S. C., Strosahl, K. D., & Wilson, K. G. (1999). *Acceptance and commitment therapy: An experiential approach to behavior change.* New York: Guilford.

Hayes, S. C., Strosahl, K. D., & Wilson, K. G. (2012). *Acceptance and commitment therapy: The process and practice of mindful change.* New York: Guilford.

Herek, G. M. (2004). Beyond "homophobia": Thinking about sexual prejudice and stigma in the twenty-first century. *Sexuality Research and Social Policy, 1*, 6–24.

Jorm, A. F., Korten, A. E., Rodgers, B., Jacomb, P. A., & Christensen, H. (2002). Sexual orientation and mental health: Results from a community survey of young and middle-aged adults. *British Journal of Psychiatry, 180*, 423–427.

Kirk, K. M., Bailey, J. M., Dunne, M. P., & Martin, N. G. (2000). Measurement models for sexual orientation in a community twin sample. *Behavior Genetics, 30*, 345–356.

Kohlenberg, R. J., & Tsai, M. (1991). *Functional analytic psychotherapy: Creating intense and curative therapeutic relationships.* New York: Plenum Press.

Laumann, E. O., Gagnon, J. H., Michael, R. T., & Michaels, F. (1994). *The social organization of sexuality: Sexual practices in the United States.* Chicago: University of Chicago Press.

McHugh, L., & Stewart, I. (Eds.). (2012). *The self and perspective taking: Contributions and applications from modern behavioral science.* Oakland, CA: New Harbinger Publications.

Meyer, I. H. (2003). Prejudice, social stress, and mental health in lesbian, gay, and bisexual populations: Conceptual issues and research evidence. *Psychological Bulletin, 129*, 674–697.

Meyer, I. H., & Dean, L. (1998). Internalized homophobia, intimacy, and sexual behavior among gay and bisexual men. In G. M. Herek (Ed.), *Stigma and sexual orientation: Understanding prejudice against lesbians, gay men, and bisexuals.* Thousand Oaks, CA: Sage.

Moon, M. W., Fornili, K., & O'Briant, A. L. (2007). Risk comparison among youth who report sex with same-sex versus both-sex partners. *Youth and Society, 38*, 267–284.

Mosher, W. D., Chandra, A., & Jones, J. (2005). Sexual behavior and selected health measures: Men and women 15–44 years of age, United States, 2002. *Advance Data from Vital and Health Statistics, 362.* Hyattsville, MD: National Center for Health Statistics.

Otis, M. D., Rostosky, S. S., Riggle, E. D. B., & Hamrin, R. (2006). Stress and relationship quality in same-sex couples. *Journal of Social and Personal Relationships, 23*, 81–99.

Paul, J. P., Catania, J., Pollack, L., Moskowitz, J., Canchola, J., Mills, T., et al. (2002). Suicide attempts among gay and bisexual men: Lifetime prevalence and antecedents. *American Journal of Public Health, 92*, 1338–1345.

Plummer, M. D. (2010). FAP with sexual minorities. In J. Kanter, M. Tsai, & R. J. Kohlenberg (Eds.), *The practice of functional analytic psychotherapy*. New York: Springer.

Remafedi, G., French, S., Story, M., Resnick, M. D., & Blum, R. (1998). The relationship between suicide risk and sexual orientation: Results of a population-based study. *American Journal of Public Health, 88*, 57–60.

Remafedi, G., Resnick, M., Blum, R., & Harris, L. (1992). Demography of sexual orientation in adolescents. *Pediatrics, 89*, 714–721.

Rosario, M., & Schrimshaw, E. W. (2014). Theories and etiologies of sexual orientation. In D. L. Tolman & L. M. Diamond (Eds.), *APA handbook of sexuality and psychology. Volume 1: Person-based approaches*. Washington, DC: American Psychological Association.

Russell, S. T., & Joyner, K. (2001). Adolescent sexual orientation and suicide risk: Evidence from a national study. *American Journal of Public Health, 91*, 1276–1281.

Russell, S. T., Seif, H., & Truong, N. L. (2001). School outcomes of sexual minority youth in the United States: Evidence from a national study. *Journal of Adolescence, 24*, 111–127.

Rust, P. C. R. (2000). Criticisms of the scholarly literature on sexuality for its neglect of bisexuality. In P. C. R. Rust (Ed.), *Bisexuality in the United States: A reader and guide to the literature*. New York: Columbia University Press.

Savin-Williams, R. C., & Ream, G. L. (2006). Pubertal onset and sexual orientation in an adolescent national probability sample. *Archives of Sexual Behavior, 35*, 279–286.

Törneke, N. (2010). *Learning RFT: An introduction to relational frame theory and its clinical application*. Oakland, CA: New Harbinger Publications.

Udry, J. R., & Chantala, K. (2002). Risk assessment of adolescents with same-sex relationships. *Journal of Adolescent Health, 31*, 84–92.

Whisman, V. (1993). Identity crisis: Who is a lesbian anyway? In A. Stein (Ed.), *Sisters, sexperts, queers: Beyond the lesbian nation*. New York: Penguin.

Whisman, V. (1996). *Queer by choice: Lesbians, gay men, and the politics of identity*. New York: Routledge.

Ziyadeh, N. J., Prokop, L. A., Fisher, L. B., Rosario, M., Field, A. E., Camargo, C. A. J., et al. (2007). Sexual orientation, gender, and alcohol use in a cohort study of US adolescent girls and boys. *Drug and Alcohol Dependence, 87*, 119–130.

CHAPTER 2

Using ACT Interventions to Help Clients Explore the Possibilities of Gender Identity

Trish Leonard, *ACT Now Ireland*; and
Lauren Grousd, *private practice*

We are our own dragons as well as our own heroes, and we have to rescue ourselves from ourselves.

—Tom Robbins

Before we can establish our identity as an "I," we must first know ourselves in terms of our gender (Butler, 1990). Therefore, the concept of gender has a significant impact upon how we construct a conceptual self. However, we are not born with gender; we learn how to become gendered within complex social interactions that dictate how we acceptably behave as female or male. And even before we take our first breath in this world, others are often forming expectations about how we should live our lives. Expecting parents may start to ask seemingly basic questions such as "Shall we paint the nursery pink or blue?" or "Will we be attending football games or ballet recitals?"

Historically, dominant heteronormative discourses dictate these expectations, establishing certain norms as "truth" and then using them to measure or judge all experiences as appropriate or inappropriate, acceptable or unacceptable, normal or abnormal. Over time, these expectations become internalized within us and gradually expand to form complex frames of reference defining the "right" way to behave according to our assigned gender. In Western society, the most predominant of these established norms is the gender binary, which presents two options for how we live our gender: as male or female (Weeks, 2010). For most people, their individual conceptualized gender feels like it fits with their biologically assigned sex, and they live according to the expectations of the gender binary quite comfortably. However, increasing numbers of individuals reject the reductionist and rigid dualism of the gender binary and are instead embracing diverse and complex ways of living their gender (Diamond, Pardo, & Butterworth, 2011).

In this chapter, we aim to accomplish several objectives. We will explore a variety of experiences that gender-nonconforming clients may present in therapy, based upon our own experiences as clinicians and our understanding of common challenges. Although the scope here is necessarily limited, we hope to convey the dynamic and varied ways in which gender-nonconforming individuals experience their lives. We will also present interventions from acceptance and commitment therapy (ACT; Hayes, Strosahl, & Wilson, 1999) that can be particularly helpful for exploring issues of gender, focusing primarily on the ACT matrix, which we have found to be an invaluable tool (Polk & Schoendorff, 2014). Throughout, we hope to underscore the utility of applying a functional contextual framework to understanding issues of gender identity and expression and working with them in a clinical environment. The contextual and personal aspects of gender are well suited to an approach that emphasizes function and making meaning within a given context. But before we turn to ACT as a particularly useful approach for working with gender-nonconforming clients, we will discuss what we mean by "gender nonconforming."

What We Mean by Gender Nonconforming

We want to be transparent and authentic about our perspectives and how they may influence the ways in which we construct meaning for ourselves and others in this chapter. Broadly speaking, both of the authors identify as cisgender, white, nonheterosexual female clinicians, and we recognize that these identities and social positions have shaped our experiences of gender and continue to do so. We do not intend this chapter to be a definitive representation of gender-nonconforming individuals' experiences, and we consider gender-nonconforming individuals' voices to be central to any conversation about their experiences. We have endeavored to fairly represent our clients' voices here, and we encourage you, regardless of your gender identity, to seek out additional perspectives and to prioritize your own processes of mindfulness, acceptance, defusion, self-as-context, chosen values, and committed action in your work with clients around gender issues.

Having established those provisos, we will use "gender nonconforming" as an umbrella term referring to "the extent to which a person's gender identity, role, or expression differs from the cultural norms prescribed for people of a particular sex" (Coleman et al., 2011, p. 168). This term is fairly accurate in encompassing the diversity of identities and gender expressions of our clients, including those who identify as transgender, transsexual, nonbinary, genderqueer, androgynous, gender fluid, or agender or who use other terminology to describe their gender. The term "gender nonconforming" also avoids inherently pathologizing identities and forms of gender expression that fall outside of dominant social norms. In 2010, the World Professional Association for Transgender Health released a statement calling for the depathologization of gender variance worldwide, especially within governmental and medical professional organizations, in order to reduce the stigma that contributes to discrimination, violence, and poor mental and physical health outcomes for gender-nonconforming individuals. We support adopting this more expansive and normalizing terminology and will utilize it throughout this chapter.

The Role of Transition

Transition exists as a valid and valued option for many people who identify as gender nonconforming. In some cases, they have a deeply experienced drive toward transition as the only way of living a complete and authentic life. Those who reach this conclusion generally display a determination and willingness to transition, even if this means risking rejection and loss of all that they currently hold dear. Typically, the process of transition includes a number of tasks, such as changing one's social presentation of gender, undergoing hormonal treatments or surgical procedures, and legally changing one's name. For those who wish to undergo medical transition, the number of tasks is greater and includes assessment, a real-life experiment, being diagnosed with a mental disorder to access treatment, and "passing" (Devor, 2004). The pressure to fulfill these prerequisites for treatment can weigh heavily on some individuals, and the process can be incredibly demanding, from being assessed "appropriate for treatment" to successfully "passing" with an "intelligible" performance of gender.

Ultimately, transitioning is a complex, dynamic, and personal process that's unique for each individual. It is, therefore, important to facilitate clients in identifying the functions of transition as they conceive its role in their lives. We've found that encouraging psychological flexibility within our gender-nonconforming clients can allow them some room to open up to diverse possibilities for how they might live their gender identity. In providing this space for clients, therapists must, of course, look beyond the historical fusion of our profession with dominant discourses defining the experiences of gender-nonconforming individuals as gender dysphoria. If therapists retain this outdated perspective, they will fail to appreciate the growing numbers of individuals who are rejecting traditional views of gender and constructing their sense of self outside the confines of heteronormative discourses.

Those considering transition often adopt a more expansive and flexible view of gender. Some reject as limiting all labels associated with a heteronormative understanding of gender. Others may combine aspects of masculinity and femininity, adopt a more ambiguous gender identification, or hold an even more fluid and shifting sense of their gender (Diamond et al., 2011). This expanding tapestry of diverse and complex ways of living individual gender demands that therapists demonstrate an equally broad and nuanced appreciation of the complexity of experiences of gender-nonconforming lives. In line with this, our profession, and our culture more generally, must shift away from a clinical understanding of transition as a rigid progression of fixed steps and toward helping individuals conceive more expansive and flexible ways of living their gender.

ACT for Gender-Nonconforming Clients

Sadly, living within contexts that are often hostile, rejecting, and dangerous appears to be the experience of many gender-nonconforming individuals. The retrospective reports of those who identify as transgender, for instance, are wrought with distressing interpersonal difficulties, including rejection by peers, parents, and other significant adults (Lev, 2004). In some cases these reports extend to experiences of physical or emotional abuse and neglect by family members and significant caregivers (Mascis, 2011). Studies involving participants who identify as transgender also reveal profound social distress in adolescence, which may increase peer group exclusion, isolation, and avoidance of school (Green, 2007). Most such histories also reveal a deep sense of disconnection and alienation. Accompanying this sense of unnameable difference (Devor, 2004), many also experience feelings of shame and self-loathing (Schaefer & Wheeler, 2004). Over time, this can lead to issues with self-esteem (Pleak, 2009) and mental health difficulties such as depression, self-injury, and substance abuse (Boza & Nicholson Perry, 2014).

ACT has proved to be efficacious with other populations and presenting problems related to trauma, substance use, anxiety, and depression (for a review, see Ruiz, 2010), and we have found that it also provides a useful framework and set of approaches for helping gender-nonconforming clients discover ways to live meaningfully in the presence of these challenges. However, while it is likely that these clients will have experienced adversities related to their gender identification and may have struggled psychologically, it is important that therapists not limit their interventions to addressing these issues. Clients are likely to present with a variety of concerns, whether they be gender-related or not, and ACT is well positioned to facilitate an integrated understanding of and therapeutic approach for whatever seems relevant for a given client. It's also important to remember that clients' gender identity or expression may not be central to their reasons for seeking therapy and could instead function as peripheral or contextual adjuncts to a more prominent problem with anxiety, depression, or other issues.

Clinical Conceptualization and Intervention with the ACT Matrix

In the rest of this chapter, we will use the ACT matrix as a lens through which to explore ACT as it relates to the experiences of gender-nonconforming clients. The matrix offers a coherent and concise framework within which therapists and clients alike can contextualize and functionally analyze thoughts, emotions, sensations, values, and actions via the six core ACT processes (acceptance, defusion, present-moment awareness, self-as-context, values, and committed action). The ultimate aim is to help clients develop psychological flexibility so they can engage in valued ways of living.

As figure 2.1 reveals, the matrix prompts two discrimination tasks: noticing five-senses experiencing versus mental experiencing, and noticing toward versus away moves.

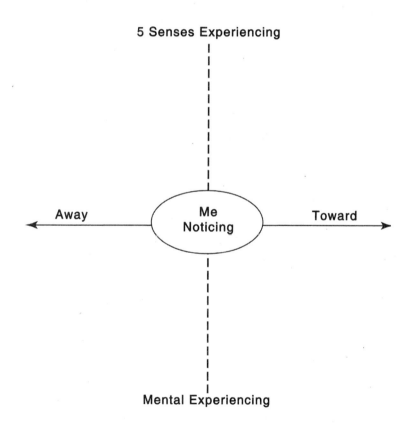

Figure 2.1. The matrix

Introducing the Matrix

Clients can use the matrix to sort their behavior and internal experiences into the four quadrants. This very act helps them identify and defuse from uncomfortable thoughts, memories, emotions, and sensations (away plus mental experiencing, in the lower left quadrant); choose pertinent values (toward plus mental experiencing, in the lower right); observe experientially avoidant behaviors and patterns (away plus five-senses experiencing, in the upper left); and identify values-congruent actions (toward plus five-senses experiencing, in the upper right). The center of the matrix represents the self-as-context perspective, indicating that there is a "me" who notices the differences between the content in each of these quadrants.

The matrix works best when clients do their own sorting. So as tempting as it might be to show them where their content "belongs" on the diagram, the therapist's role is to facilitate clients in sorting their own content. Asking, "Where would you put that on the matrix?" is a helpful way to redirect clients back into a self-as-context or observer-self perspective if they become fused with their story or otherwise get stuck in session. Polk and Schoendorff (2014) refer to this redirection as verbal aikido because the therapist takes the client's energy and redirects it onto the matrix, as opposed to becoming embroiled in arguments or debates about whether something is true or not, where it should go on the matrix, whether something is possible, and so on.

This process of sorting content (thoughts, feelings, sensations, values, behaviors) using the matrix can easily be used in concert with other ACT interventions, as we will illustrate in the following case example with a gender-nonconforming client, Mary, who is a composite of clients and clinical work each of us has encountered in our practice. Mary's example isn't intended to encompass the vast diversity of gender-nonconforming individuals' experiences. In fact, as we hope to emphasize, there is no one right answer to the question of how an individual identifies, expresses, presents, embodies, or makes meaning of gender.

Case Example: Using the Matrix with GSM Clients

Mary, now in her late forties, was designated female at birth and has identified as a butch lesbian since early adulthood. She seeks counseling to address a pattern of losing interest in sex with her partners after the initial phase of a relationship has passed. Upon reflection, Mary realizes that she identifies more as male in sexual situations and indicates that this feels frustrating and confusing because her lesbian identity has been so important to her. She starts to see that she's been avoiding sex as a way to circumvent this confusion, but her avoidance behavior has caused relationship problems and her confusion has continued. Although Mary is questioning her gender identity, she still prefers the pronouns "she" and "her."

One of our first priorities in working with Mary is to introduce the matrix. Using the matrix forces people into a self-as-context perspective as they identify and sort their internal content and external behavior into toward and away directions. In brief, self-as-context is a concept of the self as a perspective from which we can observe our own internal thoughts and feelings. (For more on self-as-context, see chapter 1.) Sometimes referred to as the observing self, it is the part of us that notices that we're noticing (Harris, 2009). Therefore, every time we ask Mary to sort her internal experiences, values, and behaviors onto the matrix, she will be utilizing her observing self. So as the work proceeds, we frequently prompt her to locate her content in this way. This provides multiple in-session rehearsals that will retrain her mind to view her experience in this way outside of session, as well.

Early on, it becomes clear that Mary frequently becomes hooked by fusion with her thoughts and by struggling with emotional, mental, and physiological discomfort. In essence, Mary is stuck. In one of her initial sessions, we ask, "What happens for you when you think about or have sex with your current partner?" To this, she responds, "I feel anxious. I feel broken. I worry that she'll leave me if I don't have sex with her. When I do have sex, I have these fantasies of doing it as a man, but I know I'll never be able to do that, and she probably wouldn't want me that way, anyway. So I sort of shut down. I go through the motions and hope she doesn't notice that I'm not really present."

Figure 2.2 shows what Mary comes up with when we ask her to sort this content onto the matrix.

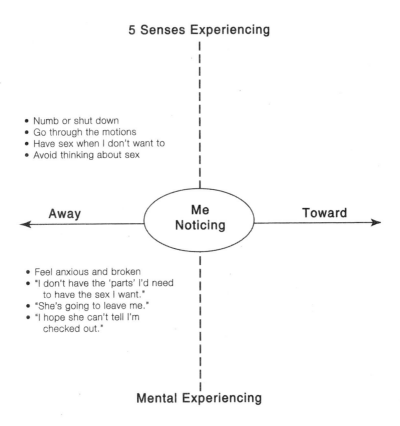

Figure 2.2. Mary sorting her thoughts on sex with her partner

Upon looking at her matrix, Mary observes, "Wow! I get so in my head during sex. This is just what I do. It doesn't work well, but I don't know what else to do." This provides multiple opportunities to examine where Mary could change her current patterns. We decide to further examine how she is "in her head." For homework, she chooses to engage in both formal and informal mindfulness practices to focus on just noticing which thoughts, feelings, sensations, and urges come up for her throughout her day.

The following week, Mary reports that she's noticing even more of a disconnect between her own sense of her gender and how others interact with her, even outside of sexual situations. "I don't like this mindfulness business," she states. "I feel worse and more confused." Rather than argue or advocate for the benefits of mindfulness or attempt to alleviate Mary's discomfort, we redirect her to the matrix, where she sorts her current experience as illustrated in figure 2.3.

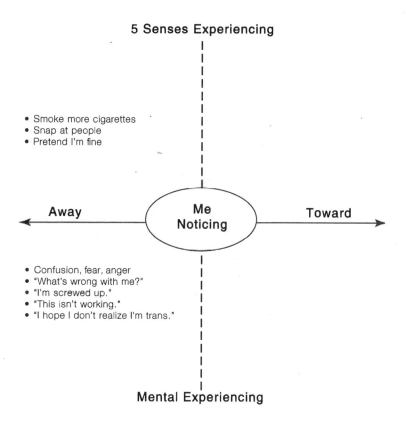

Figure 2.3. Mary sorting how she's "in her head"

Making contact with the present moment requires a willingness to do so even when it's uncomfortable. Understandably, most of us resist being uncomfortable. Clients often come to therapy wanting to eliminate their discomfort and look to their therapist for help in doing so. But what if the attempt to eliminate that discomfort is actually exacerbating it? The ACT concept of experiential avoidance describes what people do when they're unwilling to experience discomfort. In essence, they struggle to avoid or eliminate thoughts and feelings related to fear, guilt, shame, rejection, anger, anxiety, and so on by controlling their attention or behaving in certain ways.

What we want to highlight here is whether and how such avoidance strategies work for the individual in particular contexts. Workability can be assessed by the degree to which a person's strategies and actions move her in the direction of her values versus getting in the way of doing so. Do these strategies eliminate the person's discomfort in the long term? Do they cause additional problems for the person? Do they come at a cost to her sense of fulfillment and meaning in life? Does she rigidly employ them regardless of context? In other words, what is the function of a particular action or behavior in a particular context?

When Mary looks at the combined patterns in her matrix, she can see what form her experiential avoidance takes, as well as its function. In exploring the workability of Mary's away moves—actions in the upper left quadrant—she comments that they feel like temporary fixes to her. When we ask what thoughts and feelings come up for her when she shuts down, Mary states that it helps her get through having sex, but then she feels fearful and anxious afterward, wondering whether her partner noticed and feeling bad about having sex when she didn't really want to. We then ask what she does when these thoughts and feelings come up for her, and she says that she often tries to act like nothing is wrong, which leads her to feel even more anxious and angry. Then she tends to smoke more cigarettes (she's trying to quit) and become snappy and irritable with people, including her partner.

This cycle is not news to Mary. She is readily able to describe it and assess that it isn't helping her in the long run, even though she does experience some short-term relief through distraction and opting out of challenging situations. By introducing the idea that the actual problem is the struggle to avoid painful emotional states, rather than the emotions themselves, we can validate that her experiences of fear, loneliness, and dysphoria are understandable under the circumstances. They confirm that she's human. Then we can introduce the idea of allowing these feelings to be there and doing what matters to her anyway.

Now that Mary has more awareness of her avoidant patterns, she can look at the other side of the coin—or the matrix, in this case. The alternative to engaging in away moves is to take action in the service of her values by engaging in toward moves. Mary is well versed in the material in the lower left quadrant of her matrix because of the frequency with which she gets hooked by it. So in order to help her identify potential toward moves, we turn to clarifying her values. To that end, we ask her to consider the following questions:

- What's important to you about this situation or part of your life?

- What kind of person do you want to be in the face of this situation?

- How do you want to show up in this context?

- What do your feelings tell you about what you really care about?

- In an ideal world, what kind of relationship would you like to have?

She ponders these questions over the next week and plots her answers on the matrix, as shown in figure 2.4.

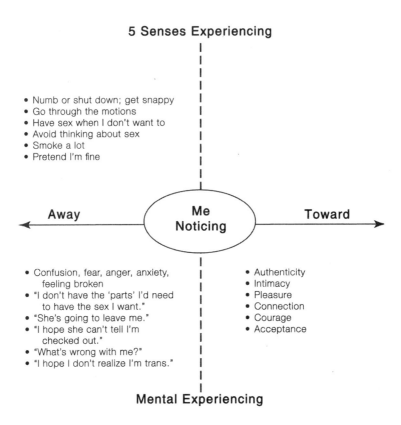

Figure 2.4. Mary clarifies her values via the matrix

In exploring the relationships between the two left-hand quadrants, Mary identifies where her actions have been unworkable, providing some relief from discomfort in the short term but tending to exacerbate her pain in the long term. She's eager to explore alternatives. Before we begin, we remind her that the difficult thoughts and feelings she's identified are likely to remain. Then we suggest that the workable alternative is to drop the struggle with difficult inner experiences and to instead make room for them while identifying ways of being in the world that feel meaningful.

The upper right quadrant is where we can help Mary explore a variety of behavioral options that are aligned with her values and also identify ways to get back on track when she finds herself astray.

Asking, "What would it look like if you were acting from the lower right quadrant?" can be a useful way to start the conversation.

Mary replies that she thinks she should do the opposite of her avoidance behaviors: that she should stop fighting and breaking up with her partners, and stop avoiding sex, including thinking about it and talking about it. However, not engaging in these behaviors is different from acting in the service of her values. So to encourage Mary to engage in committed, values-based action—behavior firmly in the upper right quadrant—we ask her to consider the following questions:

- What would it look like if you were being your most authentic self?

- What could you do that would bring you closer to your partner?

- What would connection look like in this part of your life?

- How could you be courageous in the face of these thoughts and feelings?

- What could you do in an effort to bring more pleasure into your sexual or romantic life?

In response to these questions, Mary generates the following possible toward moves:

- *Do some reading or research about gender nonconformity and sex to help me understand other people's experiences, identities, and practices.*

- *Find and attend a support group for people who identify as gender nonconforming or questioning.*

- *Talk with my partner about her sexual desires and boundaries.*

- *Practice mindfulness daily, either formally or informally, to contact and make room for my thoughts and feelings.*

- *Experiment with using toys during sex, even though that has brought up feelings of dysphoria in the past.*

- *Explore whether or how top surgery or hormone therapy might support a sense of a more integrated self for me.*

We then utilize a values-based goal-setting exercise to help Mary put her values into action and navigate any feelings of being overwhelmed that arise in relation to taking valued action.

This composite case example illustrates how we use the matrix with clients. To a large degree, we focus on helping them internalize the matrix approach and practice engaging in the six ACT processes. Our ultimate aim is that they increasingly use these skills to respond flexibly to both their internal content and the external circumstances of everyday life while living in the service of their values. For most clients, this means being courageous enough to face their fears, moving authentically through the world, connecting meaningfully with themselves and others, and valuing their own needs and desires. There is no one right answer to what this should look like.

Key Considerations in Working with Gender-Nonconforming Clients

It's not necessary to know everything about gender identity and expression prior to working with gender-nonconforming clients. Given the constantly evolving landscape of gender, this would be a difficult goal. However, we have found certain considerations to be particularly important in providing competent, compassionate, and effective support for gender-nonconforming clients. These key approaches include being sensitive to a history of trauma, helping clients transcend restrictive social constructs around gender, and remaining self-aware.

Being Sensitive to Trauma History

Clients who have experienced trauma can sometimes feel overwhelmed and experience secondary trauma when making contact with triggers in the present moment. Unfortunately, gender-nonconforming individuals continue to be subject to high rates of violence, harassment, and discrimination, which may be exacerbated by racism and other forms of oppression. Providing trauma-informed care by acknowledging the social injustice of this reality, validating clients' concerns about safety and attempts to establish safety, and providing psychoeducation about trauma and healing are vitally important when working with gender-nonconforming clients with a history of trauma. Additional therapeutic approaches, including Somatic Experiencing (Levine, 2015), eye movement desensitization and reprocessing (Shapiro, 2001), and dialectical behavior therapy (Linehan, 1993), can help these clients develop distress tolerance skills and learn to ground themselves, augmenting the mindfulness component of ACT work.

Transcending Restrictive Social Constructs

We also try to help clients hold potentially restricting societal rules around gender lightly so they can more fully explore ways of living their gender that work for them within their context. And in addition to challenging existing gender-related rules or concepts within clients, we also aim to undermine rules that may be imposed by dominant societal concepts of gender. This approach can be challenging in cases where we're required to diagnose clients with gender dysphoria in order for them to access treatment. Labeling and defining such clients while also trying to help them find their way outside of the limiting effects of medical language typically requires a fine balancing act. It can be helpful to look at such diagnoses functionally, in terms of how they fit with clients' overall goals and can bring them closer to their values. Engaging these clients in self-as-context work can be helpful in creating space for them to step back and view how the diagnosis is just one aspect of their sense of self.

Remaining Self-Aware

We've found it beneficial to stay as aware as possible of our own thoughts, feelings, and values and how they might restrict or expand the possibilities we see for a client's gender experience. By doing this, we can identify instances when we may be leading clients toward some specific path or outcome. Staying as grounded as possible in present-moment connection and awareness also helps us redirect when we realize that we're getting stuck in a problem-solving mode of mind.

In addition, we try to be on the lookout for more subtle ways our internalized concepts around gender influence the routes we explore. For example, when guiding gender-nonconforming clients in identifying their values, it's important to steer clear of gendering these values, assigning them as typically male or female. Consider Leo, who identified as female-to-male transgender. In session, he related that his psychiatrist was trying to "teach him to be a man" by encouraging him to work out at the gym, drink pints of beer, and toughen up in his responses to other men. But this way of being in the world didn't fit with Leo's own values of being compassionate, openly emotional, and expressing what he termed "his feminine side." A lot of the work with clients like Leo involves allowing a broader exploration of their unique values as a human being, regardless of gender, while also facilitating defusion from "values" their learning history may have promoted as typically male or female. One of our guiding philosophies in our work with gender-nonconforming clients is that there is no single or correct way to live one's gender. In providing space for our clients to explore the full range of possibilities open to them, we must maintain an expansive view of gender.

Conclusion

Using ACT with gender-nonconforming clients can be especially effective in helping them live authentically without prescribing what that looks like. Again, there is no one right answer. ACT provides approaches that allow therapists to validate and acknowledge clients' challenges, social and cultural contexts, emotional responses, and ways of navigating their lives safely, while also increasing the variety of potentially meaningful and fulfilling responses they can bring to those challenges. Ultimately, ACT enables therapists to support clients in developing more self-determination and a greater sense of self-efficacy, rather than potentially pathologizing their identity or keeping them stuck in a sense of hopelessness or victimhood.

References

Boza, C., & Nicholson Perry, K. (2014). Gender-related victimization, perceived social support, and predictors of depression among transgender Australians. *International Journal of Transgenderism, 15*, 35–52.

Butler, J. (1990). *Gender trouble: Feminism and the subversion of identity*. New York: Routledge.

Coleman, E., Bockting, W., Botzer, M., Cohen-Kettenis, P., DeCuypere, G., Feldman, J., et al. (2011). Standards of care for the health of transsexual, transgender, and gender-nonconforming people, version 7. *International Journal of Transgenderism, 13*, 165–232.

Devor, A. H. (2004). Witnessing and mirroring: A fourteen stage model of transsexual identity formation. *Journal of Gay and Lesbian Psychotherapy, 8*, 41–67.

Diamond, L. M., Pardo, S. T., & Butterworth, M. R. (2011). Transgender experience and identity. In S. J. Schwartz, K. Luyckx, & V. L. Vignoles (Eds.), *Handbook of identity theory and research. Volume 2: Domains and categories*. New York: Springer.

Green, R. (2007). Gender development and reassignment. *Psychiatry, 6*, 121–124.

Harris, R. (2009). *ACT made simple: An easy-to-read primer on acceptance and commitment therapy*. Oakland, CA: New Harbinger Publications.

Hayes, S. C., Strosahl, K. D., & Wilson, K. G. (1999). *Acceptance and commitment therapy: An experiential approach to behavior change*. New York: Guilford.

Lev, A. I. (2004). *Transgender emergence: Therapeutic guidelines for working with gender-variant people and their families*. Binghamton, NY: Haworth Press.

Levine, P. A. (2015). *Trauma and memory: Brain and body in a search for the living past: A practical guide for understanding and working with traumatic memory*. Berkeley, CA: North Atlantic Books.

Linehan, M. M. (1993). *Cognitive-behavioral treatment of borderline personality disorder*. New York: Guilford.

Mascis, A. N. (2011). Working with transgender survivors. *Journal of Gay and Lesbian Mental Health, 15*, 200–210.

Pleak, R. R. (2009). Formation of transgender identities in adolescence. *Journal of Gay and Lesbian Mental Health, 13*, 282–291.

Polk, K. L., & Schoendorff, B. (Eds.). (2014). *The ACT matrix: A new approach to building psychological flexibility across settings and populations*. Oakland, CA: New Harbinger Publications.

Ruiz, F. J. (2010). A review of acceptance and commitment therapy (ACT) empirical evidence: Correlational, experimental psychopathology, component, and outcome studies. *International Journal of Psychology and Psychological Therapy*, 10, 125–162.

Schaefer, L. C., & Wheeler, C. C. (2004). Guilt in cross gender identity conditions: Presentations and treatment. *Journal of Gay and Lesbian Psychotherapy*, 8, 117–127.

Shapiro, F. (2001). *Eye movement desensitization and reprocessing (EMDR): Basic principles, protocols, and procedures.* New York: Guilford.

Weeks, J. (2010). *Sexuality*, 3rd edition. New York: Routledge.

World Professional Association for Transgender Health, Board of Directors. (2010, May 26). Press release. Retrieved December 16, 2015, from http://www.wpath. org/uploaded_files/140/files/de-psychopathologisation%205–26–10%20on%20 letterhead.pdf.

CHAPTER 3

Coming Out with Compassion

Aisling Curtin, *ACT Now Ireland*;
Danielle (Danny) Ryu,
PGSP-Stanford PsyD Consortium; and
Lisa Diamond, *University of Utah*

One of the more unique aspects of the experiences of gender and sexual minorities (GSM) is "coming out." In heteronormative cultures where the assumption is that every individual is heterosexual and cisgender (having a gender identity aligned with the sex assigned at birth), individuals with culturally consonant gender identities and sexual orientations don't need to come out. In fact, just referring to someone as having a sexual orientation is often interpreted as a reference to that person being gay, lesbian, or bisexual. In this chapter, we seek to provide context for what coming out can mean and how this may vary across gender and sexual minorities. In addition, we seek to provide therapeutic tools clinicians can use to help GSM clients navigate their unique coming out trajectories.

The coming out process can be influenced by contextual factors, and these may affect the therapeutic relationship. Thus, it's essential to create a safe and compassionate therapeutic environment, particularly when the underlying culture the client lives in is openly threatening toward GSM populations. Therefore, we've endeavored to provide guidance on creating more accepting and compassionate contexts in which GSM individuals can authentically express themselves, both in the therapy room and in the world. Each of the coauthors of this chapter has come out as a gender and/or sexual minority. In writing this chapter, we hope to provide what we wish had been written when we were navigating our own unique identity processes as GSM individuals.

What Is Coming Out?

"Coming out" is generally synonymous with making something known that was previously hidden, or releasing oneself from the bounds of confinement. Interestingly, many dictionary definitions, such as Cambridge Dictionaries Online (2015), refer to "coming out" as a process involving informing others when one is gay, which obviously covers only a small range of GSM experiences. Further, there is often a misconception that coming out is an event, whereas in reality it is a nonlinear lifelong process that looks different for everyone, is context dependent, and may not apply to all GSM.

In addition, the process of coming out as a gender minority may or may not be related to sexual orientation, and the concept may have vastly different meanings and applications in the gender minority (GM) community. Even in writing this chapter, the concept of coming out had different implications and functions for the first and second authors, the former identifying as a sexual minority, and the latter identifying as both a gender and sexual minority. This disconnect is one that parallels the complexity that can imbue the use (or disuse) of coming out narratives in different GSM communities.

As it relates to gender, "coming out" may not fit as easily into the closeted versus not-closeted dichotomy that has, at times, felt empowering and accurate for sexual minorities (SM). For some gender minority individuals, coming out isn't necessarily a choice because people are constantly being gendered (accurately or not). In this way, the coming out concept may be less useful, or it may entail a constant correction of pronouns and labels. As with other aspects of gender identity, coming out doesn't necessitate any visible changes and could simply indicate a form of communicating and clarifying more accurate and affirming language with regard to identity. For other individuals, the process may involve drastic changes to appearance and behavior, the acceptance and understanding of one's gender identity as different than it was previously, or both. Some GM people may be content with how they're read and not feel the need to come out or explain their identity to others, while others may take pride in their GM status and explicitly integrate that into their identity (e.g., identifying as "a trans guy" as opposed to just "a guy"). Other GM individuals may not want to disclose their GM identity at all, preferring to be read as and to exist as cisgender after transitioning. Ultimately, "coming out" can only be defined by whomever is coming out and is a process that may or may not resonate with all clients. (We'll discuss taking a flexible approach to understanding clients' experiences in the section entitled "The Act of Unknowing").

We believe that it isn't the clinician's place to direct clients' coming out processes. Taking this stance may require challenging any underlying assumption that being "out" (in the variety of ways it can be defined) is the final and best destination. While satisfying and self-compassionate living often involves authenticity and genuineness, it is ultimately the client's decision as to how they'd like to approach the nuances of disclosing any of their identities. The clinician's job is to help clients live in alignment with their values, which may or may not involve coming out, and to create an environment of nonjudgment and compassion that facilitates self-acceptance.

Mohini

In her blog post entitled "Accepting Absolutely Everything," Tara Brach (2012) shares the true story of a regal white tiger named Mohini that speaks to the potential challenges of coming out. After years of living in a twelve-by-twelve-foot cage, Mohini was released into a more expansive and natural environment. Nonetheless, she chose to live the remainder of her life pacing a twelve-by-twelve-foot corner of her new enclosure until she'd worn away all of the grass in the area. The story and Tara's recounting of it highlight how all of us can spend our lives limiting ourselves much more than we need to.

The first author shares this story with most clients she works with, both within and outside the GSM community. It can be incredibly powerful and effective for people to write down the actions they're engaging in when they're stuck in their twelve-by-twelve, and also to identify what a new, more expansive environment would look like. This may provide a sense of the direction to move toward within the therapeutic context. (Visit http://www.newharbinger.com/34282 for a downloadable MP3 audio file and instructions about how to share this story to enhance a sense of common humanity and help clients cultivate self-compassion.)

Considerations Around Coming Out for Sexual Minorities

It is sometimes assumed that SM individuals are uniformly alienated or ostracized from their families of origin, but this is not the case. In fact, research has demonstrated incredible diversity in their family ties (e.g., Legate, Ryan, & Weinstein, 2011). However, for many SM individuals, a critical and difficult question is whether and when to disclose their sexuality to family members. Studies generally suggest that most self-identified lesbian, gay, or bisexual individuals have disclosed their sexuality to at least one family member, with 60 to 77 percent of respondents reporting that they are "out" to their parents (Bryant & Demian, 1994). Telling some family members but not others is fairly common (as reviewed in Green, 2000). In general, mothers and sisters are told more often and earlier than other family members, largely because they are perceived as being potentially more accepting (as reviewed in Savin-Williams, 2001). Other factors that shape the timing and breadth of disclosure include the degree of predisclosure intimacy, openness, support, contact, and conflict in these relationships; issues of economic dependence; the family's cultural background and religious values; and overall appraisals of the costs and benefits associated with both continued secrecy and the disruption disclosure may bring about (e.g., Baiocco, Fontanesi, Santamaria, Ioverno, Baumgartner, et al., 2014; Baiocco, Fontanesi, Santamaria, Ioverno, Marasco, et al., 2014; Green, 2000). To give an example of the last factor, cisgender SM females have been shown to receive more health benefits from disclosing their sexual orientation than cisgender SM males (Rothman, Sullivan, Keyes, & Boehmer, 2012), which may make disclosure appear more beneficial to members of that population.

Of course, simply revealing one's minority sexuality to family members isn't the same as establishing an open and honest dialogue about it. Surveys indicate that even among lesbian, gay, and bisexual individuals who are "out" to their parents, many don't discuss the issue directly (Kaiser Foundation, 2001). In some cases, parents may know and quietly tolerate the situation (D'Augelli, Grossman, & Starks, 2005; Herdt & Beeler, 1998) and yet make their disapproval subtly known, for example by refusing to acknowledge or validate the person's romantic relationships.

Disclosure to family members takes on different meanings for SM individuals in later stages of life. As Herdt and Beeler (1998) indicate, when young adults disclose their same-sex sexuality to their parents and other family members, reactions often revolve around thoughts about the future, sometimes involving grief around lost expectations and fantasies, as well as fears about their loved one's risk of being harassed or victimized. On the other hand, when people come out later, in middle age, many of these concerns about the future are largely moot. They have already traversed major milestones involving career, intimate relationships, and potentially even children. In such cases, disclosure to family members raises more issues about the past than the future, and family members may have to substantially revise and reconsider their narratives of their family's history (Beeler & DiProva, 1999): Was everything involving the SM family member a fabrication? What else might be unknown, not only about this individual but about other family members? How can something so important go unnoticed? As Herdt and Beeler (1998) point out, in some cases reckoning with and undoing decades of duplicity may prove to be a more pressing issue than wrestling with the sexuality itself.

Some families never accept a SM family member's sexuality, which raises an important question: Why disclose at all? For SM individuals who have a history of conflict and poor communication with family members and anticipate a reaction of sharp disapproval, secrecy might make more sense than disclosure (Green & Mitchell, 2002). Secrecy might even prove to be psychologically adaptive because it allows these individuals to protect and cherish their own personal truth and integrity (Baiocco, Fontanesi, Santamaria, Ioverno, Baumgartner, et al., 2014; Baiocco, Fontanesi, Santamaria, Ioverno, Marasco, et al., 2014; Laird, 1993, 1998; Legate et al., 2011; Rothman et al., 2012). Hence, instead of uniformly encouraging full disclosure, it may be preferable for clinicians (and friends and activists) to encourage SM individuals to carefully connect to their values and decide the best course of action given their unique context (Green, 2000; Legate et al., 2011).

Considerations Around Coming Out for Gender Minorities

For GM individuals, coming out to family and friends can be quite different, for a variety of reasons. Gender is omnipresent and shapes people's basic processing of information, including the characteristics they infer in others' actions as soon as gendered pronouns are assigned (Prewitt-Freilino, Caswell, & Laakso, 2012; Stern & Karraker, 1989). Because gender is so pervasive, making a change in labels or pronouns may represent a huge conceptual shift and role change for everyone involved.

In the same vein, these shifts can be particularly difficult for family members, who may bring a fused understanding of their loved one's gender to any interaction (MacNish & Gold-Peifer, 2014; Norwood, 2012). Family members may find it especially challenging to overcome their instincts and previous understandings of gender simply due to the fact that cis-normative and heteronormative family discourse is extremely gendered (e.g., mother, father, daughter, son, and so on). Additional complexity can arise when family members have chosen the name that the GM person no longer aligns or identifies with (Whitley, 2013). Loss or mourning may be rooted in both a shared experience of the past and questions about possible futures (Emerson, 1996). This speaks to one possible difference between coming out as GM versus SM (though the two aren't mutually exclusive): while both types of coming out entail a loss of an imagined future (e.g., parents imagining their son's future wife), coming out as GM may also entail a loss of past experiences (e.g., "My joy in raising my little girl is gone").

GM individuals belong to a variety of communities. Some of these communities may identify them with their true and lived gender, while others, such as family members, friends, teachers, or colleagues, may misgender them by using names and pronouns given at birth. This can be an incredibly harmful and stressful experience (Chang & Chung, 2015; Galupo, Henise, & Davis, 2014; Wentling, 2015). In fact, a disproportionate percentage of homeless and transient populations consist of GM young people who have been rejected by their families, resulting in a "chosen family"—a network of nonbiological relatives and friends who provide the kind of closeness and support typically implied by heteronormative concepts of family, which are inaccessible to many GSM individuals (e.g., Choi, Wilson, Shelton, & Gates, 2015; Garofalo, Deleon, Osmer, Doll, & Harper, 2006).

Furthermore, coming out, even to oneself, may result in rejection by or departure from formerly supportive identity-based communities, without a clear replacement. For example, a trans man who formerly identified as a lesbian and found community with queer women may no longer be welcome in that community, but he may not feel safe or identify with the cisgender male community either. This highlights the intersectionality of cultural identities, which can be a central factor in decisions about coming out to family. Lastly, a topic that merits considerable attention and discussion is the way in which difficulties around family of origin and coming out intersect with cultural understandings of sexuality and gender.

The Act of Unknowing

"Knowing" and answers are, more often than not, at the forefront of clinical competence, yet knowledge can be a double-edged sword. The second author, Danny Ryu, has grappled with the dialectic between knowing and not-knowing (or, more actively, unknowing) and has written this section based on that experience:

I began my training as a student therapist in a sexual and gender identities clinic wanting to *know*: I wanted to know how to build an alliance, how to foster an environment that facilitates both safety and growth, and so on. I wanted answers.

You probably want answers too. Perhaps you want to know how you can use mindfulness with GSM clients, how not to offend your clients, and so on. As competent clinicians, it's our responsibility to "know" as much as possible, yet along with that responsibility, we often carry the false presumption that if we just know enough, we will master whatever form of competence we tackle. But what if you don't know, or at least don't feel like you know? Lappalainen and colleagues (2007) found that trainees in acceptance and commitment therapy (ACT), in comparison to trainees in cognitive behavioral therapy (CBT), saw better symptom improvement in their clients even though they initially felt less knowledgeable about ACT and more fearful throughout in comparison to the CBT trainees.

This study tells us that feelings of not knowing and discomfort about being unsure are not, in themselves, indicators of incompetence. Taking this a step further, I propose that the not-knowing itself, as well as an active "unknowing," can be among the most valuable and powerful clinical tools, particularly when working with GSM clients. GSM people are constantly confronted, at times violently, by others' "need" to know—a need that can be grounded in limiting and often inaccurate concepts of what GSM people should or should not be, as well as how they should or should not look. Many GSM people are all too familiar with these attitudes on the part of friends, family members, coworkers, and even strangers: the need to know ("Are you a boy or a girl?"), claims of being knowledgeable (e.g., holding proscriptive definitions of "male" and "female"), and sometimes even an asserted right to know (e.g., a claimed right to ask about GM people's genitalia and bodies). Most GSM individuals, including GSM clients, live in a world in which they are frequently required to declare their identities, and at times those identities are declared for them. A few examples of being forced to declare your gender identity or have that identity declared for you include bathrooms marked "men" and "women," binary gendered sections in clothing stores, airport security machines that differentiate between "male" or "female" body scans, and the ever-present reflexive use of "ma'am" and "sir."

Defusing from Knowing

Consider what "knowledge" you currently hold about GSM communities. I invite you to loosen your grip on this "knowing" and, in doing so, to defuse yourself from the ideas you have about how gender should be expressed or defined, what the coming out process should look like, and your concepts of how you should be as a clinician utilizing ACT and mindfulness with GSM clients. In line with the ACT practice of defusion, I encourage you to experience yourself as the context in which your knowing exists and to observe it flexibly, allowing for fluidity, change, and not-knowing. With this loosened grip, you can then allow your clients to guide you through their identity and unique journey, with the understanding that they may not know where they're going, that they may not have a singular destination, and that every step along the way is as real and valid as the next.

You may wonder how you can harness your not-knowing and unknowing as powerful tools in your clinical work with GSM clients. First, as suggested by Hendricks and Testa (2012), as well as the American Psychological Association's guidelines (2015) for psychological practice with transgender and gender-nonconforming people, I encourage you to venture outside of any gender-normative paradigms that may influence you. Further, I advocate fostering an acceptance that you cannot know how clients see themselves or what language they may use around their identity (e.g., labels, pronouns, and definitions) without hearing it from them firsthand and reflecting back what you hear.

Second, being unsure is not only normal, but essential. Consider seeing this as an opportunity to "come out" as not-knowing, while also expressing a vested interest in understanding clients' identities (or not-knowing alongside them). This may offer them the space to invite you into their experiences, identities, and journeys. By accepting your not-knowing, you can free yourself of the burden of needing to already know. This may empower you to simply and compassionately ask what pronouns or labels a client uses instead of guessing or assuming based on your read of the client's gender expression.

In that sense, just as we cannot hold clients to preconceived concepts of gender or who we think they should be, neither can we hold them to who they said they were ten minutes ago. As we loosen our grip on their identity, we allow ourselves to be alongside them as they experience themselves exactly as they are in the here and now. In the ACT chessboard metaphor (Hayes, Strosahl, & Wilson, 2012), any attempt to rearrange or get rid of the infinite black and white pieces on the chessboard of our experience will prove to be futile. So even as a therapist, aspire to experience yourself as the chessboard. In doing so, you can be in intimate contact with the chess pieces, including those that are your understanding of clients' identities, without getting fixated on the arrangement of the pieces or the outcome of the game.

Embracing Not-Knowing

As therapists, our prescriptive frames and understood truths, through no fault of our own, can become fused to us and blind us to the richness available if we engage in unknowing and open ourselves to GSM clients' unique lived experiences and intersections of identities. For GSM clients, inhabiting a space in which not-knowing is a welcomed guest and unknowing is a practiced skill could, in and of itself, be a transformative, novel, and therapeutic relational experience.

In summary, through unknowing, embracing not-knowing, and "coming out" of our fixed understandings, we are practicing ACT, bringing awareness to our self-imposed twelve-by-twelve foot limits and allowing ourselves to venture beyond. By defusing from our conceptualized selves as competent clinicians, we embody a compassionate context, rather than creating a judgmental and limiting context. As Wilson and DuFrene (2010) suggest in their exercise "Sitting Inside Significant Questions," not-knowing can be a welcomed guest, a friend, a strength, and a tool, allowing us to invite ambiguity in for tea, rather than locking it out.

I encourage you to show yourself the same compassion and patience that you freely extend to clients in their not-knowing, to be humble, and to compassionately and gently consider "coming out" (at least to yourself) as not-knowing. (Visit http://www.newharbinger. com/34282 for a downloadable exercise, "Inner Voices," that you may find useful for facilitating clients in exploring different aspects of their identity.)

FAP Case Conceptualization of Coming Out

Returning to clients' experiences of coming out as GSM individuals, as we've established, this process is highly varied and often includes negative reactions such as ostracism and both overt and subtle forms of discrimination. Therefore, utilizing a therapeutic approach that's flexible and compassionate is of the utmost importance. Functional analytic psychotherapy (FAP; Kohlenberg & Tsai, 1991) postulates that therapeutic interactions are most effective when they involve awareness, courage, and therapeutic love on the part of both therapist and client. Functional contextual language helps us clearly identify what we need to do and why, as depicted in figure 3.1.

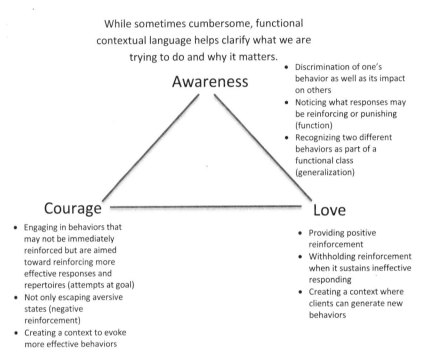

Figure 3.1. The FAP triangle of awareness, courage, and therapeutic love (Tsai & Kohlenberg, 2015)

If there is a breakdown in one or more of these processes, the therapist runs the risk of invalidating or shaming the client, and potentially reinforcing maladaptive relating or punishing improved relating by the client. Because many GSM clients will have a strong history of being punished for authentically expressing their gender or sexual identity, it is of paramount importance that therapists reinforce these clients in a genuine, authentic way that's tailored to each client. Consider Kate, a bisexual client who has previously outwardly identified as gay within GSM settings and claimed a heterosexual identity in opposite-sex intimate relationships or when spending time with straight people. In the following in-session statement, she begins to express herself more authentically. We offer several different examples of responses to her statement, incorporating varying degrees of awareness, courage, and love. (Technically speaking, FAP-consistent responses must simultaneously incorporate awareness, courage and love.)

Kate: I don't think you really understand how difficult it is for me to have to live what feels like a double life.

Therapist: You have the same fears with me as you have with everyone else. You don't think anyone will understand or accept you. [Awareness and courage.]

Therapist: It must be really difficult for you when I trigger those feelings. [Awareness and love.]

Therapist: I probably don't know exactly what it feels like to be you, Kate. But I desperately want to know. I love it when you can be this honest with me because this helps me know what's really going on for you, and I feel far more connected than when it seems like there's something you're holding back from me. Would you be open to being more honest, just like you were here with me, with other people in your life? I know if you can do it here, you could do it out there too. [Awareness, courage, and love.]

Kate desperately strives for a sense of belonging and fears rejection. So whenever she says anything in session that's true for her yet might not be pleasant for the therapist to hear, then the aim of the therapist is to reinforce Kate's authentic expression of herself and look at how Kate can bring more of this to other relationships.

Adapted ACT Exercises for Coming Out

Acceptance and commitment therapy focuses on connecting more fully with the present moment and what matters most and then moving toward a values-based life. ACT offers mindfulness and acceptance skills for what lies outside of our personal control and suggests engaging in values-guided committed action for what is within our personal control. The first author, Aisling, has adapted or created a number of ACT exercises to assist GSM clients in the process of coming out. Supplemental materials and transcripts for all of these exercises (other than the matrix approach) are available for download at http://www.newharbinger.com/34282.

Using the ACT Matrix to Identify Function

The ACT matrix (Polk & Schoendorff, 2014) can be a very powerful tool to use with GSM clients who are considering coming out to significant people or in significant contexts in their lives. The matrix can be very helpful in assessing whether the aim of coming out is to move toward a value, such as authenticity or advocacy, under appetitive control, or whether the motivation is under aversive control, such as wanting to get away from an unwanted internal experience, such as shame, or external experience, such as pressure from a partner or the GSM community. (For more details on how to use the matrix with GSM clients, see chapter 2.)

Yes Versus No

Tara Brach is well-known for her writings on radical acceptance (2003). As helpful as this approach is, in our experience this kind of acceptance can be a hard pill for many clients to swallow. They often wonder why they would possibly want to open up to all of their pain and suffering, both internal and external. This exercise helps clients experience what it feels like to deliberately greet their unwanted experiences in relation to coming out in two ways: first with the words and energy of "no," and then with the words and energy of "yes." For most clients, the first approach, a "no" reaction, is extremely time-consuming and draining. When you turn to the second part of the exercise, invite clients to notice how their experience changes when they respond to unwanted content with "yes." In this part of the exercise, both clinician and client need to be on the lookout for what we call "fake acceptance," by which we mean saying words associated with "yes" but carrying the energy of "no." Be sure to clarify that acceptance doesn't mean clients must like, love, or want difficult experiences; it just means being open to those experiences exactly as they are, without making deliberate attempts to minimize or change them. (For a downloadable audio recording of this exercise and a transcript, visit http://www.newharbinger.com/34282.)

Self-Compassionate Perspective Taking

It can be useful for clients to reconnect to a moment when they expressed their gender or sexual identity and were rejected, and then bring self-compassion to that moment retrospectively. Invite them to begin by going back into that experience and feeling it fully. Then ask them to take a step back, into the observer perspective, by imagining looking into their own eyes in this past moment of rejection. Once they've entered this perspective, ask them to identify the "reality gap": the discrepancy between what they wanted and what they got in that moment. It can be healing for them to retrospectively extend compassion toward themselves in a way that they couldn't or didn't at that time. To conclude, help clients explore how they can continue to bring this kindness and compassion into their daily life. (For a downloadable audio recording of this exercise and a transcript, visit http://www.newharbinger.com/34282.)

Inside Versus Outside Control

Much pain and suffering arises when people put the bulk of their time and effort into trying to control the uncontrollable. Because the process of coming out often involves other people and their reactions, which are largely outside of clients' control, it can be immensely helpful to provide clients with a visual representation of this distinction. (For full guidance on this approach and a client worksheet, visit http://www.newharbinger.com/34282 and download the related materials.)

To Come Out or Not to Come Out...

This exercise (inspired by Villatte, Villatte, & Hayes, 2015) makes use of ACT's underpinnings—relational frame theory (RFT; see chapter 1)—to help clients be more open to their experience without struggling with it. Specifically, it employs comparative relations, with clients imagining the same scenario before and after coming out. The following script offers a brief example of how you might conduct it. (Visit http://www.newharbinger.com/34282 to download an extended audio recording of the exercise.)

> *It might be worth noticing how you respond when you think of the two alternatives. Take a moment to imagine walking into a family gathering as your life stands now, when you haven't yet come out to your family. Take some time to picture yourself walking into the event and all the faces that you'll see, and to imagine the thoughts you'll be having... Slow this down and gently notice how it feels— your emotions, the physical sensations in your body, your thoughts, and so on.*
>
> *Now let's do the same thing with the same family event, but imagine that you've come out. Picture yourself arriving at that event... And once again open yourself up to whatever you feel. Notice the physical sensations you have...the emotions you experience...the thoughts that flow through your mind. Slow it down... What do you notice?*

No Mud, No Lotus

At some point in their lives, most, if not all, GSM individuals experience adverse reactions, both internally and externally, when they openly express their gender or sexual identity. These adverse reactions, while not desired, can offer an effective inroad to accessing values. It can be incredibly powerful for you, the clinician, to thoughtfully and empathetically disclose a similarly difficult personal experience and to share what you learned from this experience. (The experience need not be related to gender or sexual orientation.)

After sharing, you can help clients explore how their own difficult experience connects with their values, doing so either through a guided mindfulness exercise or through an open, honest dialogue incorporating FAP's principles of awareness, courage, and therapeutic love. (You'll find a transcript for the mindfulness exercise, a sample dialogue, and an additional self-reflective practice with the downloadable accessories to this book, which are available at http://www.newharbinger.com/34282.)

When conducting this exercise, it's important to do so in a way that doesn't invalidate the client's experience. So, we strongly recommend that you engage in the downloadable self-reflective practice prior to doing this exercise with clients.

Conclusion

Both the definition and the process of coming out vary widely among GSM individuals. Therefore, it is of paramount importance to treat clients as experts in their own experience in this regard, and to avoid perpetuating the limiting, proscriptive labels and categorizations that GSM people face daily. Every person's process is unique, and all people are shaped by their distinct learning history and lived experience. It is, of course, important that clinicians be informed about recent research findings and newly developed clinical tools. However, the most important clinical tool we can offer GSM clients is a compassionate space in which they are fully accepted, exactly as they are. This kind of solid therapeutic relationship provides an optimal foundation for self-acceptance and being able to live life in a way that aligns with their core values—which may or may not involve disclosing their gender or sexual identity.

References

American Psychological Association. (2015). *Guidelines for psychological practice with transgender and gender nonconforming people.* Retrieved December 14, 2015, from http://www.apa.org/practice/guidelines/transgender.pdf.

Baiocco, R., Fontanesi, L., Santamaria, F., Ioverno, S., Baumgartner, E., & Laghi, F. (2014). Coming out during adolescence: Perceived parents' reactions and internalized sexual stigma. *Journal of Health Psychology*, epub ahead of print.

Baiocco, R., Fontanesi, L., Santamaria, F., Ioverno, S., Marasco, B., Baumgartner, E., et al. (2014). Negative Parental Responses to "coming out" and Family Functioning in a Sample of Lesbian and Gay Young Adults. *Journal of Child and Family Studies, 24*, 1490–1500.

Beeler, J., & DiProva, V. (1999). Family adjustment following disclosure of homosexuality by a member: Themes discerned in narrative accounts. *Journal of Marital and Family Therapy, 25*, 443–459.

Brach, T. (2003). *Radical acceptance: Embracing your life with the heart of a Buddha.* New York: Bantam Books.

Brach, T. (2012, May 1). Accepting absolutely everything [Blog post]. Retrieved December 14, 2015, from http://blog.tarabrach.com/2012/05/accepting-absolutely-everything.html.

Bryant, A. S., & Demian, N. (1994). Relationship characteristics of American gay and lesbian couples: Findings from a national survey. *Journal of Gay and Lesbian Social Services, 1*, 101–117.

Cambridge Dictionaries Online. (2015). Come out. [Def C2]. Retrieved December 14, 2015, from http://dictionary.cambridge.org/dictionary/english/come-out.

Chang, T. K., & Chung, Y. B. (2015). Transgender microaggressions: Complexity of heterogeneity of transgender identities. *Journal of LGBT Issues in Counseling, 9*, 217–234.

Choi, S. K., Wilson, B. D., Shelton, J., & Gates, G. J. (2015). *Serving our youth 2015: The needs and experiences of lesbian, gay, bisexual, transgender, and questioning youth experiencing homelessness.* Los Angeles: Williams Institute with True Colors Fund.

D'Augelli, A. R., Grossman, A. H., & Starks, M. T. (2005). Parents' awareness of lesbian, gay, and bisexual youths' sexual orientation. *Journal of Marriage and Family, 67*, 474–482.

Emerson, S. (1996). Stages of adjustment in family members of transgender individuals. *Journal of Family Psychotherapy, 7*, 1–12.

Galupo, M. P., Henise, S. B., & Davis, K. S. (2014). Transgender microaggressions in the context of friendship: Patterns of experience across friends' sexual orientation and gender identity. *Psychology of Sexual Orientation and Gender Diversity, 1*, 461–470.

Garofalo, R., Deleon, J., Osmer, E., Doll, M., & Harper, G. W. (2006). Overlooked, misunderstood, and at-risk: Exploring the lives and HIV risk of ethnic minority male-to-female transgender youth. *Journal of Adolescent Health, 38*, 230–236.

Green, R. J. (2000). "Lesbians, gay men, and their parents": A critique of LaSala and the prevailing clinical "wisdom." *Family Process, 39*, 257–266.

Green, R. J., & Mitchell, V. (2002). Gay and lesbian couples in therapy: Homophobia, relational ambiguity, and social support. In A. S. Gurman & N. S. Jacobson (Eds.), *Clinical handbook of couple therapy*. New York: Guilford.

Hayes, S. C., Strosahl, K. D., & Wilson, K. G. (2012). *Acceptance and commitment therapy: The process and practice of mindful change*, 2nd edition. New York: Guilford.

Hendricks, M. L., & Testa, R. J. (2012). A conceptual framework for clinical work with transgender and gender nonconforming clients: An adaptation of the minority stress model. *Professional Psychology: Research and Practice, 43*, 460–467.

Herdt, G., & Beeler, J. (1998). Older gay men and lesbians in families. In C. Patterson & A. R. D'Augelli (Eds.), *Lesbian, gay, and bisexual identities in families: Psychological perspectives*. New York: Oxford University Press.

Kaiser Foundation. (2001). *Inside-out: Report on the experiences of lesbians, gays, and bisexuals in America and the public's view on issues and policies related to sexual orientation*. Menlo Park, CA: Kaiser Foundation.

Kohlenberg, R. J., & Tsai, M. (1991). *Functional analytic psychotherapy: A guide for creating intense and curative therapeutic relationships*. New York: Plenum.

Laird, J. (1993). Lesbian and gay families. In F. Walsh (Ed.), *Normal family processes*, 2nd edition. New York: Guilford Press.

Laird, J. (1998). Invisible ties: Lesbians and their families of origin. In C. J. Patterson & A. R. D'Augelli (Eds.), *Lesbian, gay, and bisexual identities in families: Psychological perspectives*. New York: Oxford University Press.

Lappalainen, R., Lehtonen, T., Skarp, E., Taubert, E., Ojanen, M., & Hayes, S. C. (2007). The impact of CBT and ACT models using psychology trainee therapists: A preliminary controlled effectiveness trial. *Behavior Modification, 31*, 488–511.

Legate, N., Ryan, R., & Weinstein, N. (2011). Is coming out always a "good thing"? Exploring the relations of autonomy support, outness, and wellness for lesbian, gay, and bisexual individuals. *Social Psychological and Personality Science, 3*, 145–152.

MacNish, M., & Gold-Peifer, M. (2014). Families in transition: Supporting families of transgender youth. In T. Nelson & H. Winawer (Eds.), *Critical Topics in Family Therapy*. New York: Springer.

Norwood, K. (2012). Transitioning meanings? Family members' communicative struggles surrounding transgender identity. *Journal of Family Communication, 12*, 75–92.

Polk, K. L., & Schoendorff, B. (Eds.). (2014). *The ACT matrix: A new approach to building psychological flexibility across settings and populations*. Oakland, CA: New Harbinger Publications.

Prewitt-Freilino, J. L., Caswell, T. A., & Laakso, E. K. (2012). The gendering of language: A comparison of gender equality in countries with gendered, natural gender, and genderless languages. *Sex Roles, 66*, 268–281.

Rothman, E. F., Sullivan, M., Keyes, S., & Boehmer, U. (2012). Parents' supportive reactions to sexual orientation disclosure associated with better health: Results from a population-based survey of LGB adults in Massachusetts. *Journal of Homosexuality, 59*, 186–200.

Savin-Williams, R. C. (2001). *Mom, Dad, I'm gay: How families negotiate coming out.* Washington, DC: American Psychological Association.

Stern, M., & Karraker, K. H. (1989). Sex stereotyping of infants: A review of gender labeling studies. *Sex Roles, 20*, 501–522.

Tsai, M., & Kohlenberg., R. J. (2015). Functional analytic psychotherapy (FAP): Deepening your clinical skills of awareness, courage, therapeutic love, and behavioral interpretation. [PowerPoint slides]. Retrieved through personal communication.

Villatte, M., Villatte, J., & Hayes, S. C. (2015). *Mastering the clinical conversation: Language as intervention.* New York: Guilford.

Wentling, T. (2015). Trans* disruptions: Pedagogical practices and pronoun recognition. *Transgender Studies Quarterly, 2*, 469–476.

Whitley, C. T. (2013). Trans-kin undoing and redoing gender: Negotiating relational identity among friends and family of transgender persons. *Sociological Perspectives, 56*, 597–621.

Wilson, K., & DuFrene, T. (2010). *Things might go terribly, horribly wrong: A guide to life liberated from anxiety.* Oakland, CA: New Harbinger Publications.

CHAPTER 4

Compassion-Focused Therapy in the Treatment of Shame-Based Difficulties in Gender and Sexual Minorities

Nicola Petrocchi, *John Cabot University, Rome*;
Marcela Matos and Sérgio Carvalho,
University of Coimbra; and
Roberto Baiocco, *Sapienza, University of Rome*

And as long as you are in any way ashamed before yourself, you do not yet belong with us.

—Friedrich Nietzsche

S hame is a particularly intense and often incapacitating emotion involving feelings of inferiority, social unattractiveness, defectiveness, powerlessness, and self-consciousness, along with urges to escape, hide, or conceal one's deficiencies (Tracy, Robins, & Tangney, 2007). It has been recognized as a critical force in human psychosocial functioning and development, with a central impact on sense of self, social relationships, and behavior (Gilbert, 1998). Highlighting the interpersonal facet of this emotion, Jordan (2004) defined shame as "a sense of unworthiness to be in connection, an absence of hope that empathic response will be forthcoming from another person" (p. 122). Although shame is somewhat ubiquitous, gender and sexual minorities (GSM) are particularly afflicted by high levels of shame and shame-related issues (McDermott, Roen, & Scourfield, 2008).

According to the minority stress model (Meyer, 2003), GSM populations face unique experiences, such as stigma and discrimination, related to their GSM identity. This model suggests that in addition to distal chronic stressors, such as discrimination, there are also proximal chronic stressors, which relate to the internalization of sexual prejudice (e.g., internalized homophobia), anticipation of distal stressful events (e.g., rejection sensitivity), and concealment of one's sexual identity. All of these factors are strongly related to shame (Allen & Oleson, 1999) and have been found to perniciously affect the mental and physical health of GSM individuals (Meyer, 2003).

Research has consistently shown that shame leads to poor mental health, especially among GSM populations (Bybee, Sullivan, Zielonka, & Moes, 2009). Furthermore, recent evidence shows that early shame experiences can function as traumatic memories, eliciting intrusions, hyperarousal symptoms, and avoidance, and become central to people's self-identity and life story. Traumatic shame memories have also been found to increase current feelings of shame and vulnerability to psychopathological symptoms, primarily depression (Matos & Pinto-Gouveia, 2010).

Shame is also detrimental to the physical health of gay individuals. In a study examining the incidence of infectious and neoplastic diseases among 222 gay men, those who concealed the expression of their sexual identity (mostly due to shame; Meyer, 2003) experienced a significantly higher incidence of cancer and several infectious diseases over a five-year follow-up period (Cole, Kemeny, Taylor, & Visscher, 1996). Similarly, HIV-positive gay men who blame themselves for negative events (a characteristic highly linked to shame; Petrocchi, Ottaviani, & Couyoumdjian, 2014) showed more rapid damage to the immune system (indicated by declining CD4 levels) than those who didn't manifest this attributional style (Segerstrom, Taylor, Kemeny, Reed, & Visscher, 1996).

Shame has also negative relational effects, for example, causing people to have difficulty experiencing mutual and authentic connections. When GSM individuals feel shameful, they may conceal parts of themselves from others, including romantic partners, out of fear of rejection or ridicule. This often leads to lack of mutuality in relationships and exacerbates disconnection (Hartling, Rosen, Walker, & Jordan, 2004), withdrawal, or avoidance of people and communities, generating loneliness. In fact, shame is negatively related to perceived social support and commitment in relationships (Greene & Britton, 2015).

However, even when GSM individuals decide to stop concealing their identity, the stressors associated with the process of coming out can have a deleterious impact on their physical and psychological health. One common form these stressors take is family rejection, which may entail displays of anger, a blaming attitude, or even disgust, with consequences ranging from depression, developing a negative GSM identity, and substance abuse to, in extreme cases, suicide (Baiocco, Fontanesi, et al., 2014). This was confirmed by a recent investigation on a large sample of Italian and Spanish young adults, which found that lesbian, gay, and bisexual people experience significantly higher levels of suicidal ideation than heterosexuals—about twice as much (Baiocco, Ioverno, Longiro, Baumgartner, & Laghi, 2014). Sexual orientation was the strongest predictor, after depression, of suicidal ideation. Moreover, Feinstein, Goldfried, and Davila (2012) found that internalized homonegativity mediates the relationship between victimization and risk for suicidal ideation.

On the other hand, a supportive and positive family environment is associated with positive mental health outcomes for young adults, including low levels of internalized sexual stigma, depression, and suicidal idealization and high levels of social support and self-esteem (Ryan, Russell, Huebner, Diaz, & Sanchez, 2010). Early positive affiliative interactions and memories of experiencing safeness, warmth, and nurture during childhood are associated with well-being and health and a heightened capacity for self-acceptance and self-nurturing, and ultimately, these early experiences protect against psychopathology, including depression (Cacioppo, Berston, Sheridan, & McClintock, 2000).

Recently, processes that protect against shame and shame memories, such as self-compassion and psychological flexibility, have been explored in relation to sexual orientation. Self-compassion entails being kind and understanding, rather than critical, toward oneself in situations involving pain and failure, and recognizing such experiences as part of the human condition. It also involves maintaining a mindful and accepting awareness of painful thoughts and feelings (Neff, 2003). Psychological flexibility refers to a willingness to contact the present moment fully and without defense, which also entails compassionate acceptance of one's experiences (Hayes, Pistorello, & Levin, 2012). In particular, self-compassion has proven highly beneficial in regard to several indicators of mental and physical well-being, such as psychopathology, positive affect, life satisfaction, happiness, resilience, emotion regulation, and adaptive coping (see Barnard & Curry, 2011, for a review).

In a recent study comparing heterosexual and gay men, Matos, Carvalho, Cunha, Galhardo, and Sepodes (2015) found that those who identified as gay reported that their shame memories were more central to their self-identity and life story; they also had higher levels of internal shame and depressive symptoms. In addition, they had fewer memories of experiencing warmth and safeness within their family during childhood and reported lower levels of self-compassion and psychological flexibility. And although both shame memories and affiliative memories were associated with internal shame, depressive symptoms, self-compassion, and psychological flexibility in both groups, the magnitude of correlations was stronger in the gay sample. For these men, shame and a relative paucity of affiliative memories were strongly associated with internal shame and depressive symptoms and negatively correlated with self-compassion and psychological flexibility. Importantly, in the gay men both self-compassion and psychological flexibility mediated the impact of shame memories and affiliative memories on internal shame and depressive symptoms.

The role of self-compassion in fostering well-being for GSM populations has been further confirmed by recent research that identified self-compassion as a significant predictor of life satisfaction in gay men while controlling for age, income, and openness about sexual orientation (Jennings & Philip Tan, 2014). Recently developed psychotherapeutic approaches, such as compassion-focused therapy (CFT; Gilbert, 2010), are specifically designed to help people develop and work with experiences of inner warmth, safeness, and soothing via compassion and self-compassion. CFT, and especially compassionate mind training, which involves specific activities designed to develop compassionate attributes and skills, could therefore represent a useful intervention for GSM shame-based difficulties.

CFT Conceptualization of Shame-Related Issues and Implications for Treatment

Compassion-focused therapy and compassionate mind training arose from clinical observations of people with high levels of shame and self-criticism, who usually have great difficulty being kind to themselves, feeling self-warmth, or being self-compassionate when they experience setbacks and suffering. Problems of shame and self-criticism are often rooted in a history of abuse, bullying, high expressed emotions in the family, invalidation, or lack of affection (Schore, 1998). Individuals who were subjected to these kinds of early experiences can become highly sensitive to threats of rejection or criticism and may quickly become self-blaming and self-attacking as a way to correct themselves, retain a sense of control, and avoid future adverse events, such as humiliation and rejection (Gilbert, 2010). It has also been suggested that people who fear rejection or criticism by others may engage in perfectionistic striving or seek high rank in an effort to put themselves beyond rebuke, to maintain social control, and to defend against fears of inferiority (Gilbert, 1998). Due to their state of insecure dominance, they don't experience failures with a sense of acceptance and compassion; rather, they experience them as disasters that threaten them with feelings of powerlessness, inferiority, and vulnerability at deep, implicit levels. Thus, people who are prone to self-criticism and feelings of shame experience both their external and internal worlds as hostile, and this is often the case for lesbian and gay individuals with high levels of internalized homonegativity (Feinstein et al., 2012).

Self-devaluation, inner hostility, and self-invalidation are all key processes by which pathological suffering arises and normal recovery processes are hindered. In fact, the CFT perspective suggests that self-evaluating systems, including self-criticism and self-compassion, operate through brain processes similar to those that are stimulated when other people are critical or compassionate, generating the same emotional and physiological responses (Longe et al., 2010). This mechanism might explain why self-criticism and inner shame play a major role in many forms of psychological difficulties (Gilbert, 2010). In the case of lesbian and gay individuals with high internalized homonegativity, their self-attacking tendencies exacerbate stress responses already triggered by an ostracizing external world, amplifying negative affect and ultimately increasing the chances that they will develop some sort of psychopathology.

Individuals prone to high levels of shame and self-criticism often find it difficult to generate feelings of contentment, safeness, or warmth in their relationships with others and themselves, especially when they face frustrations or suffering. CFT approaches this problem by focusing on the evolved functions that underpin certain types of feelings and styles of social relating (Gilbert, 2010). Research into the neurophysiology of emotion suggests that there are at least three types of emotion regulation system (Depue & Morrone-Strupinsky, 2005): the threat and protection system, the incentive and resource-seeking system, and the soothing, contentment, and safeness system. (For a detailed description of how the three systems are conceptualized and used in CFT see Gilbert, 2010.)

The Threat and Protection System

The function of the threat and protection system is to help us notice threats quickly and provoke emotions such as anxiety, anger, disgust, and shame, which alert us to a need to take action to protect ourselves and motivate us to do so. The behavioral results include fight, flight, and submission, with serotonin playing a role in the synaptic regulation of threat responses (LeDoux, 1998). Excessive activity of this system is considered to be the cause of many aspects of psychopathology (Gilbert, 1998). The CFT formulation explores how early life events can sensitize an individual's threat and protection system, leading to the development of safety strategies, including submissive strategies, such as appeasing, engaging in self-blame and self-criticism, and avoiding interpersonal conflicts. These kinds of strategies increase vulnerability to anxiety and depression (Gilbert, 2010); therefore, CFT clinicians seek to establish whether they are present in order to validate their functions and origins, which can help decrease shame.

This approach facilitates the emergence of self-compassion because it helps clients recognize that their pathologies and symptoms are not their fault and have often arisen in association with safety strategies. From this standpoint, clients can begin to compassionately reflect on the fact that they needed to develop these safety strategies, and validate themselves for doing so. From the CFT perspective, once individuals stop criticizing themselves for their symptoms, they are freer to move toward taking responsibility and learning to cope with those symptoms.

The Incentive and Resource-Seeking System

In humans, the function of the incentive and resource-seeking system is to generate positive, energizing feelings, such as excitement, curiosity, enthusiasm, and pride, that motivate us to seek out resources, such as food, sex, and friendships. This system is connected to our desires, which guide us toward important life goals. The feelings associated with this system are linked to arousal and feeling energized and even hyped-up, and are mediated by the dopaminergic system (Depue & Morrone-Strupinsky, 2005). This system and the threat system can be linked in complex ways. For example, when obstacles to our desires and goals become a threat, thwarting the incentive and resource-seeking system, the threat system becomes active, giving rise to feelings of anxiety, frustration, and anger. Moreover, some people pursue status, material possessions, and achievement in order to feel safe and avoid feelings of rejection, subordination, or inferiority. They may want to prove themselves and constantly achieve in order to feel accepted and okay. Status-seeking, competitiveness, and attempting to avoid rejection are all linked to the incentive system (Gilbert, 2010).

The Soothing, Contentment, and Safeness System

In Buddhist psychology, positive feelings linked to satisfying desires (such as those elicited when the incentive seeking system is activated) give us pleasure but not happiness because they're dependent on acquiring rewards, resources, and achievements. In contrast, happiness comes from cultivating a calm, nonstriving, mindful, and compassionate orientation. Research into the neurophysiology of emotion seems to confirm this conceptualization. When animals don't have to be attentive to threats and dangers or deal with them, and when they have sufficient resources, they can enter states of quiescence and contentment (Depue & Morrone-Strupinsky, 2005). The positive emotions of the soothing system, in contrast to those of the incentive system, are associated with a sense of peacefulness, well-being, and soothing—in other words, a state of not seeking.

The soothing system, which is synaptically mediated by endorphins and oxytocin, isn't just the absence of threat or low activity in the threat system. It is a separate system that developed alongside the evolution of attachment behavior and is linked to feelings of social safeness, such as being loved and wanted by others (Carter, 1998). Activation of this system is triggered by caring parental behaviors, especially physical proximity, and has a soothing effect on infants' physiology. For adults, feelings connected to affiliation, warmth, and affection continue to exert soothing effects through their physiological profile (increased activity of the vagus nerve and corresponding higher heart rate variability; Porges, 2007), which facilitates down-regulation of the threat system, thereby reducing anger, anxiety, and sadness. Activation of the soothing system can also shut down excessive activity of the incentive system (seeking, doing, and achieving).

Balancing the Three Emotion Regulation Systems

These three systems can become unbalanced, and one of the primary goals of CFT is rebalancing them. People with high levels of shame and self-criticism often have increased activity of the threat system, the incentive system, or both. They find it difficult to feel content or safe within themselves and in their interpersonal relationships. From the viewpoint of CFT, the soothing system is insufficiently accessible to them, perhaps because it was understimulated during early life, or perhaps because it has been chronically deactivated by repetitive trauma experiences, leading to a functional prevalence of the threat system.

Given this developmental, social, and neurophysiological model, it becomes clear why CFT focuses on activation of the soothing system in therapy. This system is particularly sensitive to interpersonal cues of social safeness, acceptance, and being cared for, as manifested in tone of voice, facial expressions, and tactile signals. It is also key in regulating the threat system and the incentive system. Thus, the first role of the CFT therapist is to help clients experience safeness within their therapeutic interactions so they can tolerate and feel safe with whatever is explored in the therapy (Gilbert, 1998). The next step is to assist clients in developing a compassionate relationship with themselves to replace patterns that involve blaming, condemning, and criticizing themselves.

In CFT, therapists clarify that compassion is not pity, nor does it mean being soft or weak. Compassion is "sensitivity to the suffering of self and others, with a deep commitment to try to relieve it" (Dalai Lama, 1995, p. 16). From the CFT perspective, learning to be compassionate requires that people learn how to be open to and tolerate their painful feelings, and that they develop more acceptance of their emotions, desires, and other experiences, especially when they are painful. Therefore, compassion doesn't mean turning away from emotional difficulties and discomfort; rather, it involves bringing courage, honesty, and commitment to learning to cope with difficulties, with the ultimate goal being to heal and alleviate these difficulties. In this way, activating compassionate motivations is a strong mechanism of change because it helps people disengage from self-criticism and shame, which often give rise to negative internal feedback loops that exacerbate and maintain emotional suffering. Thus, one of the main goals of CFT is helping clients recognize when they're shifting into a mind-set dominated by the threat system (e.g., by ruminating, engaging in self-criticism, or attacking the self, whether psychologically or physically). Recognizing that this is happening allows clients to take the next step: deliberately refocusing and activating compassionate motivations toward themselves and others.

Compassion-Focused Practices

In CFT, compassion is understood in terms of specific attributes and skills that can be cultivated and enhanced with practice. Thus, a central tool in CFT is compassionate mind training: a set of compassion-focused exercises designed to stimulate brain systems connected to affiliation and soothing, which physiologically down-regulate the threat system.

Compassion-focused exercises can be orientated in different ways: developing compassion for other people, developing self-compassion, and opening up to receiving compassion from other people. These different "flows" of compassion can be trained using different psycho-therapeutic practices, such as attention refocusing, breathing exercises to downregulate the sympathetic nervous system, empty chair work to enact different parts of the self (for example, the compassionate self), and expressive writing, such as writing a compassionate letter.

A core practice in CFT is referred to as compassionate imagery; this approach encompasses a series of visualizations that help clients generate compassionate feelings for themselves. In this practice, therapists help clients create and explore an image of their ideal of compassion. Clients may, for example, explore what their ideal "compassionate other" might look like in terms of facial expressions, tone of voice, gestures, and so on. Therapists guide clients through the imagery exercises, helping them become aware of the emotions associated with various images. Sometimes clients prefer nonhuman images, such as an animal, a tree, or the ocean. If so, these images should be imagined as sentient, with specific compassionate qualities, such as wisdom, strength, warmth, and nonjudgment. Clients often imagine that their image has been through situations similar to what they have experienced, as opposed to being some higher deity that has never dealt with the conflicts and tragedies of human experience. Thinking about what makes the compassionate image ideal for them is an important part of the exercise. As in a process of guided discovery, clients can think about what they really wish for in terms of feeling compassion from another, such as protection, understanding, to be known fully, strength, or wisdom.

Humans have evolved to seek out care from others (Hrdy, 2009) and our brain systems are particularly sensitive to signals of social safeness and affiliation from others. The thoughts and feelings surrounding the experience of being emotionally represented with love and pleasure in others' minds triggers a sense of safeness and of being valued that is crucial to emotion regulation. Thus, imagining this motivation (having deep concern and wishes for us) arising from a compassionate image and being directed toward us is a crucial component of these exercises. Several studies have shown the efficacy of this imagery intervention in achieving positive psychological outcomes (see, for example, Lincoln, Hohenhaus, & Hartmann, 2013).

Case Example: Held and Soothed by a Transgender Deity

We will now offer a case history describing how CFT's compassionate imagery intervention helped Federico, a twenty-six-year-old gay man seeking therapy for depressive symptoms. He reported a history of severe bullying, which he experienced before moving to Rome to attend university. During his junior high school years, a group of older students repeatedly insulted him and beat him up in front of other students. As a result, he experienced constant and deep feelings of fear and shame at school.

At home, he couldn't vent or turn to family members for support. His parents were the first to show what he termed "silent disgust" for his sexual orientation, which they systematically denied. In fact, the main rule in his home was, "If we don't talk about problems, they don't exist." On the few occasions when Federico tried to discuss his sexuality with his parents, they became silent and depressed, which generated a deep sense of guilt and self-blame within him. As a consequence, he learned how to conceal his tendencies, continuously monitoring his own gestures and tone of voice and attacking himself whenever he felt his self-control strategies weren't sufficient to protect his parents (this type of gender self-policing is a common consequence of stigma and self-stigma in GSM individuals; Herek, Gillis, & Cogan, 2015).

Federico felt that there was something intrinsically wrong with him and that it was the cause of his parents' depression, as well as the constant harassment he endured from other people. Ultimately, he felt that he was the cause of his own unhappiness. The only way he found to cope with these feelings of guilt, shame and unworthiness was trying to be a perfect student in order to give his parents all the satisfaction he couldn't give them in other ways (by being "normal").

In therapy, during the case formulation it became clear that this excessive striving toward success was a safety strategy Federico had developed to protect himself from painful feelings of shame and guilt; in other words, it was linked to the threat protection system. However, as an unintended consequence of this strategy, Federico became increasingly anxious and scared of failing and used self-criticism in an attempt to motivate himself—in his words, to help him "push harder and avoid being swallowed in the black whirlpool of feeling like a lonely piece of crap." He was unable to experience any feelings of self-warmth, self-compassion, or internal reassurance. Importantly, he also couldn't access any memory of reassuring figures who saw and validated his difficulties, or who reminded him that he didn't choose to be gay—that he simply was born this way, and that it was okay. Ultimately, he felt it was his fault if people, including his parents, didn't accept him, and believed that he couldn't complain or feel sad about something he had caused.

When the man he was dating, who suffered from bipolar disorder, left him due to a depressive episode, Federico blamed himself for not having been good enough to prevent his boyfriend's relapse. And in addition to feeling sad about the end of the relationship, he also felt disgusted by his own low mood and sense of abandonment, which were interfering with his productivity at school. Only during his own therapy did Federico become fully aware of the severity of his boyfriend's diagnosis. Cognitive restructuring helped him realize that there was nothing more he could have done to prevent his boyfriend's depressive episode and the end of the relationship. Yet even as Federico came to know that his feelings of sadness and apathy were normal human reactions to his loss, he wasn't able to feel completely comforted by this thought. In fact, he deeply felt that it was neither right nor safe to mourn and that his friends would abandon him. As he said, "People know me as an always happy guy. They wouldn't like my sadness." He feared that, as a result, there wouldn't be anyone to help stop him from spiraling down into depression. This invalidating and self-critical attitude toward his own suffering was clearly exacerbating his depressive mood.

Compassion-focused imagery helped Federico overcome his excessive self-blaming and fear of negative emotions, and also increased his ability to validate and compassionately take care of what he termed his "abandoned and fragile part." After he realized that criticizing himself for feeling sad and apathetic only worsened his depressive state, his therapist guided him in imagining an ideal compassionate image—an entity imbued with completely compassionate qualities. This ideal entity would know everything about Federico's inner life and would completely understand and accept the difficulty and complexity of his situation. Moreover, it would hold a deep and strong commitment to him and a sincere desire to relieve his suffering and help him feel safe, heal, and cope. It would also show great warmth, acceptance, and wisdom, having itself lived similar life experiences, allowing it to deeply know how it feels to live Federico's experience from the inside—not from some sort of separate, divine mind that is out of touch with human struggles.

During the first compassionate visualization, Federico cracked a smile and then revealed that the only way he could conceive of a completely nonjudging, compassionate, and strong entity was to imagine a "weird and colorful" transgender deity. He visualized this image warmly smiling at him, reassuring him that there isn't a right or wrong way to feel and to live, and that even being a man and a woman at the same time, as the deity was, could be seen as "one of the many colors of this inscrutable design that is living in this planet," as Federico put it. He clarified to the therapist that being in front of the image made him feel a little more okay, understood, and protected and said he felt that this compassionate image could be there with him, patiently holding him silently when he needed to vent his pain and cry.

This compassionate imagery approach greatly helped Federico overcome his downward spiral into depression. His therapist invited him to visualize this compassionate deity at least once a day, especially late at night, when Federico was often sad and anxious because he couldn't call anyone for support. Over time, he gradually came to feel that it was okay for him to be sad in bed for a while. At those times, visualizing the deity's warm smile allowed him to stop feeling anxious and self-critical about his sadness and helped him sleep without nightmares and a pervasive sense of being under attack by his own negative emotions. Thanks to this approach, along with other CFT practices, Federico's depressive episode remitted after three months.

Conclusion

Building on evolutionary theory and the neuroscience of affect regulation, CFT proposes that whatever intervention a therapist uses, it should be employed with a clear picture of how self-related processes, such as self-compassion and self-criticism, can ease or exacerbate emotional suffering. This is particularly relevant for the treatment of sexual minorities, among whom internalized homonegativity often takes the form of self-invalidation, shame, and self-criticism, perhaps explaining why GSM individual are at increased risk for poorer mental and physical health outcomes than heterosexuals (Mereish & Poteat, 2015). With its strong focus on decreasing self-attacking attitudes and increasing the ability to self-soothe, CFT may well represent a critical advancement in treating sexual minorities and bolstering their mental and physical health. CFT has already been proved to be effective in the treatment of several psychopathological conditions (for a review see Leaviss & Uttley, 2015). Future clinical investigations are warranted to specifically test the efficacy of CFT in reducing shame-based difficulties among LGBT individuals.

Acknowledgments

The authors acknowledge Professor Paul Gilbert for his precious guidance, valuable suggestions, and continuous encouragement during the preparation of this manuscript. Part of the research presented in this chapter has been supported by the second author (Marcela Matos), postdoctoral grant number SFRH/BPD/84185/2012, sponsored by FCT (Portuguese Foundation for Science and Technology).

References

Allen, D. J., & Oleson, T. (1999). Shame and internalized homophobia in gay men. *Journal of Homosexuality, 37*, 33–43.

Baiocco, R., Fontanesi, L., Santamaria, F., Ioverno, S., Marasco, B., Bamugartner, E., et al. (2014). Negative parental responses to coming out and family functioning in a sample of lesbian and gay young adults. *Journal of Child and Family Studies, 24,* 1490–1500.

Baiocco, R., Ioverno, S., Longiro, A., Baumgartner, E., & Laghi, F. (2014). Suicidal ideation among Italian and Spanish young adults: The role of sexual orientation. *Archives of Suicide Research, 19,* 75–88.

Barnard, L., & Curry, J. (2011). Self-compassion: Conceptualizations, correlates, and interventions. *Review of General Psychology, 15,* 289–303.

Bybee, J. A., Sullivan, E. L., Zielonka, E., & Moes, E. (2009). Are gay men in worse mental health than heterosexual men? The role of age, shame and guilt, and coming-out. *Journal of Adult Development, 16,* 144–154.

Cacioppo, J. T., Berston, G. G., Sheridan, J. F., & McClintock, M. K. (2000). Multilevel integrative analysis of human behavior: Social neuroscience and the complementing nature of social and biological approaches. *Psychological Bulletin, 126,* 829–843.

Carter, C. (1998). Neuroendocrine perspectives on social attachment and love. *Psychoneuroendocrinology, 23,* 779–818.

Cole, S., Kemeny, M., Taylor, S., & Visscher, B. (1996). Elevated physical health risk among gay men who conceal their homosexual identity. *Health Psychology, 15,* 243–251.

Dalai Lama. (1995). *The power of compassion: A collection of lectures by His Holiness the XIV Dalai Lama,* trans. G. T. Jinpa. New York: HarperCollins.

Depue, R., & Morrone-Strupinsky, J. (2005). A neurobehavioral model of affiliative bonding: Implications for conceptualizing a human trait of affiliation. *Behavioral and Brain Sciences, 28,* 313–395.

Feinstein, B., Goldfried, M., & Davila, J. (2012). The relationship between experiences of discrimination and mental health among lesbians and gay men: An examination of internalized homonegativity and rejection sensitivity as potential mechanisms. *Journal of Consulting and Clinical Psychology, 80,* 917–927.

Gilbert, P. (1998). What is shame? Some core issues and controversies. In P. Gilbert & B. Andrews (Eds.), *Shame: Interpersonal behaviour, psychopathology, and culture.* New York: Oxford University Press.

Gilbert, P. (2010). *Compassion focused therapy: Distinctive features.* New York: Routledge.

Greene, D. C., & Britton, P. J. (2015). Predicting relationship commitment in gay men: Contributions of vicarious shame and internalized homophobia to the investment model. *Psychology of Men and Masculinity, 16,* 78–87.

Hartling, L. M., Rosen, W. B., Walker, M., & Jordan, J. V. (2004). Shame and humiliation: From isolation to relational transformation. In J. V. Jordan, M. Walker, & L. M. Hartling (Eds.), *The complexity of connection.* New York: Guilford.

Hayes, S. C., Pistorello, J., & Levin, M. (2012). Acceptance and commitment therapy as a unified model of behavior change. *Counseling Psychologist, 40,* 976–1002.

Herek, G. M., Gillis, J. R., & Cogan, J. C. (2015). Internalized stigma among sexual minority adults: Insights from a social psychological perspective. *Stigma and Health, 56,* 18–34.

Hrdy, S. (2009). *Mothers and others: The evolutionary origins of mutual understanding.* Cambridge, MA: Belknap Press.

Jennings, L., & Philip Tan, P. (2014). Self-compassion and life satisfaction in gay men. *Psychological Reports, 115,* 888–895.

Jordan, J. V. (2004). Shame and humiliation: From isolation to relational transformation. In J. V. Jordan, M. Walker, & L. M. Hartling (Eds.), *The complexity of connection.* New York: Guilford.

Leaviss, J., & Uttley, L. (2015). Psychotherapeutic benefits of compassion-focused therapy: An early systematic review. *Psychological Medicine, 45,* 927–945.

LeDoux, J. (1998). *The emotional brain: The mysterious underpinnings of emotional life.* New York: Touchstone.

Lincoln, T., Hohenhaus, F., & Hartmann, M. (2013). Can paranoid thoughts be reduced by targeting negative emotions and self-esteem? An experimental investigation of a brief compassion-focused intervention. *Cognitive Therapy and Research, 37,* 390–402.

Longe, O., Maratos, F., Gilbert, P., Evans, G., Volker, F., Rockliff, H., et al. (2010). Having a word with yourself: Neural correlates of self-criticism and self-reassurance. *Neuroimage, 49,* 1849–1856.

Matos, M., Carvalho, S., Cunha, M., Galhardo, A., & Sepodes, C. (2015). *Psychological flexibility and self-compassion: An antidote against shame in homosexual men.* Manuscript submitted for publication.

Matos, M., & Pinto-Gouveia, J. (2010). Shame as a traumatic memory. *Clinical Psychology and Psychotherapy, 17,* 299–312.

McDermott, E., Roen, K., & Scourfield, J. (2008). Avoiding shame: Young LGBT people, homophobia, and self-destructive behaviours. *Culture, Health, and Sexuality, 10,* 815–829.

Mereish, E., & Poteat, V. (2015). A relational model of sexual minority mental and physical health: The negative effects of shame on relationships, loneliness, and health. *Journal of Counseling Psychology, 62,* 425–437.

Meyer, I. (2003). Prejudice, social stress, and mental health in lesbian, gay, and bisexual populations: Conceptual issues and research evidence. *Psychological Bulletin, 129,* 674–697.

Neff, K. (2003). The development and validation of a scale to measure self-compassion. *Self and Identity, 2,* 223–250.

Petrocchi, N., Ottaviani, C., & Couyoumdjian, A. (2014). Dimensionality of self-compassion: Translation and construct validation of the self-compassion scale in an Italian sample. *Journal of Mental Health, 23,* 72–77.

Porges, S. W. (2007). The polyvagal perspective. *Biological Psychology, 74,* 116–143.

Ryan, C., Russell, S., Huebner, D., Diaz, R., & Sanchez, J. (2010). Family acceptance in adolescence and the health of LGBT young adults. *Journal of Child and Adolescent Psychiatric Nursing, 23,* 205–213.

Schore, A. N. (1998). Early shame experiences and infant brain development. In P. Gilbert & B. Andrews (Eds.), *Shame: Interpersonal behavior, psychopathology, and culture*. New York: Oxford University Press.

Segerstrom, S. C., Taylor, S. E., Kemeny, M. E., Reed, G. M., & Visscher, B. R. (1996). Causal attributions predict rate of immune decline in HIV-seropositive gay men. *Health Psychology, 15*, 485–493.

Tracy, J. L., Robins, R. W., & Tangney J. P. (Eds.) (2007). *The self-conscious emotions: Theory and research*. New York: Guilford.

CHAPTER 5

Mindfulness and Acceptance for Malignant Shame

Matthew D. Skinta, *Palo Alto University*; and
Paul D'Alton, *University College Dublin*

Whatever is unnamed, undepicted in images, whatever is omitted from biography, censored in collections of letters, whatever is misnamed as something else, made difficult-to-come-by, whatever is buried in the memory by the collapse of meaning under an inadequate or lying language—this will become not merely unspoken, but unspeakable.

—Adrienne Rich

Shame profoundly affects gender and sexual minorities (GSM) and arises from living in a heterocentric, cisgender world in which societal beliefs that GSM individuals are somehow disordered or pathological are still widespread (e.g., Encarnación, 2014). Among GSM populations, shame not only occurs at high rates, but also correlates with greater psychological distress, substance use, and sexual risk behaviors, particularly among bisexuals (Hequembourg & Dearing, 2013). Furthermore, a large body of literature supports an association between the internalization of shaming messages and the negative self-identity challenges experienced by GSM individuals (e.g., Brown, Low, Tai, & Tong, 2015; Page, Lindahl, & Malik, 2013). In this chapter, we will review a behavioral model of emotion and shame grounded in relational frame theory (RFT; Hayes, Barnes-Holmes, & Roche, 2001) and acceptance and commitment therapy (ACT; Hayes, Strosahl, & Wilson, 1999), and illustrate how this model can be utilized via a case example that introduces a novel defusion exercise.

A Behavioral Perspective on Shame and Emotion

From an evolutionary perspective, emotions are a legacy that ensures our survival, allowing us to adapt to changing environments and survive impending threats to our physical well-being (Levenson, 2014). The universality of certain basic human emotions (happiness, sadness, anger, fear, surprise, and disgust) has been supported by cross-cultural research, particularly in the work of Paul Ekman (1973). Findings are more contradictory, however, when the scope is narrowed to the specific, contingent ways in which individuals express emotions (Hess & Thibault, 2009; Mesquita, Barrett, & Smith, 2010). A factor that makes emotions even more complex for verbal, thinking humans is that we don't require external events to experience powerful and challenging emotional experiences. In fact, vividly imagining a threat can cause the same physiological, affective, and cognitive responses as an actual threat (Sapolsky, 2004). Furthermore, the words people use to describe their emotional states may primarily reflect their learning history and interactions with verbal communities, as well as the causes they ascribe to their emotional states (Sabini & Silver, 2005). Ultimately, any behavioral account of an emotion, shame included, requires that we attend to the functional aspects of the emotion within a specific context.

Understanding Shame

Shame is one of the self-conscious emotions; that is, the object of the emotion is the self. In general, contemporary psychological theorists argue that people experience guilt when they have a negative evaluation of their behavior or actions, whereas shame involves a negative evaluation of the self (Barrett, 1995; Tangney, Stuewig, & Mashek, 2007), specifically when there is a threat of isolation or rejection from their social group (e.g., Gilbert, 2010). Shame isn't unique to any diagnostic label and has been linked to depression (Orth, Berking, & Burkhardt, 2006), PTSD (Wilson, Drozdek, & Turkovic, 2006), substance abuse (Dearing, Stuewig, & Tangney, 2005), and suicide (Hastings, Northman, & Tangney, 2000). The specific impact of shame on GSM individuals probably varies by gender or sexual identity, as past research has suggested that specific patterns of substance use or psychiatric disorders are more likely depending on whether individuals are gay, bisexual, lesbian, or transgender (Cochran & Mays, 2009). However, shame may play a significant part in addictive behaviors and substance use disorders across GSM populations (Matthews, Lorah, & Fenton, 2006). Although these behaviors may be used in an attempt to escape or soften difficult feelings, they often become yet another source of shame in the cycle, as does compulsive sexual behavior (Quadland & Shattls, 1987).

The relationship between the embodied experience of an emotion such as shame and people's internal cognitive experience is complex (e.g., Colombetti, 2013). In the early years of the HIV epidemic, it was observed that sexual minority men who concealed their sexuality experienced significantly more rapid progression to AIDS (Cole, Kemeny, Taylor, Visscher, & Fahey, 1996), indicating that shame and self-stigma exert a powerful dampening effect on the immune system. Shame also contributes toward HIV risk behaviors among transgender women (Hughto, Reisner, & Pachankis, 2015).

Perspective Taking and Shame

Research has shown that the human brain responds to social rejection in a manner similar to how it responds to physical pain (Kross, Berman, Mischel, Smith, & Wager, 2011; MacDonald & Leary, 2005). This focus on the self and other, which involves the capacity for perspective taking and sets shame apart from emotions such as anger and joy, emerges later in development, somewhere around three years of age (M. Lewis, 1997). Recent research into perspective taking provides a better vantage point from which we can understand what's happening at this age that allows for a "self" to develop. This has implications for how therapy might most effectively amend those perspectives on the self (for a fuller treatment, see McHugh & Stewart, 2012).

Relational frame theory is a contextual behavioral approach to science in which the usual object of behaviorism—the behavior of an organism—must be considered within a particular context (Martell, Addis, & Jacobson, 2001). At the most basic level, an RFT perspective suggests that we learn how to experience our self as a result of interactions within our verbal communities, gradually developing a consistent perspective with reference to a speaker (ourselves or others). Through continued use and correction, a child learns that "I" refers only to the person speaking, whereas "you" refers to the person the speech is directed at, and, likewise, that "here" refers only to one's current physical location, whereas "there" may be any other physical space, and that "now" indicates this present moment, whereas "then" can apply to any past or future point in time.

These three frames, I-you, here-there, and now-then, are referred to as deictic frames, meaning "shown directly" (Barnes-Holmes et al., 2001). These are the building blocks of perspective taking, which is the learned ability to consider perspectives other than one's lived experience in the moment (I-here-now). Although emotions can serve as important sources of information and guide us, shame inherently involves difficulty in shifting away from one's I-here-now experience. For example, if a gay man feels ashamed about his sexuality now, he's likely to believe that he'll continue to feel this terrible emotion in the future, and to believe that others will also feel ashamed of him.

Conversely, self-compassion inherently involves psychological flexibility. For example, consider if that same man were to bring self-compassion to the process of coming out. Although he may have feelings of shame, along with fears and painful thoughts about how others may respond, a self-compassionate stance would allow him to look at himself through the eyes of his loved ones and imagine that they may deeply value him and hold him with love and care, and that they might feel warmth when thinking of him and wish for him to be happy in life. In this way, and as described more fully below, self-compassion often requires making an emotional connection with the perspective that one's future self (I-there-then) or significant others might feel warmth, love, and kindness about whatever shame or painful thoughts the person is experiencing in the moment.

Communal and Malignant Shame

Research on shame and its impact on gender and sexual minorities has primarily focused on individual experiences and impacts. The impact of shame on GSM communities is an important lens to consider, given the widespread experience of shame among GSM individuals and the degree to which many cultures view sexual or gendered behaviors as moral events. One way we might conceptualize communal shame is that it is the shame of a group-based identity. Communal shame has primarily been considered in regard to national identities associated with past atrocities (e.g., German citizens in the wake of the Holocaust; Liu & Dresler-Hawke, 2006). Regarding GSM populations, research on internalized stigma measures reveals the common perception of a sense that the group one belongs to might be experienced as shameful (e.g., Testa, Habarth, Peta, Balsam, & Bockting, 2015). Communal shaming messages are common both within GSM communities, such as when a young trans client rejects a referral to a peer support group because of her perception that other trans women are likely to be sex workers, as well as from outside these communities, as seen in the history of HIV-prevention campaigns with embedded shaming messages (e.g., Odets, 1995) and current debates about pre-exposure prophylaxis and the argument that mitigating the risk of HIV might only disinhibit sex-focused gay men more (e.g., Elsessor et al., 2015).

Malignant shame carries this concept one step further. A term developed to describe the postcolonial Irish response to communal shame, "malignant shame" refers to shame about feeling shame, leading people to make attempts to reject the affective experience of shame (O'Connor, 1995). In the first author's experience with treating GSM clients in large, urban cities on the US West Coast, shame often first arises in therapy as something clients are embarrassed to have. For these clients, who have typically left dangerous or persecutory locations behind and cast any fundamentalist religious upbringings aside, acknowledging that shame still plays an active role in their experience of daily life is a further source of shame. This effect may be magnified when therapists are also members of a gender or sexual minority community, as there is a risk that they might avoid topics that elicit their own experience of shame (Tangney & Dearing, 2003). This may be particularly likely among GSM therapists who believe they should be comfortable with shame.

ACT for Shame Among GSM Clients

Among behavioral interventions, acceptance and commitment therapy has been most examined for the treatment of shame. ACT focuses on the verbal processes that underlie experiential avoidance and fusion. "Experiential avoidance" refers to avoidant behaviors, both internal and external, that occur in response to unwanted internal stimuli. "Fusion" refers to a person's attachment to or identification with these stimuli. For example, a gay man might frequently have the thought *I'll be rejected if people know how much I crave feeling loved*, and this thought could occur even in the absence of experiences with rejection. Fusion with this thought might lead him to avoid sharing his needs with romantic or sexual partners, reducing the likelihood that his needs will be met. He might also choose not to set sexual boundaries with partners through risk-reduction strategies, opening himself up to the possibility of contracting HIV or other sexually transmitted infections (Wolitski & Fenton, 2011).

ACT promotes psychological flexibility through the cultivation of six key processes:

- **Acceptance** of unwanted emotions, thoughts, and experiences

- **Defusion** from the default mode of assuming every thought is literally true and believable

- **Present-moment awareness**, or a nonjudgmental focus on the here and now

- **Self-as-context**, or perspective taking, as evidenced by flexibility in applying the relational frames of I-you, here-there, and now-then

- **Values** that can be used to guide behaviors

- **Committed action** in the service of those values, in ways that are workable and while being willing to experience whatever discomfort those actions may entail

In the following sections, we will explore one way of conceptualizing how ACT might be applied to working with shame in GSM clients, and then we'll turn to a case example demonstrating what this might look like in session.

Minority Stress and the Psychological Inflexibility Hexaflex

One of the most popular and productive frames for exploring the impact that broad societal devaluation of gender and sexual minorities has upon individuals is Meyer's minority stress theory (Institute of Medicine, 2011; Meyer, 2003). This theory posits that only a comprehensive assessment of proximal to distal sources of stigma can reveal the full weight of societal bias. The components of Meyer's model include self-stigma (e.g., internalized homophobia, internalized transphobia), expectations of rejection, stress due to concealment, and discriminatory or prejudicial actions.

It is fairly straightforward to integrate this model into ACT, which focuses on the challenges posed by psychological inflexibility, wherein life becomes unworkable due to avoidance of emotionally painful thoughts and emotions, a high degree of fusion with rules or beliefs about the world that restrict behavior, and a lack of awareness or infrequent contact with valued behaviors. Indeed, minority stress theory can be plotted out on the classic ACT psychological inflexibility hexaflex (Hayes, & Strosahl, & Wilson, 2012), as depicted in figure 5.1.

Present-moment awareness is inhibited by the intrusion of memories of past discrimination or violence. Self-as-context, or perspective taking, is inhibited by assumptions about others' responses being dangerous. In a pattern often referred to as the "best little boy in the world" syndrome (Pachankis & Hatzenbuehler, 2013), many gay men have historically managed the experience of shame through overachieving—constantly striving, through accomplishments, awards, and aplomb, to secure a sense of worthiness that their inner critic assures them is not real (Downs, 2012), such that in place of committed action they engage in concealment and overachievement, and in place of an orientation toward values they may experience a lack of clarity about what a meaningful life might look like. On the left side of the hexaflex, cognitive fusion with homophobic or transphobic stereotypes further limits flexibility, and experiential avoidance often manifests as a fear of rejection or unpredictable responses of others.

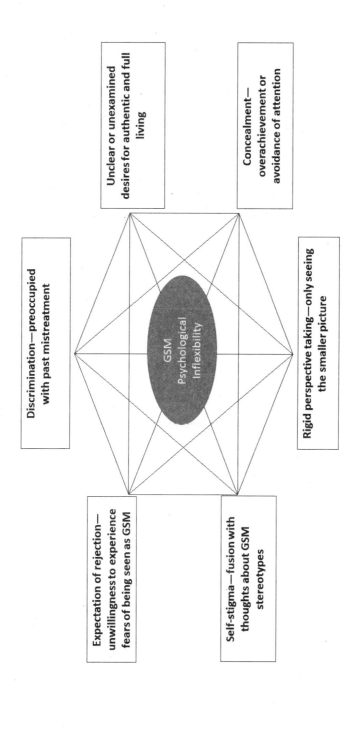

Figure 5.1. The minority stress psychological inflexibility hexaflex

Most importantly, this model of GSM psychological inflexibility suggests concrete steps ACT practitioners can take to help increase well-being and reduce shame in GSM clients, which we will outline shortly. First, however, we will provide a framework for understanding what self-compassion is and how it might be promoted.

Treating Shame and Promoting Psychological Flexibility

Articulation is the antidote to shame, or at the very least represents opening up to a different way of being. As Helen Lewis has said, "At the moment that the person himself says, 'I am ashamed,' shame affect is likely to be diminishing" (1971, p. 197). Yet this tends to be exactly the challenge in psychotherapy with people who experience shame, as shame demands to be concealed, often by being enveloped in other, more acceptable emotions. Furthermore, the mind will produce thoughts and messages designed to support the perception of threat. However, such thoughts need not be a problem, given that decoupling clients' responses from their unworkable thoughts grants them greater freedom for growth and change (Levin, Luoma, & Haeger, 2015). Building on Kristin Neff's work on self-compassion (2003, 2009), therapists can facilitate this shift by helping clients develop mindfulness, a sense of common humanity, and self-kindness—qualities that can be defined and mapped onto the core ACT processes (Luoma & Platt, 2015; Yadavaia, Hayes, & Vilardaga, 2014).

Mindfulness: Through present-moment awareness, observing the flow of shameful thoughts about the self related to one's gender or sexual identity can help weaken fusion.

Sense of common humanity: The sense of a shared human experience of shame inherently strengthens perspective-taking skills and helps people cultivate an awareness of the variety of ways they can be viewed by themselves and others. It can be transformative to consider viewing one's own life through the eyes of a loving, caring other (Shapira & Mongrain, 2010). Similarly, it can be incredibly powerful for GSM clients to consider the perspectives of other GSM individuals, cultivating an awareness that there are a number of experiences others in this minority group can relate to (Meyer, 2015; Russell & Richards, 2003).

Self-kindness: This involves practicing greater acceptance of both oneself and difficult private events, such as fearful thoughts about possible discrimination, feelings of shame or despair, or memories of rejection, and making a conscious choice to engage in more meaningful life experiences, even if doing so brings up this difficult content.

In addition to helping clients develop these qualities, therapists might also consider fostering community connectedness. Described at times as a part of the minority stress model, integration into broader GSM communities is a powerful resilience factor (Fokkema & Kuyper, 2009; Meyer, 2015). It promotes perspective taking and heightens awareness of shared, common struggles related to shame and marginalization. In addition, attaching meaningfulness to these shared struggles can increase committed, values-based action and provide relief from self-critical thoughts (Russell & Richards, 2003). Drawing all of this together, in figure 5.2 we present an ACT hexaflex depicting the GSM psychological flexibility that can arise through these processes.

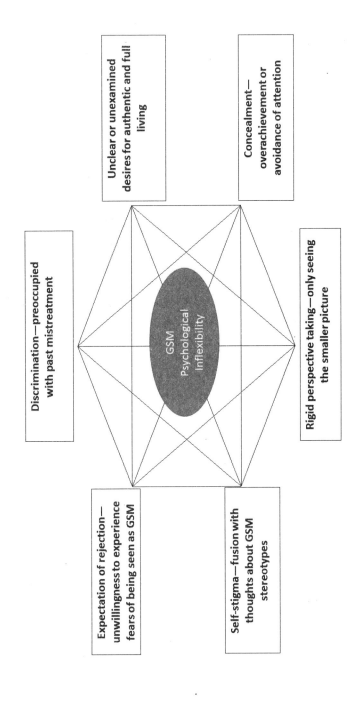

Figure 5.2. The GSM psychological flexibility hexaflex

Case Example: Coping with Shame through Sex

Now we'll present a case example illustrating a dynamic some gay men develop: managing shame through sexual compulsivity. With the advent of hookup apps that utilize smartphone geolocations, the relative ease of finding sexual partners offers a unique temptation. It makes it possible for a person to have a sexual encounter relatively quickly when feeling overwhelmed by negative affect, including shame. However, because sex is intense, alternate means of self-soothing begin to lose their salience. This can lead to a cycle in which sex is followed by an increase in feelings of shame, sadness, or loneliness, which then leads to seeking sex again for a momentary boost in positive affect (Martin, Chernoff, Buitron, & McFarr, 2006; Quadland & Shattls, 1987). In our experience, shame and experiencing their sexuality as out-of-control are common reasons that gay men seek therapy.

Andrew is a twenty-eight-year old Caucasian gay man. He is currently in law school, has never had a relationship that lasted more than a few months, and often spends an entire day or stays up late at night seeking multiple sex partners, which has occasionally impacted his performance on exams. He is typically the bottom, or receptive partner, and finds that sex without a condom feels more intense when he's hoping to lose himself in the moment. His shame afterward is accompanied by intense fear of exposure to HIV, though he has recently begun taking Truvada (tenofovir disoproxil) as pre-exposure prophylaxis (PrEP) to reduce the risk of transmission. He sometimes finds himself crying after sex, and when dating, he often feels like he ruins things if he has sex with a new partner too quickly, so he stops returning the person's calls.

Andrew: I almost didn't come today. I mean, it's okay now that I'm here, but I kept thinking about what you probably thought of me after our last session.

Therapist: What kind of thoughts did you have?

Andrew: I think of this time when I was little and my stepdad was throwing away anything in my room he thought wasn't masculine enough. He just kept yelling that something was wrong with me.

Therapist: We've talked about this thought coming up before and how hard it is when you start arguing with yourself in an attempt to make it to go away—how that might even make the thought feel more difficult to carry.

Andrew: It's exactly like that, but I don't want to carry it with me.

Therapist: I want to try something with you. Sometimes when we develop these kinds of thoughts, it's like a line on a sheet of paper. (*Draws a line, as below.*)

Therapist: The brain is great at drawing connections and terrible at erasing them. So when we argue with our thoughts—for example, "But I'm *not* like this!"—we just keep touching that same thought: "Not like what?" "Like this." The thought just picks up weight. (*Adds to the drawing to show a vicious cycle, as below.*)

Therapist: So what we really want to do is find some new places for our thoughts to go—maybe add some branches so it's not just one big feedback loop, getting stronger and stronger. (*Makes a new drawing with a bunch of branching lines, as follows.*)

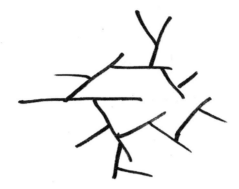

Andrew: Okay, I get the feedback loop part, and adding branches sounds great. So how do I do that?

Therapist: You can use something I call "Comma-And." To do this, I start with a thought, then I add a comma, an "and," and whatever else might come to mind that also feels believable.

Andrew: What if it's just something else bad?

Therapist: That's okay, too. Remember, the goal is to have lots of directions, not to try to force or control things. So while I'd love it if you considered some positive thoughts about yourself, let's stick with whatever feels true for you right now. You had mentioned thinking, "Something is wrong with me." I wonder if there's a stickier thought there? Something like "I'm unlovable" or "I'm broken"?

Andrew: (*Starts to cry a bit.*) Yeah, the thought "No one can love me." That hits closer to home.

Therapist: And?

Andrew: And my friends value me…

Therapist: And?

Andrew: See, this is where it doesn't work. I was about to say "Men are fine just using me for sex."

Therapist: Well, if you'll bear with me, I'd like you to write for a bit. Go ahead and write down what you just said: "No one can love me, and my friends value me, and men are just fine using me for sex." (*Pauses.*) Okay, now just keep writing in the same way. (*Pauses to allow Andrew to write, occasionally offering an "and?" prompt, until Andrew has half a page of statements.*) Okay, I'd like you to stop. Would you be willing to go back to the top of the page and read everything back to me?

Andrew: (*Reads.*) "No one can love me, and my friends value me, and men are fine just using me for sex, and it's not worth asking for my needs to be met, and I just want to be loved, and my brother tells me that he loves me, and I'm really good at my job, and I like to help people who are hurting, and I get so lonely sometimes, and my mom tells me I matter so much to her, and my dog loves me, and it's not like lots of guys don't like sex, and someone who loves me will see all of me, and…"

Therapist: I want you to look back at that first thought: "No one can love me." How believable does it feel now compared to when you first wrote it down?

Andrew: It feels a little looser. It's still in there, but it doesn't seem like the only thing that's there.

Therapist: I want you to sit with this for a moment—to really notice how this feels in your heart and in your gut as you consider that thought a little more lightly…I really want you to keep at this. I'd like you to consider doing this during the week as difficult thoughts come up. You can read them to me next week, or even to yourself in the mirror. Thoughts are often less sticky when we say them out loud.

In this example, the defusion exercise Comma-And eventually incorporated each of the elements of self-compassion as conceptualized in ACT. Mindfulness was invoked by prompting Andrew to attend to his emotions in the moment. Furthermore, by labeling his experience of the initial thought as looser, he increased his awareness of the experience of fusion that was occurring prior to the exercise. Andrew also referred to how he thinks others see him—something that commonly occurs when people do this exercise. This facilitates developing a sense of common humanity, as clients engage in perspective taking and notice less rigid facets of the self. Finally, by engaging in such a difficult exercise and noticing the relief that comes with holding his self-critical thoughts more lightly, Andrew begins to open the door to self-kindness while also embodying a more authentic expression of his values.

Conclusion

The experience of shame is multifaceted and cuts directly to the very core of the self. Shame is often countered with frantic efforts to escape that most dangerous and unrelenting critic: one's own mind. These efforts may be externally focused, taking forms such as overachieving, substance abuse, or compulsive sexuality, or internally focused, such as ruminating over self-critical thoughts. ACT offers an effective avenue for reducing the burden of shame by fostering an accepting and nonjudgmental stance toward the self, including clients' most self-critical thoughts, and by increasing clients' perspective-taking abilities and deepening their awareness of their common humanity. For GSM clients, the latter can be enhanced by connecting more authentically with their GSM community and understanding that many others share their experience of suffering related to shame. Finally, the ACT processes of present-moment awareness and defusion allow people to accept their worst thoughts and fears as simply thoughts and fears, rather than buying into them.

For therapists who often work with GSM individuals or who are themselves GSM, shame is a challenging area that requires active self-care so they can work from a place of compassion, present-moment awareness, and warmth. Ultimately, by creating the context necessary for psychological flexibility to flourish in our GSM clients, we allow ourselves to grow in self-compassion alongside them.

References

Barnes-Holmes, Y., Barnes-Holmes, D., Roche, B., Healy, O., Lyddy, F., Cullinan, V., et al. (2001). Psychological development. In S. C. Hayes, D. Barnes-Holmes, & B. Roche (Eds.), *Relational frame theory: A post-Skinnerian account of human language and cognition.* New York: Kluwer Academic.

Barrett, K. C. (1995). A functionalist approach to shame and guilt. In J. P. Tangney & K. W. Fischer (Eds.), *Self-conscious emotions: The psychology of shame, guilt, embarrassment, and pride.* New York: Guilford.

Brown, J., Low, W. Y., Tai, R., & Tong, W. T. (2015). Shame, internalized homonegativity, and religiosity: A comparison of the stigmatization associated with minority stress with gay men in Australia and Malaysia. *International Journal of Sexual Health,* published online July 13.

Cochran, S. D., & Mays, V. M. (2009). Burden of psychiatric morbidity among lesbian, gay, and bisexual individuals in the California Quality of Life Survey. *Journal of Abnormal Psychology, 118,* 647–658.

Cole, S. W., Kemeny, M. E., Taylor, S. E., Visscher, B. R., & Fahey, J. L. (1996). Accelerated course of human immunodeficiency virus infection in gay men who conceal their homosexual identity. *Psychosomatic Medicine, 58,* 219–231.

Colombetti, G. (2013). *The feeling body: Affective science meets the enactive mind.* Cambridge, MA: MIT Press.

Dearing, R. L., Stuewig, J., & Tangney, J. P. (2005). On the importance of distinguishing shame from guilt: Relations to problematic alcohol and drug use. *Addictive Behaviors, 30,* 1392–1404.

Downs, A. (2012). *The velvet rage: Overcoming the pain of growing up gay in a straight man's world,* 2nd edition. Philadelphia: Da Capo Press.

Ekman, P. (1973). Universal facial expressions in emotion. *Studia Psychologica, 15,* 140–147.

Elsessor, S. A., Oldenburg, C. E., Biello, K. B., Mimiaga, M. J., Safren, S. A., Egan, J. E., et al. (2015). Seasons of risk: Anticipated behavior on vacation and interest in episodic antiretroviral pre-exposure prophylaxis (PrEP) among a large national sample of US men who have sex with men (MSM). *AIDS and Behavior,* epub ahead of print.

Encarnación, O. G. (2014). Gay rights: Why democracy matters. *Journal of Democracy, 25,* 90–104.

Fokkema, T., & Kuyper, L. (2009). The relation between social embeddedness and loneliness among older lesbian, gay, and bisexual adults in the Netherlands. *Archives of Sexual Behavior, 38,* 264–275.

Gilbert, P. (2010). *Compassion focused therapy: Distinctive features.* New York: Routledge.

Hastings, M. E., Northman, L. M., & Tangney, J. P. (2000). Shame, guilt, and suicide. In T. Joiner & M. D. Rudd (Eds.), *Suicide science: Expanding the boundaries.* Norwell, MA: Kluwer Academic.

Hayes, S. C., Barnes-Holmes, D., & Roche, B. (Eds.). (2001). *Relational frame theory: A post-Skinnerian account of human language and cognition.* New York: Kluwer Academic.

Hayes, S. C., Strosahl, K. D., & Wilson, K. G. (1999). *Acceptance and commitment therapy: An experiential approach to behavior change.* New York: Guilford.

Hayes, S. C., Strosahl, K. D., & Wilson, K. G. (2012). *Acceptance and commitment therapy: The process and practice of mindful change,* 2nd edition. New York: Guilford.

Hequembourg, A. L., & Dearing, R. L. (2013). Exploring shame, guilt, and risky substance use among sexual minority men and women. *Journal of Homosexuality, 60,* 615–638.

Hess, U., & Thibault, P. (2009). Darwin and emotion expression. *American Psychologist, 64,* 120–128.

Hughto, J. M. W., Reisner, S. L., & Pachankis, J. E. (2015). Transgender stigma and health: A critical review of stigma determinants, mechanisms, and interventions. *Social Science and Medicine, 147,* 222–231.

Institute of Medicine. (2011). *The health of lesbian, gay, bisexual, and transgender people: Building a foundation for better understanding.* Washington, DC: National Academies Press.

Kross, E., Berman, M. G., Mischel, W., Smith, E. E., & Wager, T. D. (2011). Social rejection shares somatosensory representations with physical pain. *Proceedings of the National Academy of Sciences, 108,* 6270–6275.

Levenson, R. W. (2014). The autonomic nervous system and emotion. *Emotion Review, 6,* 100–112.

Levin, M. E., Luoma, J. B., & Haeger, J. A. (2015). Decoupling as a mechanism of change in mindfulness and acceptance: A literature review. *Behavior Modification, 39,* 870–911.

Lewis, H. B. (1971). Shame and guilt in neurosis. *Psychoanalytic Review, 58,* 419–438.

Lewis, M. (1997). The self in self-conscious emotions. *Annals of the New York Academy of Sciences, 818,* 119–142.

Liu, J. H., & Dresler-Hawke, E. (2006). Collective shame and the positioning of German national identity. *Psicologia Politica, 32,* 130–153.

Luoma, J. B., & Platt, M. G. (2015). Shame, self-criticism, self-stigma, and compassion in acceptance and commitment therapy. *Current Opinion in Psychology, 2,* 97–101.

MacDonald, G., & Leary, M. R. (2005). Why does social exclusion hurt? The relationship between social and physical pain. *Psychological Bulletin, 131,* 202–223.

Martell, C. R., Addis, M. E., & Jacobson, N. S. (2001). *Depression in context: Strategies for guided action.* New York: Norton.

Martin, D., Chernoff, R., Buitron, M., & McFarr, L. (2006, February). Sexual-risk behavior chain analysis in persistently high-risk gay men. In R. Durvasula (Chair), *Personality Disorders in HIV—Research and Clinical Perspectives.* Symposium conducted at the annual meeting of the American Psychological Association, Toronto, ON.

Matthews, C. R., Lorah, P., & Fenton, J. (2006). Treatment experiences of gays and lesbians in recovery from addiction: A qualitative inquiry. *Journal of Mental Health Counseling, 28,* 111–132.

McHugh, L., & Stewart, I. (Eds.). (2012). *The self and perspective taking: Contributions and applications from modern behavioral science.* Oakland, CA: New Harbinger Publications.

Mesquita, B., Barrett, L. F., & Smith, E. R. (Eds.). (2010). *The mind in context.* New York: Guilford.

Meyer, I. H. (2003). Prejudice, social stress, and mental health in lesbian, gay, and bisexual populations: Conceptual issues and research evidence. *Psychological Bulletin, 129,* 674–697.

Meyer, I. H. (2015). Resilience in the study of minority stress and health of sexual and gender minorities. *Psychology of Sexual Orientation and Gender Diversity, 2,* 209–213.

Neff, K. (2003). Self-compassion: An alternative conceptualization of a healthy attitude toward oneself. *Self and Identity, 2,* 85–101.

Neff, K. (2009). The role of self-compassion in development: A healthier way to relate to oneself. *Human Development, 52,* 211–214.

O'Connor, G. (1995). Recognizing and healing malignant shame. In T. Ziff (Ed.), *Distant relations: Chicano, Irish, Mexican art and critical writing.* New York: Smart Art Press.

Odets, W. (1995). *In the shadow of the epidemic: Being HIV-negative in the age of AIDS.* Durham, NC: Duke University Press.

Orth, U., Berking, M., & Burkhardt, S. (2006). Self-conscious emotions and depression: Rumination explains why shame, but not guilt, is adaptive. *Personality and Social Psychology Bulletin, 32,* 1608–1619.

Pachankis, J. E., & Hatzenbuehler, M. L. (2013). The social development of contingent self-worth in sexual minority young men: An empirical investigation of the "best little boy in the world" hypothesis. *Basic and Applied Social Psychology, 35,* 176–190.

Page, M. J., Lindahl, K. M., & Malik, N. M. (2013). The role of religion and stress in sexual identity and mental health among lesbian, gay, and bisexual youth. *Journal of Research on Adolescence, 23,* 665–677.

Quadland, M. C., & Shattls, W. D. (1987). AIDS, sexuality, and sexual control. *Journal of Homosexuality, 14,* 277–298.

Russell, G. M., & Richards, J. A. (2003). Stressor and resilience factors for lesbians, gay men, and bisexuals confronting antigay politics. *American Journal of Community Psychology, 31,* 313–328.

Sabini, J., & Silver, M. (2005). Why emotion names and experiences don't neatly pair. *Psychological Inquiry, 16,* 1–10.

Sapolsky, R. M. (2004). *Why zebras don't get ulcers,* 3rd edition. New York: Holt.

Shapira, L. B., & Mongrain, M. (2010). The benefits of self-compassion and optimism exercises for individuals vulnerable to depression. *Journal of Positive Psychology, 5,* 377–389.

Tangney, J. P., & Dearing, R. L. (2003). *Shame and guilt.* New York: Guilford.

Tangney, J. P., Stuewig, J., & Mashek, D. J. (2007). Moral emotions and moral behavior. *Annual Review of Psychology, 58,* 345–372.

Testa, R. J., Habarth, J., Peta, J., Balsam, K., & Bockting, W. (2015). Development of the Gender Minority Stress and Resilience Measure. *Psychology of Sexual Orientation and Gender Diversity, 2,* 65–77.

Wilson, J. P., Drozdek, B., & Turkovic, S. (2006). Posttraumatic shame and guilt. *Trauma, Violence, and Abuse, 7,* 122–141.

Wolitski, R. J., & Fenton, K. A. (2011). Sexual health, HIV, and sexually transmitted infections among gay, bisexual, and other men who have sex with men in the United States. *AIDS and Behavior, 15,* 9–17.

Yadavaia, J. E., Hayes, S. C., & Vilardaga, R. (2014). Using acceptance and commitment therapy to increase self-compassion: A randomized controlled trial. *Journal of Contextual Behavioral Science, 3,* 248–257.

CHAPTER 6

Treating Disordered Eating in Gay Men and Other GSM Clients Using DBT and ACT

Joseph C. Walloch, *University of Nevada, Reno;* and Mary L. Hill, *Georgia State University*

Body dissatisfaction (BD) and disordered eating (DE) are becoming more common among gay and bisexual men (Hospers & Jansen, 2005). More importance is often placed on appearance in gay male culture than among straight men, with gay men being more likely to be evaluated by themselves and others based on physical appearance (Smolak & Murnen, 2001). Fortunately, mindfulness- and acceptance-based treatments such as dialectical behavior therapy (DBT; Linehan, 1993) and acceptance and commitment therapy (ACT; Hayes, Strosahl, & Wilson, 1999) can help gay men address these issues so they can engage more fully in their lives and increase their quality of life.

This chapter presents information regarding BD and DE and the unique experiences of gay men related to these issues, and introduces DBT and ACT as potentially useful evidence-based treatments for this population. Although the chapter focuses primarily on gay men, information concerning other gender and sexual minorities (GSM) who may share similar cultural and psychological experiences is also presented.

Throughout, we'll use a case example to illustrate how to employ these treatments with GSM clients, and to demonstrate how this approach can be individualized, including in culturally sensitive case conceptualizations. The client in this case example is Ahmed, a twenty-four-year old Middle Eastern gay man who has struggled with DE for five years, starting in his senior year of high school after he came out as gay. Now he is constantly preoccupied with food, weight, and BD, engages in occasional binge eating, and exercises excessively on a regular basis. He maintains relationships with a few friends but often feels lonely and unattractive. Ahmed wants a stable romantic relationship and has had satisfactory dating experiences, but he is still single. He believes that he needs to be flawless in order to attract a partner.

Body Dissatisfaction and Social Context

BD relates to negative evaluations of weight and body characteristics (e.g., size and shape) and involves a perceived discrepancy between a person's evaluation of his body and his ideal (Cash & Szymanski,

1995). BD is affected by social factors, with preferences in body shape and size being predominantly influenced by one's culture (Grogan, 2008). Therefore, it is necessary to look not only at the experiences of individuals vis-à-vis their bodies but also at the cultural context in which the individual functions. BD is common among gay men who, like women, can trace their BD to gendered power relations instigated and maintained by men (Wood, 2004). Consequently, the body becomes a site of social struggle, not only between men and women, but also between the dominant heterosexual construct of masculinity and the subordinate, gay male culture

In Meyer's minority stress model, "gay people, like members of other minority groups, are subjected to chronic stress related to this stigmatization" (1995, p. 38). Gay men who have greater expectations of being stigmatized for being gay are hypothesized to desire a powerful, fit physique as a defense against the experience of prejudice from others or their own internalized shame (Strelan & Hargreaves, 2005).

BD and DE

Disordered eating occurs when a number of unhealthy attitudes and behaviors related to eating, exercise, and BD coincide (Fairburn, 2008). Eating disorders, which lie on the severe end of the DE spectrum, are characterized by persistent disturbances in eating and related behaviors that lead to significant impairment. These behaviors are associated with serious medical and psychological problems, such as anxiety and depression, and death due to medical complications or suicide (Ogden, 2010). However, the etiology and consequences of DE are commensurate with those of eating disorders (Thomas, Vartanian, & Brownell, 2009); therefore, we will refer to both eating disorders and subthreshold eating pathology as DE.

BD, DE, and GSM

Rates of DE among bisexual men are also elevated, with levels similar to those among gay men (Strother, Lemberg, Stanford, & Turberville, 2012). For sexual minority women, the research is limited

111

and conflicting (see Bankoff & Pantalone, 2014). For example, several studies have shown that straight women endorse more DE and BD than lesbian women (e.g., Owens, Hughes, & Owens-Nicholson, 2003; Polimeni, Austin, & Kavanagh, 2009). However, other studies have found that levels of DE among sexual minority women are equivalent to or higher than those of straight women (Austin et al., 2009; Maloch, Bieschke, McAleavey, & Locke, 2013).

The literature concerning DE and BD has primarily focused on cisgender individuals, whose gender identity matches their sex assigned at birth. The research is limited and mixed in terms of increased risk of DE and BD among transgender individuals. Two studies suggest that those who identify as transgender are likely to engage in DE (Algars, Alanko, Santtila, & Sandnabba, 2012; Diemer, Grant, Munn-Chernoff, Patterson, & Duncan, 2015), and that they engage in DE to accentuate characteristics of their gender or as a means of self-control. However, another study found that individuals who identified as male-to-female trans women reported a significantly lower drive for thinness and fewer DE symptoms than cisgender individuals (Khoosal, Langaham, Palmer, Terry, & Minajagi, 2009).

Because the research in this area is inconsistent and still in its infancy, it is important for future studies to identify potential risk and protective factors related to BD and DE among different GSM groups. However, the preliminary findings we've outlined do suggest that it's important to consider an individual's unique historical and situational context in order to better understand the development and maintenance of BD and DE. Sexual orientations and gender presentations that are incongruent with the dominant culture may increase distress among those individuals, which may in turn manifest as BD and DE if they have other vulnerabilities to these problems.

Mindfulness- and Acceptance-Based Interventions for DE

Several theoretical models and interventions have attempted to better conceptualize and treat DE. Wilson (1996) called for increased attention to acceptance-based methods for treating DE; and in the intervening years, these approaches have come to seem particularly salient for GSM clients, who have historically been oppressed, because they "may resonate with clients from nondominant cultural and/or marginalized backgrounds who, due to understandable mistrust of the mental health system, may assume that they will be blamed in therapy for their current circumstances" (Fuchs, Lee, Roemer, & Orsillo, 2013, p. 3).

Two of the evidence-based mindfulness- and acceptance-oriented cognitive behavioral therapies for treating disordered eating are DBT and ACT. These approaches emphasize the importance of context (Hofmann, Sawyer, & Fang, 2010) and are suitable for addressing common comorbidities with DE, such as anxiety and stigma. These therapies share several interrelated central themes: acceptance, mindfulness, an expanded view of psychological health, and the goal of creating a life worth living.

Preliminary research suggests that both DBT and ACT are promising treatments for DE (see Masuda & Hill, 2013). Many studies have shown that a form of DBT tailored to DE (DBT-ED; Safer, Telch, & Chen, 2009) reduces bingeing, purging, and urges to eat in response to negative mood and increases weight satisfaction. ACT also appears to be beneficial and effective for a range of DE concerns (see Manlick, Cochran, & Koon, 2013; Masuda & Hill, 2013). ACT emphasizes acknowledging and accepting whatever is not within one's power to control (Fuchs et al., 2013; Kater, 2010), such as stigmatizing messages related to one's GSM identity (Walloch, Cerezo, & Heide, 2012), as well as one's emotional response to stigma (e.g., anger or sadness) while still choosing to pursue one's values. This is especially useful for GSM clients who continue to experience pressure from within their communities as well as prejudice from the dominant society.

Furthermore, ACT may promote pursuing changes to societal problems, such as stigma and prejudice, utilizing the same processes used in DE treatment. For example, an individual may experience fear and self-defeating thoughts in relation to wanting to facilitate social justice and still choose to pursue that value. Preliminary data for ACT targeted at stigma suggest that it is effective in reducing self-stigma around sexual orientation (Yadavaia & Hayes, 2012).

The majority of participants with DE in DBT and ACT studies have been women; however, these interventions seem viable for gay men and other GSM clients who engage in DE. To date, there have been three small treatment studies investigating the benefits of using ACT for DE with GSM clients (Hill, Masuda, Melcher, Morgan, & Twohig, 2015; Hill, Masuda, Moore, & Twohig, 2015; Walloch, 2014). Because the research is limited, it's imperative that future research endeavors focus on GSM clients with these issues.

DBT Foundations

DBT is a mindfulness- and acceptance-based cognitive behavioral therapy originally developed to treat chronically suicidal individuals who met diagnostic criteria for borderline personality disorder on the premise that these clients use self-injurious behaviors to regulate their emotions (Linehan, 1993). This use of maladaptive behaviors is thought to be due to a lack of skills in identifying and employing more adaptive methods for regulating emotions.

DBT is a comprehensive treatment grounded in a biopsychosocial theory of emotion dysregulation and combines three theoretical positions: behavioral science, dialectical philosophy, and Zen practice (Linehan, 1993). Behavioral science, the principles of behavior employed as a technology of change, is integrated with a technology of acceptance (with techniques drawn from both Zen and Western contemplative practices), and these poles are balanced within the dialectical framework (Dimeff & Koerner, 2007). The goals of treatment are to increase clients' motivation to change, improve their access to the larger environment, structure the environment to be reinforcing, and improve the therapist's competence in conducting DBT and motivation to persist in carrying out treatment (Linehan, 2015).

From the DBT perspective, pervasive emotion dysregulation manifests from a transaction between biological dysfunction in one's emotion regulation system (e.g., heightened emotional sensitivity) and an invalidating environment (Linehan, 1993). An invalidating environment is one that regularly discounts an individual's communication of thoughts and emotions (Linehan, 1993). Living in invalidating environments has serious consequences, among them that individuals may develop maladaptive strategies to regulate or eliminate intense emotions, including DE. In order to decrease or eliminate these maladaptive strategies, clients learn emotional acceptance, distress tolerance, and adaptive emotion regulation skills, with various in-session treatment strategies, such as validation, problem-solving, and dialectics, being used to address salient behavioral targets (Linehan, 2015).

DBT for Gay Men with DE

Adaptations to the standard DBT biosocial theory have been proposed for the unique clinical presentations of those with DE. Like those with borderline personality disorder, they may have biological vulnerabilities in terms of regulating emotions; however, they may also have vulnerabilities in their hunger-satiety system, and if this vulnerability interacts with an invalidating environment, DE may result (Wisniewski & Kelly, 2003). Although this hypothesis was developed to explain DE in straight women, the rationale may also be applicable for gay men and other GSM clients. For example, gay men, like straight women, live in a culture that invalidates a healthy, accepting stance toward their appearance, and in both groups appearance is often associated with self-worth and sexual desirability.

DBT Applications with GSM

Standard DBT strategies (see Linehan, 1993, 2015) can be adapted to address DE in GSM clients in culturally sensitive ways that are mindful of minority stress. Returning to the case study of Ahmed, he is initially skeptical of treatment and is concerned that his therapist won't understand his experiences and current struggles. Ahmed says he feels his emotions very intensely and that it's difficult for him to calm down. He also mentions that because he diets regularly, he subsequently feels famished and has unbearable urges to binge.

PRESENTING THE BIOSOCIAL THEORY

When meeting with Ahmed for the first time, his clinician should explain the biosocial theory (Linehan, 1993) and how both the interaction with an invalidating environment and one's predisposition to heightened emotional sensitivity are hypothesized to contribute to the development of DE. When doing so, it will be important for the clinician to highlight the fact that gay men often experience invalidation from both their home environments and society more broadly. Presenting the theory in this way can help build rapport, trust, and understanding. This type of presentation can also aid in normalizing the consequences that many GSM individuals face, which will help validate Ahmed's unique experience and provide some solace in knowing that he is not alone in his struggle.

COMMITMENT STRATEGIES

During initial sessions, DBT therapists use various strategies to promote clients' commitment to change (Linehan, 1993). In Ahmed's case, he's ambivalent about getting treatment and hesitant to make changes. Although his DE provides temporary relief from sadness, loneliness, and anxiety, he acknowledges that it isn't sustainable. The following dialogue provides an example of how his therapist could use commitment strategies, such as freedom to choose amidst an absence of alternatives, playing the devil's advocate, and examining the pros and cons. (For more details on these approaches, see Linehan, 1993.)

Ahmed:　　I'm not sure that therapy is the best thing for me right now. I don't have much time, and I don't binge that much. Plus, I like how I look after working out.

Therapist:　　You don't have to change anything. You can continue to do what you're doing, but you'll have to be okay with not having a boyfriend, feeling lonely, and spending money on binge food. It's your choice.

116

Ahmed: I definitely don't want to continue feeling this way, and I don't want to waste money on food. I can't to go on like this. I do need to change.

Therapist: Knowing that you need to change and actually changing are two different things. This treatment takes a lot of work, and you'll have to be devoted to it. There are other therapies out there that won't require as much from you.

Ahmed: Yeah, but I really do need to stop.

Therapist: Before you make this commitment, let's look at the pros and cons of other treatments and the pros and cons of DBT.

VALIDATION

Validation, which entails communicating that individuals' behaviors are understandable given their experiences, is an essential communication style and the principal acceptance strategy in DBT (Linehan, 1993). Validation is particularly beneficial for GSM clients who have been and continue to be invalidated by their family and by society at large. There are six levels of validation, with level 6 being the highest, and DBT calls for therapists to validate at the highest level whenever possible (Linehan, 1993). A comprehensive discussion of each level is beyond the scope of this chapter (for more information, see Linehan, 1997). However, we will offer a brief explanation of levels 4 through 6 here, with examples, as these may be crucial when working with GSM clients.

Level 4: Describe the individual's behavior as understandable given his learning history or biology. Ahmed's previous therapist wasn't sensitive to his experiences as a gay male. Knowing this, his current therapist can validate at level 4 by saying, "It makes sense that you're concerned that I may not understand you, just like your last therapist. Let's be open with one another so that doesn't happen again."

Level 5: Identify and communicate ways the individual's behavior is understandable in his current circumstances. In response to Ahmed's use of exercise to try to attract a boyfriend, his therapist can validate at level 5 by saying, "It's understandable that you want to look good for other guys. Many people want to find a partner, and it makes sense that you're longing for that kind of connection."

Level 6: Be radically genuine. Level 6 requires that therapists respond to their clients as they would to anyone else in their life and treat them as equals. This may be especially important for GSM individuals, who are often treated as "less than." In Ahmed's case, his therapist might validate at level 6 by saying, "It makes sense that you're ashamed about your bingeing. This is a major problem, man. Why in the world would you want to continue doing this?"

URGE SURFING

Individuals who are preoccupied with food and engage in dietary restraint during the day are more inclined to overeat or binge in the evenings, often doing so alone in order to avoid shame. Urge surfing, which is a common mindfulness skill used in DBT for substance use (DBT-SUD; McMain, Sayrs, Dimeff, & Linehan, 2007) and DE (DBT-ED; Safer et al., 2009), originated in the relapse prevention literature (Marlatt, 1985). Ahmed's therapist could introduce this skill after teaching him other core mindfulness skills (see Linehan, 2015) and then encourage him to maintain a nonjudgmental stance toward his emotions and urges to binge until they decrease or pass.

ACT Foundations

Like DBT, ACT is a transdiagnostic mindfulness- and acceptance-based cognitive behavioral therapy. It has a growing body of empirical support for effectiveness in treating a variety of problems, including DE (see A-Tjak et al., 2015; Manlick et al., 2013). ACT is the application of the psychological flexibility model (Levin, Hildebrandt, Lillis, & Hayes, 2012), in which thoughts, emotions, and behaviors are considered in terms of their functional relationships with the context in which they occur. Psychological flexibility is a model of health made up of six interrelated processes: defusion, acceptance, self-as-context, contact with the present moment, values, and committed action (Hayes, Wilson, Gifford, Follette, & Strosahl, 1996). Psychological flexibility increases people's ability to experience psychological discomfort in order to pursue important life goals (Hayes, Pistorello, & Levin, 2012). A complete presentation of the psychological flexibility model is beyond the scope of this chapter. Instead, we will provide a brief overview the model and how ACT techniques can be applied to DE. Figure 6.1 illustrates the six core ACT processes in the traditional ACT hexaflex (Hayes, Luoma, Bond, Masuda, & Lillis, 2006), along with how some of these processes relate specifically to DE.

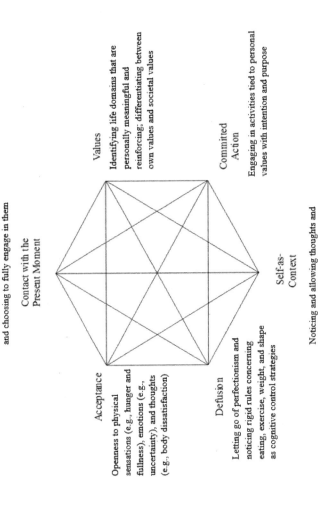

Values
Identifying life domains that are personally meaningful and reinforcing; differentiating between own values and societal values

Committed Action
Engaging in activities tied to personal values with intention and purpose

Contact with the Present Moment
Increasing awareness of one's experiences and choosing to fully engage in them

Self-as-Context
Noticing and allowing thoughts and emotions to be experienced without allowing them to define the self (e.g., finding a sense of self beyond appearance or weight)

Acceptance
Openness to physical sensations (e.g., hunger and fullness), emotions (e.g., uncertainty), and thoughts (e.g., body dissatisfaction)

Defusion
Letting go of perfectionism and noticing rigid rules concerning eating, exercise, weight, and shape as cognitive control strategies

Figure 6.1. Psychological flexibility specific to DE

ACT for DE

The goal of promoting behaviors consistent with values can be broken down into smaller goals: helping clients clarify their values, assisting them in identifying the functions of their problematic behaviors, and helping them assess the degree to which those behaviors inhibit their pursuit of values. In ACT, the emphasis is on increasing valued activities in the moment or in the short term, rather than changing or eliminating ways of thinking and feeling and then pursuing values (Hayes et al., 1996). So for clients with DE, instead of waiting for a time when they aren't experiencing eating-related anxiety, aren't concerned about gaining weight, or aren't experiencing DE cognitions, they can learn to pursue their values even while experiencing those thoughts and emotions. Engaging in effective action while experiencing seemingly inconsistent thoughts is important because these clients may not fully believe "logical" thoughts about their weight and eating (e.g., "I shouldn't care about my weight") and therefore may still experience emotional discomfort (e.g., anxiety when eating or experiencing BD).

ACT Case Conceptualization

In ACT, problems are conceptualized functionally in terms of how behavioral patterns are maintained in a given context and how they affect overall functioning and quality of life. For clients with DE, case conceptualization begins with identifying the function of their eating-related behaviors and determining the short-term and long-term consequences, particularly as they related to the client's values. For many individuals, DE serves as a way to feel better in the moment, gain attention, or distract themselves from uncomfortable thoughts and emotions. However, there are many long-term consequences, including physical pain or damage due to DE, social isolation, interpersonal conflicts with concerned loved ones, and interference with education and career goals. In therapy, it's necessary to discuss the consequences of a given client's DE without blaming. Instead, it's helpful to normalize individuals' experiences, acknowledging that DE has worked to help them immediately escape or avoid discomfort, and that it makes sense that they would continue to engage in DE, even if the costs are significant.

Some clients may have insight into the function of their DE; others may need assistance from the therapist. When gathering information regarding the functions of a client's DE, it may be useful to ask about historical contexts; for example, what occurred around the time when the client first began to engage in DE? It's also important to identify the current situational context and functions of DE, as this can shed light on maintaining factors. To this end, it's useful to work with clients to explore their DE patterns, identifying the antecedents of DE and both the immediate and long-term consequences.

For example, Ahmed's DE emerged shortly after he came out, and it may have developed as a way to escape difficult emotions and situations that commonly occur when people come out, such as feared or actual rejection by friends and family. To assess his current patterns of DE, Ahmed's therapist asks him about the last time he engaged in DE, what occurred prior to that episode, and what he thought, felt, and did during and after the episode. Ahmed reports that he regularly restricts his eating during the day and overexercises, even though he's tired and hungry, explaining, "I don't want to gain weight because no one wants to date a fat guy, so I have to diet and exercise. Plus, I'm proud that I can overcome needs to eat and rest. At the same time, I know that I'm hurting my body, and I've missed out on some social events either because I felt like I had to work out or because I didn't want to be around people who were eating."

ACT case conceptualization also requires making tentative hypotheses about fusion with thoughts and identities, unwillingness to accept difficult internal experiences, disconnection from the present moment, lack of clear values, and disconnection from valued life domains. In Ahmed's case, he values social relationships and connection with others, including a romantic relationship. Because he fears judgment from others and compares himself negatively to his peers, he focuses on his physical appearance rather than his loneliness and fear, and on activities that allow him to experience a sense of accomplishment and pride. By focusing on being physically "flawless," which may be an identity with which he is cognitively fused, Ahmed can also reduce fears of uncertainty and potential rejection by future partners. Although this immediately reduces his internal distress, it also causes his life to revolve around food, exercise, and appearance, leaving him disconnected from his personal values. Furthermore, if this pattern remains unchanged, he'll feel compelled to continue to diet and exercise excessively in order to not experience dissonance with the identity he's fused with and to avoid future judgment and rejection by himself and others.

ACT for Gay Men with DE

ACT interventions are directly tied to case conceptualization. There aren't set rules about specific techniques to use or the course of therapy. Therefore, therapists must keep the purpose of different ACT techniques in mind, rather than just using ACT concepts in session for the sake of "doing ACT." Treatment should be tailored to the individual and will vary depending on a given client's motivation, level of insight, and unique presenting concern.

VALUES

Promoting values and values-based action is the primary goal in ACT. And when clients lack motivation to change, focusing on promoting full and vital living as a treatment goal, rather than targeting problem behaviors directly, can be useful. This may mean focusing treatment on values clarification and the degree to which a client is living in a way consistent with those values, and then collaboratively creating specific goals related to promoting valued action.

For example, because Ahmed has identified physical health, friendships, and a romantic relationship as important, relevant goals for him could include making small changes regarding food and exercise or consulting with a dietician to gain knowledge about balanced, healthy eating; increasing meaningful interactions with friends; identifying what qualities are important to him in a romantic relationship; and engaging in actions related to meeting a partner, such as completing an online dating profile.

MINDFULNESS AND ACCEPTANCE

If problematic avoidance of thoughts, feelings, memories, or physiological sensations becomes apparent, a discussion of the costs of trying to avoid these experiences might be helpful. For example, Ahmed may recognize that his attempts to avoid psychological discomfort via DE haven't worked in the long term (e.g., he continues to experience BD, anxiety, and loneliness) and have, in fact, created additional problems (e.g., additional anxiety, feelings of frustration, physical pain from lack of nutrition and overexercise, and social isolation).

After clients recognize the futility of efforts to avoid distressing thoughts and emotions, they are ready to learn the behavioral alternatives: acceptance and mindfulness (Hayes et al., 1996). Although acceptance won't necessarily eliminate the initial psychological pain, it will eliminate the additional suffering that comes with ineffective attempts to avoid pain and disconnection from values.

In addition to mindfulness of the breath, thoughts, and emotions (Hayes, Strosahl, & Wilson, 2012), mindful eating and mindfulness of common DE triggers can be particularly helpful for those who struggle with DE. It can help them learn to bring more nonjudgmental awareness to their experiences of hunger, satiety, eating, and emotional or situational triggers that precede DE, such as anxiety or BD. This mindful awareness allows clients to choose whether or not to engage in DE, rather than immediately and reactively engaging in problematic eating and related behaviors. They can also learn, through experience, that they are able to openly experience difficult thoughts and emotions without using DE to escape or avoid them.

Teaching mindfulness and acceptance skills is only considered useful if doing so helps clients move in valued directions. Their unique experiences are also important. For example, instead of telling clients that DE is an ineffective avoidance strategy, the therapist should gather information about the function and consequences of a particular client's DE and help him recognize for himself that it is problematic.

Conclusion

The etiology and presentation of DE among gay men and other GSM is complex. This complexity is linked to perceptions of self that are shaped by the broader social context in which these individuals live—a context that affords straight and cisgender individuals more privilege. Being a member of a group that's at high risk for struggling with DE, as gay men are, adds to the problem. It is crucial to consider historical and situational contexts that may contribute to BD and DE in GSM. DBT and ACT have been shown to be effective in treating DE, and both consider the functions of DE, such as emotion regulation, and the role of contextual factors, and also integrate mindfulness, acceptance, and values into treatment.

References

Algars, M., Alanko, K., Santtila, P., & Sandnabba, N. K. (2012). Disordered eating and gender identity disorder: A qualitative study. *Eating Disorders, 20,* 300–311.

A-Tjak, J. G. L., Davis, M. L., Morina, N., Powers, M. B., Smits, J. A. J., & Emmelkamp, P. M. G. (2015). A meta-analysis of the efficacy of acceptance and commitment therapy for clinically relevant mental and physical health problems. *Psychotherapy and Psychosomatics, 84,* 30–36.

Austin, S. B., Ziyadeh, N. J., Corliss, H. L., Rosario, M., Wypij, D., Haines, J., et al. (2009). Sexual orientation disparities in purging and binge eating from early to late adolescence. *Journal of Adolescent Health, 45,* 238–245.

Bankoff, S. M., & Pantalone, D. W. (2014). Patterns of disordered eating behavior in women by sexual orientation: A review of the literature. *Eating Disorders, 22,* 261–274.

Cash, T., & Szymanski, M. L. (1995). The development and validation of the Body-Ideals Questionnaire. *Journal of Personality Assessment, 64,* 466–477.

Diemer, E. W., Grant, J. D., Munn-Chernoff, M. A., Patterson, D. A., & Duncan, A. E. (2015). Gender-identity, sexual orientation, and eating-related pathology in a national sample of college students. *Journal of Adolescent Health, 57,* 144–149.

Dimeff, L. A., & Koerner, K. (Eds.). (2007). *Dialectical behavior therapy in clinical practice: Applications across disorders and settings.* New York: Guilford.

Fairburn, C. G. (2008). Eating disorders: The transdiagnostic view and the cognitive behavioral theory. In C. G. Fairburn (Ed.), *Cognitive behavior therapy and eating disorders.* New York: Guilford.

Fuchs, C., Lee, J. K., Roemer, L., & Orsillo, S. M. (2013). Using mindfulness- and acceptance-based treatments with clients from nondominant cultural and/or marginalized backgrounds: Clinical considerations, meta-analysis findings, and introduction to the special series. *Cognitive and Behavioral Practice, 20*, 1–12.

Grogan, S. (2008). *Body image: Understanding BD in men, women, and children.* New York: Routledge.

Hayes, S. C., Luoma, J. B., Bond, F. W., Masuda, A., & Lillis, J. (2006). Acceptance and commitment therapy: Model, processes, and outcomes. *Behaviour research and therapy, 44*, 1–25.

Hayes, S. C., Pistorello, J., & Levin, M. E. (2012). Acceptance and commitment therapy as a unified model of behavior change. *Counseling Psychologist, 40*, 976–1002.

Hayes, S. C., Strosahl, K. D., & Wilson, K. G. (1999). *Acceptance and commitment therapy: An experiential approach to behavior change.* New York: Guilford.

Hayes, S. C., Strosahl, K. D., & Wilson, K. G. (2012). *Acceptance and commitment therapy: The process and practice of mindful change,* 2nd edition. New York: Guilford.

Hayes, S. C., Wilson, K. G., Gifford, E. V., Follette, V. M., & Strosahl, K. D. (1996). Experiential avoidance and behavioral disorders: A functional dimensional approach to diagnosis and treatment. *Journal of Consulting and Clinical Psychology, 64*, 1152–1168.

Hill, M. L., Masuda, A., Melcher, H., Morgan, J., & Twohig, M. (2015). Acceptance and commitment therapy for women diagnosed with binge eating disorder: A case-series study. *Cognitive and Behavioral Practice, 22*, 367–378.

Hill, M. L., Masuda, A., Moore, M., & Twohig, M. P. (2015). Acceptance and commitment therapy for individuals with problematic emotional eating: A case-series study. *Clinical Case Studies, 14*, 141–154.

Hofmann, S. G., Sawyer, A. T., & Fang, A. (2010). The empirical status of the "new wave" of cognitive behavioral therapy. *Psychiatric Clinics of North America, 33*, 701–710.

Hospers, H. J., & Jansen, A. (2005). Why homosexuality is a risk factor for eating disorders in males. *Journal of Social and Clinical Psychology, 24*, 1188–1201.

Kater, K. (2010). New pathways: Applying acceptance and commitment therapy to the treatment of eating disorders. In M. Maine, B. M. McGilley, & D. W. Bunnell (Eds.), *Treatment of eating disorders: Bridging the research-practice gap.* San Diego, CA: Elsevier.

Khoosal, D., Langaham, C., Palmer, B., Terry, T., & Minajagi, M. (2009). Features of eating disorders among male-to-female transsexuals. *Sexual and Relationship Therapy, 24*, 217–229.

Levin, M. E., Hildebrandt, M. J., Lillis, J., & Hayes, S. C. (2012). The impact of treatment components suggested by the psychological flexibility model: A meta-analysis of laboratory-based component studies. *Behavior Therapy, 43*, 741–756.

Linehan, M. M. (1993). *Cognitive-behavioral treatment of borderline personality disorder*. New York: Guilford.

Linehan, M. M. (1997). Validation and psychotherapy. In A. Bohart & L. Greenberg (Eds.), *Empathy reconsidered: New directions in psychotherapy*. Washington DC: American Psychological Association.

Linehan, M. M. (2015). *DBT skills training manual*, 2nd edition. New York: Guilford.

Maloch, J. K., Bieschke, K. J., McAleavey, A. A., & Locke, B. D. (2013). Eating concerns in college women across sexual orientation identities. *Journal of College Counseling, 16*, 275–288.

Manlick, C. F., Cochran, S. V., & Koon, J. (2013). Acceptance and commitment therapy for eating disorders: Rationale and literature review. *Journal of Contemporary Psychotherapy, 43*, 115–122.

Marlatt, G. A. (1985). Cognitive assessment and intervention procedures for relapse prevention. In G. A. Marlatt & J. R. Gordon (Eds.), *Relapse prevention: Maintenance strategies in the treatment of addictive behaviors*. New York: Guilford.

Masuda, A., & Hill, M. L. (2013). Mindfulness as therapy for disordered eating: A systematic review. *Neuropsychiatry, 3*, 433–447.

McMain, S., Sayrs, J. H. R., Dimeff, L. A., & Linehan, M. M. (2007). Dialectical behavior therapy for individuals with borderline personality disorder and substance dependence. In L. A. Dimeff & K. Koerner (Eds.), *Dialectical behavior therapy in clinical practice: Applications across disorders and settings*. New York: Guilford.

Meyer, I. H. (1995). Minority stress and mental health in gay men. *Journal of Health and Social Behavior, 36*, 38–56.

Ogden, J. (2010). *The psychology of eating: From healthy to disordered behavior*, 2nd edition. Malden, MA: Wiley-Blackwell.

Owens, L. K., Hughes, T. L., & Owens-Nicholson, D. (2003). The effects of sexual orientation on body image and attitudes about eating and weight. *Journal of Lesbian Studies, 7*, 15–33.

Polimeni, A., Austin, S. B., & Kavanagh, A. M. (2009). Sexual orientation and weight, body image, and weight control practices among young Australian women. *Journal of Women's Health, 18*, 355–362.

Safer, D. L., Telch, C. F., & Chen, E. Y. (2009). *Dialectical behavior therapy for binge eating and bulimia*. New York: Guilford.

Smolak, L., & Murnen, S. (2001). Gender and eating problems. In R. Striegel-Moore & L. Smolak (Eds.), *Eating disorders: Innovative directions in research and practice*. Washington, DC: American Psychological Association.

Strelan, P., & Hargreaves, D. (2005). Reasons for exercise and body esteem: Men's response to self-objectification. *Sex Roles, 53*, 495–503.

Strother, E., Lemberg, R., Stanford, S. C., & Turberville, D. (2012). Eating disorders in men: Underdiagnosed, undertreated, and misunderstood. *Eating Disorders, 20*, 346–355.

Thomas, J. J., Vartanian, L. R., & Brownell, K. D. (2009). The relationship between eating disorder not otherwise specified (EDNOS) and officially recognized eating disorders: Meta-analysis and implications for *DSM*. *Psychological Bulletin, 135*, 407–433.

Walloch, J. C. (2014). *Acceptance and commitment therapy for the treatment of body image dissatisfaction and maladaptive eating attitudes and behaviors in gay men: A pilot study.* Unpublished doctoral dissertation, California School of Professional Psychology at Alliant International University, San Francisco.

Walloch, J. C., Cerezo, A., & Heide, F. (2012). Acceptance and commitment therapy to address eating ·disorder symptomatology in gay men. *Journal of LGBT Issues in Counseling, 6*, 257–273.

Wilson, G. T. (1996). Acceptance and change in the treatment of eating disorders and obesity. *Behavior Therapy, 27*, 417–439.

Wisniewski, L., & Kelly, E. (2003). The application of dialectical behavior therapy to the treatment of eating disorders. *Cognitive and Behavioral Practice, 10*, 131–138.

Wood, M. J. (2004). The gay male gaze: Body image disturbance and gender oppression among gay men. *Journal of Gay and Lesbian Social Services, 17*, 43–62.

Yadavaia, J. E., & Hayes, S. C. (2012). Acceptance and commitment therapy for self-stigma around sexual orientation: A multiple baseline evaluation. *Cognitive and Behavioral Practice, 19*, 545–559.

PART II

Building and Rebuilding Relationships

CHAPTER 7

Healing the Wounds of Rejection: Deepening Vulnerability and Intimacy with Functional Analytic Psychotherapy

Matthew D. Skinta and Kimberly Balsam,
Palo Alto University; and
R. Sonia Singh, *Bowling Green State University*

To *feel* anything
deranges you. To be seen
feeling anything strips you
naked. In the grip of it
pleasure or pain doesn't
matter. You think what
will they do what new
power will they acquire *if*
they see me naked like
this. If they see you
feeling. You have no idea
what. It's not about *them.*
To be seen *is* the penalty.

—Anne Carson, RED DOC>

G ender and sexual minority (GSM) clients have usually experienced a variety of interpersonal pressures early in life. While this may take overt forms, such as familial rejection of gender-nonconforming children (e.g., Landolt, Bartholomew, Saffrey, Oram, & Perlman, 2004), it can also manifest covertly, within individuals, in the form of concealment, fear of rejection, and social isolation in an attempt to mitigate minority stress (Hatzenbuehler, McLaughlin, & Xuan, 2012). Later, this guardedness may appear upon entering the therapy room and may also interfere with attempts to forge romantic or other meaningful relationships outside of therapy (e.g., Szymanski & Hilton, 2013). Client guardedness is a challenge in therapy. Evidence-based therapies are not like cookbooks, resulting in effective outcomes when applied mechanically; they must be delivered within the context of a warm, empathic relationship (Thwaites & Bennett-Levy, 2007). Outcomes are enhanced when therapists go beyond the manual and attend to the relationship (e.g., Kohlenberg, Kanter, Bolling, Parker, & Tsai, 2002).

Unfortunately, training programs that emphasize evidence-based therapies rarely provide explicit guidance in using the relationship between therapist and client as a therapeutic tool, including within behavioral case conceptualization (Castonguay, Constantino, McAleavey, & Goldfried, 2010). Furthermore, therapists may not receive appropriate training in GSM issues, which can be particularly problematic given that GSM clients have generally been sensitized to perceived rejection and shaming within therapeutic interactions. This may leave therapists feeling on edge or uncertain in the relationship, and possibly ill equipped to attend to these interpersonal challenges. This difficulty is evidenced by data indicating that personality disorders may be overdiagnosed among GSM clients (e.g., Falco, 1991; Gonsiorek, 1982).

In this chapter, we provide background on how GSM lives often involve contexts that punish attempts at intimacy and vulnerability, along with a model for using basic behavioral principles, as articulated by functional analytic psychotherapy (FAP; Kohlenberg & Tsai, 1991), as a powerful remedy. We include a case example to illustrate what this approach might look like in session.

Interpersonal Vulnerabilities Among GSM Clients

Despite recent changes in social acceptance of diverse gender and sexual identities, GSM populations continue to be socially oppressed. Indeed, although 2015 saw some high-profile advancements in social and institutional policies, such as the US Supreme Court's marriage equality decision, Ireland's passage of marriage equality by popular referendum, and the establishment of equality based on sexual and gender identity in Nepal's new constitution, discrimination against this group remains embedded in contemporary life. The impact of this social oppression on GSM people is conceptualized as minority stress (see Meyer, 2003), which is defined as the additional burden of stress that results from living with a minority identity. Minority stress theory is a primary lens through which we can understand the stressors GSM individuals face (Institute of Medicine, 2011). It organizes these sources of stress into four categories: discriminatory events, self-stigma, expectations of rejection, and concealment of a GSM identity (Meyer, 2003). Even on more subtle levels, GSM individuals typically don't experience the degree of social valuation and recognition for their lives, relationships, families, and identities as other members of society do, which can have deleterious impacts on development and thriving over the life span (Kertzner, 2007).

Within this oppressive social context, interpersonal relationships are an area of particular vulnerability for GSM people (Hatzenbuehler, 2009) because GSM-related stigma is experienced in relation to others. Given the pervasiveness of negative attitudes about GSM identities, it's understandable that GSM individuals may become secretive and distant in their relationships. These experiences begin in the family because, in contrast to individuals with other minority identities, GSM individuals often grow up in families that don't share their minority status and therefore tend to develop an awareness of their difference from important others early in life. And whereas individuals from racial or cultural minority groups may receive messages from their family of origin, both covert and overt, about coping with oppression and taking pride in their minority identity, this isn't the case for most GSM people. Role models at school, in the community, and in the culture are also lacking. This feeling of dissimilarity can result in a sense of alienation and create vulnerabilities for mental health problems (e.g., Starks, Newcomb, & Mustanski, 2015).

For GSM individuals, interpersonal challenges go beyond merely being different. Norms for gender and sexual conformity are strong and were even stronger when most GSM clients were children. These norms are apparent throughout society but are often most salient within family structures. Deviation from these norms can go beyond rejection to overt punishment, including verbal, physical, and sexual abuse. Indeed, GSM people are much more likely than their cisgender, heterosexual peers to have experienced childhood victimization at home and in the community—a difference that is evident even when adult siblings are compared to each other (see Balsam, Beauchaine, Mickey, & Rothblum, 2005). Beyond the family, GSM people are at elevated risk for verbal, physical, and sexual victimization in both childhood and adulthood. Being bullied in childhood is also a common experience for GSM people (Pilkington & D'Augelli, 1995), perhaps especially among those who are gender nonconforming (Toomey, Ryan, Diaz, Card, & Russell, 2010). It is well established that these kinds of traumatic experiences have a deleterious effect on mental and physical health. Additionally, harm from others can lead to guardedness and unwillingness to trust, both of which can impact social functioning (Janoff-Bullman & Frieze, 1983).

Another relevant aspect of GSM identities is that; unlike a number of other minority identities, they can be concealed or disclosed to varying degrees. The choice of disclosing to others, referred to as coming out, is seen as an ongoing process over the life span, rather than a single event. Within each social context, whether a particular relationship (e.g., with a new neighbor) or a situation (e.g., a new job), GSM individuals must engage in complex internal negotiations and closely monitor the social environment to make decisions about whether, how, and when to disclose their GSM identity. This ongoing stressor can be experienced as a sense of vigilance, with a need to be on guard against possible rejection in new relationships

(Balsam, Beadnell, & Molina, 2013; Hatzenbuehler, Nolen-Hoeksema, & Erickson, 2008). This rejection sensitivity (Pachankis, Goldfried, & Ramrattan, 2008), which stems from negative childhood experiences, is linked to mental health and interpersonal problems in adulthood (Feinstein, Goldfried, & Davila, 2012).

Bear in mind that all of these unique experiences related to GSM identity may vary depending on other social and cultural contextual factors, including race, ethnicity, immigrant status, socioeconomic status, and disability. For GSM people of color, for example, the degree to which GSM identity and racial or ethnic identity are personally salient varies from person to person, or for the same person across contexts. A Korean-American lesbian woman, for example, might feel more identified with her Korean culture when she's with family, who may not even know about her lesbian identity, yet more identified with her lesbian identity when she's with her white partner, who may not identify with her Korean heritage. These nuances of identity and disclosure of identity can create a sense of separateness and interpersonal detachment among GSM individuals who are multiply marginalized.

Another important issue to consider is that the label "GSM" encompasses a diverse array of sexual and gender minority identities, and within this broad assemblage people may have vastly different life experiences. For example, lesbian and gay individuals have enjoyed greater acceptance and visibility within US culture in recent years, whereas bisexual and transgender people are often left out of public discourse, which may heighten their personal sense of isolation and stigma. And although community groups and organizations often refer to themselves as serving the lesbian, gay, bisexual, and transgender community, the dominant perspectives within such organizations are often those of lesbian and gay people. Paradoxically, bisexual people face challenges and potential prejudice in coming out as GSM to society at large, and as bisexual to some segments of the GSM community. Likewise, transgender and gender nonconforming people face challenges and prejudice from both cisgender populations and lesbian, gay, and bisexual populations regarding their gender identities and expression, perhaps fueled by the complex, uncomfortable relationship between discrimination and perceived gender atypicality that is common among lesbians and gay men (e.g., van Beusekom, Baams, Bos, Overbeek, & Sandfort, 2015). Clearly, then, it is important for clinicians working with GSM clients to conduct individualized assessments of the unique stressors and interpersonal challenges related to a given individual's specific identity.

Functional Analytic Psychotherapy for GSM

Functional analytic psychotherapy is a behaviorally based approach that involves creating an intense and curative therapeutic relationship. It arose through the exploration of a simple question: Why is it that some therapists are remarkably more successful than others in terms of promoting recovery and symptom reduction, as well as more general thriving? Person-centered psychotherapy had identified characteristics such as therapeutic warmth, empathy, and unconditional positive regard as important components of effective psychotherapy, yet these factors alone didn't seem to account for the variety of therapeutic outcomes or the variable effectiveness of well-researched manualized therapies (Kohlenberg & Tsai, 1991). Ultimately, observation and careful functional analysis revealed that highly effective therapists tend to respond in particular ways to particular types of in-session behavior. Specifically, when therapists bring a combination of awareness, courage, and love to their interactions, in-session shaping of interpersonal behaviors tends to generalize to out-of-session relationships (Tsai et al., 2009).

The Components of FAP

In FAP, the basic unit of analysis is clinically relevant behavior (CRB): behaviors that manifest in session and have a bearing on clients' difficulties outside of session. CRBs that interfere with relationships or maintain clinical problems are referred to as CRB1. Behaviors that are functional or interpersonally intimate are referred to as CRB2. FAP therapists work to naturally reinforce CRB2 in session and to block or decrease the expression of CRB1 (Tsai et al., 2009). Whereas acceptance and commitment therapy (ACT; Hayes, Strosahl, & Wilson, 1999) focuses on client-defined values, FAP always holds deep, genuine, and meaningful relationships as a value to be promoted in therapy.

FAP utilizes five rules to promote behavior change in session (Tsai et al., 2009):

Rule 1: Watch for the occurrence of CRB.

Rule 2: Evoke CRB in session.

Rule 3: Reinforce CRB2 naturally.

Rule 4: Observe how therapist behavior affects the client.

Rule 5: Promote generalization of CRB2 to out-of-session situations.

Bear in mind that the five rules of FAP are guidelines, rather than a proscriptive course of therapy, and that the FAP process involves ongoing application of these rules. That said, the five rules of FAP are in keeping with basic behavioral principles, which suggest that as long as CRB occurs or is evoked and CRB2 is naturally reinforced, CRB2 will increase in frequency within session, potentially promoting out-of-session behavior change (Lizarazo, Muñoz-Martínez, Santos, & Kanter, 2015).

Minority Stress and FAP

FAP is fundamentally a contextual behavioral approach, so it demands that therapists consider the broader environments of the client's life. No functional analysis of GSM clients is complete without an acknowledgment of the complex and painful ways that most societies have expressed and continue to express bias toward GSM communities. Minority stress theory is one means of considering these factors. When individuals begin to wonder whether they possess a GSM identity, they may experience aversive contingencies from their environment, such as verbal harassment, social rejection, and physical assault (Plummer, 2010). GSM clients who present clinically with anxiety, depression, or substance use may have been affected by factors related to minority stress that aren't present among heterosexual, cisgender clients (Cochran & Mays, 2009; Feinstein et al., 2012). Patterns related to concealment, expressions of shame, avoiding discussion of traumatic losses, or avoiding topics that might elicit judgment or rejection are all effects of minority stress that may be identified as CRB1 when using a FAP approach with GSM clients.

The Five Rules of GSM-Sensitive FAP

FAP may be challenging for therapists who are inexperienced with functional analysis or with GSM communities, as the same behavior could be either CRB1 or CRB2 depending on the context and history of a specific client. To help you navigate any such challenges, in this section we discuss how to apply each of the five rules of FAP in a GSM-sensitive way.

RULE 1: BE AWARE OF GSM-SPECIFIC CRB

If a young gay man discloses that he's attracted to his male therapist and his presenting problem is sexual compulsivity and using sexuality to block interpersonal vulnerability, this would be a CRB1. However, if a client has previously stated that he fears rejecting responses or violence in response to self-disclosure to heterosexual men, and he knows his therapist identifies as heterosexual, this expression of attraction may involve vulnerability and trust, making it CRB2, which should be naturally reinforced. In short, the topography of a behavior doesn't indicate its function. Of course, the preceding examples aren't mutually exclusive. In the event that CRB1 and CRB2 are commingled, delineating and reinforcing the aspects of the behavior that represent CRB2 may be helpful in shaping a client's behavior. Finally, as with any application of FAP to a minority population, it is imperative that therapists be aware of the limitations of their knowledge and work to remedy any gaps by pursuing information from sources other than the client (Miller, Williams, Wetterneck, Kanter, & Tsai, 2015).

RULE 2: EVOKE GSM-SPECIFIC CRB IN SESSION

A powerful therapeutic technique with GSM clients is to amplify typical FAP exercises by heightening their evocative potential in regard to sexuality and gender. For example, a cisgender therapist might ask a transgender client what it's like to explore gender identity with someone who is in a position to identify with the gender assigned at birth. As another example, the first author of this chapter, who identifies as a gay man, has often asked gay male clients with relationship challenges what it's like to be interpersonally vulnerable and close to another gay man in the moment. An alternative approach is to use FAP's Loss Inventory assignment (Tsai et al., 2009), which can be given with modified instructions, asking clients to reflect upon and enumerate their unspoken losses due to being GSM. (Please visit http://www.newharbinger.com/34282 to download the exercise "GSM Loss Inventory.") In all cases, it's imperative that therapists be aware of GSM-specific developmental milestones, such as coming out, dating, hormonal or surgical interventions, or first sexual encounters, and how family members, friends, and loved ones responded to these milestones, in order to create a complex, accurate case conceptualization.

RULE 3: REINFORCE CRB2 NATURALLY

For therapists who aren't experienced with GSM clients, reinforcing CRB2s naturally can be a tricky area—and one where stigma might intrude into therapy. This could occur if the therapist either reinforces the client's self-stigmatizing beliefs or behaviors or fails to explore issues related to the client's sexual orientation or gender identity, perhaps due to the therapist's own avoidance or discomfort (Plummer, 2010).

"Natural reinforcement" refers to emotional expression reflecting the therapist's genuine experience in the moment. For example, in response to a client sharing his realization that he couldn't fake an attraction to a female partner, the therapist could foster closeness and connection by going beyond simple reflection to express genuine concern, warmth, and sadness for the client.

RULE 4: OBSERVE YOUR IMPACT

There are several ways to track the therapeutic impact of rule 3 (reinforcing CRB2). Of course, one is noticing any reduction of symptoms of psychological distress and CRB1. Another is attending to the client's communication in session, noticing any increases in vulnerable personal disclosures or statements indicating that the client has attached a greater sense of interpersonal closeness or feeling of meaningfulness to the therapeutic relationship.

Here's an example of how that might play out in session: One of the authors had a client who often laughed during uncomfortable interpersonal disclosures, including sharing that his husband made a passing comment that he had thoughts of divorcing him over a minor conflict. When this therapist responded authentically regarding how painful this situation sounded, the client softened and shared that he felt truly seen by the therapist. For the rest of his course of therapy, he no longer laughed during moments of difficult personal disclosure and was more open to staying with and vulnerably disclosing painful experiences. By attending to the success of this intervention, the therapist determined that, for this client, authentically reflecting the emotions that he'd minimized could block CRB1 and promote CRB2. This emboldened the therapist to explore reinforcing other CRB2s by empathically reflecting the client's muted negative affect.

RULE 5: PROMOTE GENERALIZATION

The ultimate measure of any therapy's effectiveness is the extent to which it leads to lasting change outside of the therapy room. An example would be when an emotionally distant client, who has begun to voice feelings of closeness, trust, and intimacy with her therapist, shares that she's taken risks in her out-of-session life that have deepened friendships or romantic relationships. A classic tool used in FAP to promote generalization is an emotional risk log, in which real-life behaviors topographically similar to in-session CRB2s are targeted for daily practice in the client's life outside of session.

Case Example: Using FAP to Help GSM Clients

This case example focuses on use of the therapeutic relationship and the five rules of FAP to increase courage, vulnerability, and intimacy in a client whose life experience had highlighted the dangers of vulnerability, leading to core concerns of guardedness and isolation, which are common themes among older sexual minority clients who seek treatment for depression.

The therapist is a gay man. The client, Pamela, is a fifty-four-year-old Caucasian lesbian woman. She has been married two times, to men in both cases, though she has always experienced sexual and romantic attraction to women and has identified as a lesbian since her most recent divorce at age thirty-six. She has one daughter, from her first marriage, who is attending a university across the country. Pamela recently ended a four-year relationship with a woman whom she felt distant from and unhappy with. For many years Pamela was an enlisted serviceperson in the military and moved frequently, and she is currently a contractor with a medical records company. She doesn't feel connected or close to any of her colleagues, and she has few long-term friends. She presented for therapy meeting criteria for a major depressive episode, which she had experienced before. She doesn't understand why the current episode isn't resolving as quickly as past episodes.

Pamela: I was so resentful for so long. I tried to be perfect and fit everything she wanted me to be, and it just ate away at me from the inside. She might have been trying to change after I told her I was leaving, but I was done already.

Therapist: It sounds like this is something you've experienced in other relationships—giving care, effort, and love to others and hoping that the other person will anticipate your needs. [Rule 1: Pamela's reflection on how her relationships go wrong may reflect an important CRB.]

Pamela: Yes! I know it doesn't make sense, but deep down it feels like if someone really loved me, they'd notice that my needs aren't being met.

Therapist: I have to admit that this makes me a bit nervous. I wonder if this will come up in our relationship here? Maybe you have a need in therapy that I can't meet for you? [Rule 2: Evoking CRB by describing the potential parallel between Pamela's other relationships and the therapeutic relationship.]

Pamela: I don't think that's a risk! You get paid to be with me, and you'll forget about me the second I leave this office. [CRB1: Minimizing the relevance of the relationship.]

Therapist: It sounds like it would be hard to let this be a real relationship. [Rule 3: Responding to CRB1 contingently, focusing on the function of the statement and not the content.]

Pamela: It just seems like it would be so painful to open up like that if this is the sort of relationship that ends one day. [CRB2: Acknowledging a desire to connect and expressing some vulnerability in regard to sharing her fear of connecting.]

Therapist: It is scary to form a new relationship, and there's this uncertainty about what will happen for us in the future. I feel that uncertainty too, and yet I still want you to trust me and share your needs so our relationship can matter. [Rule 3: Naturally reinforcing the CRB2 of expressing uncertainty and wishing to connect more deeply.]

Pamela: My heart is beating so rapidly. I want to risk it, and I know in my head that this is probably important… It just feels so scary. I'm afraid that if I tell you what I need and you don't give it to me, I'll feel even more unlovable. [CRB2: Opening up and being even more vulnerable.]

Therapist: I can see your eyes tearing up, and it looks like you're touched. Is that because I'm sharing my desire to connect with you and have this relationship matter? [Rule 4: Observing the impact of his actions with Pamela in the moment.]

Pamela: I want to know how to do this. I feel like everyone else figured this out so long ago. I'm already in my fifties, and I don't know how to do this. [CRB2: Staying connected and disclosing more.]

Therapist: I feel like what we're doing right now might relate to what you were saying earlier about dating, relationships, and friendships: that if you let me know what you need from me and risk me not giving it to you, it might feel even worse. It seems like this is a pattern that keeps coming up with other relationships. Would you be willing to practice what we've been doing outside of session? We've discussed using an emotional risk log to practice courage outside of session. Would you be willing to strive to take a risk, no matter how small, at least once a day over the next week by making what you need clear to someone close to you? [Rule 5: Promoting generalization.]

Pamela: I can do this. I think it's the only thing that will help.

In Pamela's case, over a lengthy period of time she gradually began to increase her risks, starting with clarifying and expressing her needs within friendships and work relationships. At first she was reluctant to try dating again, but after over a year in therapy she began to consider the possibility. She was anxious to get it right this time, without sliding back into old patterns of trying to appease her partner. After she finally went out on a date, the following dialogue ensued.

Pamela: So it happened. I had my first date with Margo.

Therapist: That's wonderful! I know how nervous you were. What happened? [Rule 3: Reinforcing CRB2 with a genuine and warm response to Pamela's report of a new behavior in alignment with her goals.]

Pamela: Well, I'm not sure if she's right for me. There were some things we had very much in common, and also some views of hers that didn't work for me. At one point she tried to order a chicken dish for me! I love when she's being butch, but…[CRB2: Stating a preference for dating a woman who identifies as butch is a new vulnerable disclosure for Pamela.]

Therapist: You're a vegetarian… [Misses the chance to apply rule 3: Reinforcing the vulnerable disclosure.]

Pamela: Yes! This is embarrassing to say, but ten years ago I would have just eaten the sides and pushed bits of chicken around my plate so I didn't look too fussy, but I would have resented it. This time, I spoke up and changed the order, and I told Margo that I don't eat meat. [Huge CRB2: Not only asserting a personal detail about herself that may elicit judgment, but also asserting what she needs, rather than hoping her date will anticipate it.]

Therapist: This is huge! You just jumped right in and told Margo what you needed without expecting her to figure it out or hoping she'd catch on. [Rule 3: Enthusiastically reinforcing Pamela for the risk and acknowledging its amplitude. Also rule 5: Relating this particular risk to the broader class of behaviors that is the target of therapy.]

Pamela: I was so anxious right afterward, but it wasn't a big deal at all. It turns out that Margo's longest relationship was with a vegetarian, so the incident led to sharing stories. She told me how excited she was to learn this about me, and that she was considering trying it out herself.

Therapist: Wow! So if you hadn't have taken that risk, not only might you have felt resentful, you would also have missed the chance to have a warm and connected moment with her. [Rule 5: Linking a positive outcome to the broader class of behaviors reflected by expressing her needs.]

By the end of therapy, Pamela had become fairly adept at voicing her needs. She continued to struggle with identifying when it was a good idea to do so and weighing factors such as the importance of the relationship or the cost of not voicing a particular concern. However, she also began to view being fully present and expressing her desires as an integral part of all meaningful relationships. She had deepened a small number of friendships, and for the first time in her life started traveling with friends. Although she hadn't yet forged another long-term relationship, she was dating frequently and had learned to end relationships when they weren't a good fit for her.

Conclusion

The habitual practice of guarding oneself from genuine and authentic connection comes at a high price. Life as a GSM youth is rarely completely safe, and adults' expectations in regard to gender and sexual identity are often confounded by the cross-gender behavior of transgender youth and sexual minority boys, specifically. It's understandable that behaviors that effectively mitigate the distress of moving through a dangerous world tend to become overrehearsed and reflexive. Further, taking new steps toward emotional vulnerability is often accompanied by fear, so it isn't surprising that interpersonal difficulties generally don't resolve in the absence of a safe, nurturing place to grow. While for some GSM individuals that might occur among loving friends or in a relationship, therapists should be mindful of the deeply meaningful and pivotal role the therapeutic relationship plays, especially given the greater frequency with which GSM individuals turn to psychotherapy (Murphy, Rawlings, & Howe, 2002).

Given that judgmental, rejecting, or even violent responses may dominate the personal history of GSM clients, the therapist's usual task of fostering an environment of awareness, compassion, and therapeutic love is paramount. FAP provides a lens through which therapists can not only deepen the therapeutic relationship, but also use this relationship to promote the types of vulnerable relationships that GSM clients want and need in their personal lives.

References

Balsam, K. F., Beadnell, B., & Molina, Y. (2013). The Daily Heterosexist Experiences Questionnaire: Measuring minority stress among lesbian, gay, bisexual, and transgender adults. *Measurement and Evaluation in Counseling and Development, 46*, 3–25.

Balsam, K. F., Beauchaine, T. P., Mickey, R. M., & Rothblum, E. D. (2005). Mental health of lesbian, gay, bisexual, and heterosexual siblings: Effects of gender, sexual orientation, and family. *Journal of Abnormal Psychology, 114*, 471–476.

Castonguay, L. G., Constantino, M. J., McAleavey, A. A., & Goldfried, M. R. (2010). The therapeutic alliance in cognitive-behavioral therapy. In J. C. Muran & J. P. Barber (Eds.), *The therapeutic alliance: An evidence-based guide to practice*. New York: Guilford.

Cochran, S. D., & Mays, V. M. (2009). Burden of psychiatric morbidity among lesbian, gay, and bisexual individuals in the California Quality of Life Survey. *Journal of Abnormal Psychology, 118*, 647–658.

Falco, K. L. (1991). *Psychotherapy with lesbian clients: Theory into practice*. Hove, United Kingdom: Psychology Press.

Feinstein, B. A., Goldfried, M. R., & Davila, J. (2012). The relationship between experiences of discrimination and mental health among lesbians and gay men: An examination of internalized homonegativity and rejection sensitivity as potential mechanisms. *Journal of Consulting and Clinical Psychology, 80*, 917–927.

Gonsiorek, J. (1982). The use of diagnostic concepts in working with gay and lesbian populations. *Journal of Homosexuality, 7*, 9–20.

Hatzenbuehler, M. L. (2009). How does sexual minority stigma "get under the skin"? A psychological mediation framework. *Psychological Bulletin, 135,* 707–730.

Hatzenbuehler, M. L., McLaughlin, K. A., & Xuan, Z. (2012). Social networks and risk for depressive symptoms in a national sample of sexual minority youth. *Social Science and Medicine, 75,* 1184–1191.

Hatzenbuehler, M. L., Nolen-Hoeksema, S., & Erickson, S. J. (2008). Minority stress predictors of HIV risk behavior, substance use, and depressive symptoms: Results from a prospective study of bereaved gay men. *Health Psychology, 27,* 455–462.

Hayes, S. C., Strosahl, K. D., & Wilson, K. G. (1999). *Acceptance and commitment therapy: An experiential approach to behavior change.* New York: Guilford.

Institute of Medicine. (2011). *The health of lesbian, gay, bisexual, and transgender people: Building a foundation for better understanding.* Washington, DC: National Academies Press.

Janoff-Bullman, R., & Frieze, I. H. (1983). A theoretical perspective for understanding reactions to victimization. *Journal of Social Issues, 39,* 1–17.

Kertzner, R. M. (2007). Developmental issues in lesbian and gay adulthood. In I. H. Meyer & M. E. Northridge (Eds.), *The health of sexual minorities: Public health perspectives on gay, bisexual, and transgender populations.* New York: Springer.

Kohlenberg, R. J., Kanter, J. W., Bolling, M. Y., Parker, C. R., & Tsai, M. (2002). Enhancing cognitive therapy for depression with functional analytic psychotherapy: Treatment guidelines and empirical findings. *Cognitive and Behavioral Practice, 9,* 213–229.

Kohlenberg, R. J., & Tsai, M. (1991). *Functional analytic psychotherapy: Creating intense and curative therapeutic relationships.* New York: Plenum Press.

Landolt, M. A., Bartholomew, K., Saffrey, C., Oram, D., & Perlman, D. (2004). Gender nonconformity, childhood rejection, and adult attachment: A study of gay men. *Archives of Sexual Behavior, 33,* 117–128.

Lizarazo, N. E., Muñoz-Martínez, A. M., Santos, M. M., & Kanter, J. W. (2015). A within-subjects evaluation of the effects of functional analytic psychotherapy on in-session and out-of-session client behavior. *Psychological Record, 65,* 463–474.

Meyer, I. H. (2003). Prejudice, social stress, and mental health in lesbian, gay, and bisexual populations: Conceptual issues and research evidence. *Psychological Bulletin, 129,* 674–697.

Miller, A., Williams, M. T., Wetterneck, C. T., Kanter, J., & Tsai, M. (2015). Using functional analytic psychotherapy to improve awareness and connection in racially diverse client-therapist dyads. *Behavior Therapist, 38,* 150–156.

Murphy, J. A., Rawlings, E. I., & Howe, S. R. (2002). A survey of clinical psychologists on treating lesbian, gay, and bisexual clients. *Professional Psychology: Research and Practice, 33,* 183.

147

Pachankis, J. E., Goldfried, M. R., & Ramrattan, M. E. (2008). Extension of the rejection sensitivity construct to the interpersonal functioning of gay men. *Journal of Consulting and Clinical Psychology, 76*, 306–317.

Pilkington, N. W., & D'Augelli, A. R. (1995). Victimization of lesbian, gay, and bisexual youth in community settings. *Journal of Community Psychology, 23*, 33–56.

Plummer, M. D. (2010). FAP with sexual minorities. In J. Kanter, M. Tsai, & R. J. Kohlenberg (Eds.), *The practice of functional analytic psychotherapy.* New York: Springer.

Starks, T. J., Newcomb, M. E., & Mustanski, B. (2015). A longitudinal study of interpersonal relationships among lesbian, gay, and bisexual adolescents and young adults: Mediational pathways from attachment to romantic relationship quality. *Archives of Sexual Behavior, 44*, 1821–1831.

Szymanski, D. M., & Hilton, A. N. (2013). Fear of intimacy as a mediator of the internalized heterosexism-relationship quality link among men in same-sex relationships. *Contemporary Family Therapy, 35*, 760–772.

Thwaites, R., & Bennett-Levy, J. (2007). Conceptualizing empathy in cognitive behaviour therapy: Making the implicit explicit. *Behavioural and Cognitive Psychotherapy, 35*, 591–612.

Toomey, R. B., Ryan, C., Diaz, R. M., Card, N. A., & Russell, S. T. (2010). Gender-nonconforming lesbian, gay, bisexual, and transgender youth: School victimization and young adult psychosocial adjustment. *Developmental psychology, 46*, 1580–1589.

Tsai, M., Kohlenberg, R. J., Kanter, J. W., Kohlenberg, B., Follette, W. C., & Callaghan, G. M. (Eds.). (2009). *A guide to functional analytic psychotherapy: Awareness, courage, love, and behaviorism.* New York: Springer.

Van Beusekom, G., Baams, L., Bos, H. M., Overbeek, G., & Sandfort, T. G. (2015). Gender nonconformity, homophobic peer victimization, and mental health: How same-sex attraction and biological sex matter. *Journal of Sex Research, 53*, 98–108.

148

CHAPTER 8

Elephants in the Room: Straight Therapists' Microaggressions with GSM Couples

Joanne Steinwachs, *private practice*; and
Thomas G. Szabo, *Florida Institute of Technology*

Dealing with others is dealing with ourselves dealing with others.

—Norman Fischer

Doing couples therapy is hard. Managing the complex dynamics of all of the relationships in the room—therapist to each partner, partners to each other, and partners to the therapist—is challenging. Couples often present in great distress and with urgency, and it isn't uncommon for partners to be unskillful and even hostile in session. Not surprisingly, research (Jacobson et al., 1984) suggests that preventing relationship problems is easier than treating them, that there is great ambiguity in determining what a successful outcome of couples therapy would be (staying together or separating), and that partners' goals are often at odds (e.g., favoring the status quo versus change).

Working with gender and sexual minority (GSM) couples can increase the challenges. One consideration is that efficacy evaluations of behavioral marital therapy have mostly looked at married, white, heterosexual couples (Spitalnick & McNair, 2005). When we conducted literature searches in PsycInfo using the terms "efficacy studies," "gay," "lesbian," "LGBT," and "behavioral couples therapy" in all their various combinations, we came up with zero results. In addition, therapists may face a mismatch between their gender role or identity and the couple's. Couples therapists clearly need good distress tolerance skills for this work (Rait, 2000), regardless of their clients' GSM status.

Heteronormativity and Microaggressions in Therapy

This chapter refers to gay, lesbian, bisexual, transgender, queer, and questioning people as gender and sexual minorities (GSM). Although the likelihood of overt bigotry by therapists toward GSM people seeking therapy is less than in the past, the probability of subtle homonegative or heteronormative responses from the therapist remains fairly high (Moon, 2011; Plummer, 2012), especially if there is a gender identity mismatch between therapist and client. Heteronormative responses from therapists often reflect a bias in which "any sexual identity that varies from being 'fully heterosexual' is viewed as deviant, morally wrong, and unnatural" (McGeorge & Carlson, 2011, p. 15). Such heteronormative verbal responses, even when offered in a well-meaning way, can be particularly insidious because they implicitly convey disempowerment of those whose behavior lies outside the assumed norm. McGeorge and Carlson suggest that heterosexual therapists cannot free themselves completely from a heteronormative bias. Therefore, they recommend that "heterosexual therapists who desire to practice LGB affirmative therapy need to acknowledge that they are both heterosexist and anti-heterosexist or, said slightly differently, heterosexist and LGB affirmative therapists" (p. 22).

The implicit prejudice of heteronormativity can manifest as microaggression, which communicates denigration and even contempt (MacDonald, 2013). Microaggressions have a detrimental impact on treatment of GSM clients, leading to early termination, lack of trust in therapy in general, confusion, invalidation, internalized homophobia, and lack of safety (Shelton & Delgado-Romero, 2011). Plummer (2012) suggests that most if not all therapists have worked with at least one GSM client. In spite of this, lack of specific training for straight therapists working with GSM clients increases the probability that they will commit microaggressions.

To counteract this, therapists are often given stigma awareness training, in which they learn to suppress language that implies prejudice. However, suppression of prejudice can paradoxically lead to more prejudicial thoughts and behaviors and make it difficult to remain present, negatively impacting interpersonal connections (Lillis & Levin, 2014). This can have damaging effects on the therapeutic relationship. Furthermore, most people know what is considered bigoted and can refrain from using prejudicial language. Nevertheless, implicit prejudice is likely to be present even among people who deny overt prejudice (Luoma, 2014).

Plummer (2012) suggests using a functional contextual approach. In this approach, both client and therapist behaviors are continually assessed and reassessed throughout the therapy in the light of each person's history (Kanter et al., 2009). "Every client is a micro-culture, carrying deeply rooted cultural, social, generational, and reinforcement histories, highly different from the therapist's" (Vandenburghe et al., 2012, p. 183). Therapists are also micro-cultures with their own specific histories. A contextual approach allows therapists to explore thoughts, emotions, actions, and sensations from the stance that everything a person does make sense, given that person's particular history. Importantly, this approach allows therapists to do more than just see the validity of a particular way of being; it also allows them to help clients change unworkable patterns of interaction.

Because it's common for GSM clients to experience microaggressions in therapy, (MacDonald, 2013; Shelton & Delgado-Romero, 2011), this chapter offers an approach for addressing microaggression that blends acceptance and commitment therapy and functional analytic psychotherapy, illustrated with an extended case example.

Human Language and the Inevitability of Microaggression

Researchers have long been interested in the factors that cause people with verbal skills to respond to the world in less than optimal ways. In regard to a phenomenon called "rule insensitivity" (Hayes, Brownstein, Zettle, Rosenfarb, & Korn, 1986), numerous experiments have shown that when given a rule, people often continue to respond to the rule after the situation changes and the rule no longer applies (e.g., Matthews, Shimoff, Catania, & Sagvolden, 1977; Shimoff, Catania, & Matthews, 1981). In regard to the topic of this chapter, it's easy to imagine that a therapist who's been trained to suppress prejudiced speech may overextend this rule and avoid opportunities to evoke intense, therapeutic dialogues with a GSM client due to fear of making a mistake and demonstrating bigotry.

An additional factor related to less than optimal human performance is the way language systems operate upon the worldview of a speaker. Compared to animal communication, human language is unique in that words can be used to relate events with no physical counterparts in the immediate environment. For example, the word "duck" can be related to *utka* (Russian for a type of duck) by speakers fluent in English even though they have no Russian language skills, an actual duck (or *utka*) isn't present, and they have never seen an *utka* or heard the word *utka* before the current context.

Further, these events can be related in a variety of arbitrary ways using relational cues such as superior-inferior or valuable-worthless. This relational repertoire provides language users with remarkable advantages in navigating the world. However, there are hidden costs to this ability. Humans as young as two, without any formal training, rapidly expand their networks of relational responses, many of which may be faulty and generated so quickly that they seem to occur without thought. To give an example, consider the relationship of opposition between "like me" and "not like me." "Not like me" can be in a relationship with "unfamiliar," which can coordinate with "uncomfortable" and then with "bad." For a human competent in language, this can happen in a split second. So if a therapist is a white, middle-class, married, straight man, and his client is a black, poor, transgender woman who supports herself as a sex worker, problematic relations may emerge very quickly and without any intention.

One interesting feature of language is that these verbal relations can be particularly intractable once formed. Whether applied to self or others, they can operate as straitjackets (as does heteronormativity), narrowly confining the person to behavior that coheres with the relation. Continuing with the preceding example, the therapist's various verbal descriptions of his client ("transgender," "poor," "sex worker," and so on) could interfere with his ability to accurately hear the client's disclosure of personal experiences that don't fit with the therapist's relational networks around these descriptions.

In sum, rule insensitivity, rapidly expanding relational networks, and rigidly defined repertoires in regard to the self and others conspire to make it highly likely if not inevitable that the most well-meaning individuals, including therapists, will commit microaggressions when interacting with others from the unavoidable network of heteronormativity. Although this state of affairs may seem hopeless, there is a way out. The remainder of this chapter is devoted to describing ways that therapists can use acceptance and commitment therapy and functional analytic psychotherapy to undermine the hurtful effects of language and foster healing within the therapeutic relationship.

Overview of ACT with a Focus on Microaggression

Acceptance and commitment therapy undermines negative processes of language to help people actively and mindfully engage in their here-and-now experience (Hayes, Strosahl, & Wilson, 1999). As a result, energy formerly spent in attempts to avoid or control natural distress can be devoted to determining one's values and constructing a life of meaning. For example, instead of fearfully scrutinizing our responses for microaggressions, therapists can engage fully and openly, knowing that they will make missteps and that they can take responsibility for doing so.

ACT focuses on fostering processes of psychological flexibility: attention to the present moment, acceptance, values identification, defusion from thoughts and other mental content, committed action, and flexible perspective taking. Each has an opposing process; preoccupation with the past and/or future, experiential avoidance, unclear or unexamined values, cognitive fusion, unworkable persistence or impulsivity, and rigid perspective taking (Strosahl, Hayes, Wilson, & Gifford, 2004).

ACT therapists routinely use metaphors to reorganize the functions of related events. Because metaphors call attention to new relationships between events, they can be used to transform how those events function. One example of the clinical utility of metaphor is illustrated in the following dialogue.

Therapist: Let's say you and I are moving out of our houses. We take a box into our kitchens, write the word "Kitchen," on it and put some stuff into it. Will we have the same things in our boxes?

Client: There may be some things the same, but not completely.

Therapist: But the boxes have the same words on them. Think of words as boxes. What might we find if we opened up our word boxes called "Normal Relationships" or "Healthy Sexual Expression"? We need to move carefully, especially when we start assuming that our word boxes all have the same stuff in them.

Client: That makes sense.

Therapist: Now, how did the stuff in our kitchen boxes come to be there?

Client: Maybe some of it we inherited from our family, like dishes or something. Some we bought ourselves. Some things just ended up there, like stuff in the junk drawer.

Therapist: We can inherit things that fill up our word boxes. Since I probably have a different history and inheritance, my word boxes might be a very bad fit for you. If that happens, we need a way of knowing that I might be trying to put your experience in a box that doesn't fit. One way you might notice this is feeling suddenly unsafe or uncomfortable. You might tell yourself that I don't mean any harm, and I probably don't, but letting this slide can harm our relationship. No matter how uncomfortable you or I become, I want to know when you feel I'm distorting your experience.

In this example, the complex stimulus functions of history and learning are transferred from accumulating objects to accumulating ways of responding and also to the experience of heteronormativity. This helps create psychological flexibility for both client and therapist to directly address microaggression. This is just one example of how ACT therapists can use language to undermine the rigid language rules that may accompany addressing microaggression.

Overview of FAP with a Focus on Microaggression

FAP uses behavioral principles of reinforcement in the context of interpersonal psychotherapy. FAP's theorized primary mechanism of change is "providing natural reinforcement for client improvements that occur during the session" (Kohlenberg & Tsai, 1991, p. 11). Instances of client behavior are seen as primarily falling into two classes of clinically relevant behavior (CRB). CRB1 is in-session examples of the client's inflexibility processes that impede connection, and CRB2 is more flexible behavior that facilitates interpersonal connection. Therapists watch for CRB as it occurs in the moment, in the therapeutic relationship, and respond contingently by ignoring or confronting CRB1 and reinforcing CRB2. This is thought to shape more effective interpersonal behavior that can then be generalized to the client's life.

FAP also attends to therapist behaviors, or Ts. In parallel with CRBs, T1 denotes therapist inflexibility that disrupts connection, whereas T2 refers to therapist flexibility that strengthens connection (Callaghan, 2006). Because FAP is a contextual approach grounded in functional analysis, therapist behaviors, such as becoming angry or frightened or feeling shame in session, are not necessarily T1. Therapist behaviors such as denying, evading, or ignoring these responses or pretending to be unaffected probably are T1. In contrast, disclosing these responses in a nondefensive manner would probably constitute T2 and lead to more trust and openness in the therapy relationship.

To bring these concepts to life and tie them in with the ACT processes outlined above, here are two examples of therapist's private behavior after committing a microaggression. The first is T1, and the second is T2.

Rigid perspective-taking: *I'm a terrible person and a terrible therapist.*

Experiential avoidance: *I just can't stand that I've made this...*

Cognitive fusion and rigid focus on the past or future: *... therapy-destroying mistake.*

Unworkable persistence or impulsivity: *I'll just apologize over and over or change the subject...*

Disruption of values: *...because it's more important that I not feel this than that I help my client.*

Flexible perspective-taking and acceptance: *I am a person with a history, and that history just showed up in a very painful way for my client and me.*

Cognitive defusion: *Although my mind tells me I'm a bad therapist, I can hold both my effect and my intent...*

Acceptance: *...and be open to how it has impacted this person I care about...*

Committed action: *...by slowing down, acknowledging what happened, creating a context where my client can be fully heard,...*

Values: *...and being open to my client's pain to deepen our connection...*

Present-moment awareness: *...right now, in this moment.*

FAP sets forth five rules to guide therapeutic interactions (Weeks, Kanter, Bonow, Landes, & Busch, 2011). Instead of rigid "musts," these are organizing principles. (For a complete discussion of these rules, see chapter 7.)

Rule 1: Watch for CRB.

Rule 2: Evoke CRB.

Rule 3: Reinforce CRB2.

Rule 4: Assess the effects of your behavior on the client.

Rule 5: Provide functional interpretations that promote generalization.

Regarding rule 4, we suggest asking explicitly about the effects of your behavior, starting in the first session. Establishing a context for honest client feedback is crucial to creating space in which therapist microaggressions can be addressed. An effective way to embed rule 4 is to ask clients to complete session bridging questionnaires (appendix D in Tsai et al., 2009). Another is to make explicit the probability that you will commit microaggressions. Here's an example of how you might address this topic.

Therapist: Let's talk about intent and effect. I often get into a struggle with other people when these two things show up. Let's imagine I say something you experience as hurtful and you let me know. And then I say, "I didn't mean to hurt you."

Client: Yeah, but I'm still hurt.

Therapist: And we could argue about it.

Client: Yeah, forever.

Therapist: It's interesting though. If you say to me, "What you just said hurt me," is it possible that I would think you mean, "You meant to hurt me"?

Client: Sure, maybe.

Therapist: And I could then push back, because that wasn't my intent.

Client: Yeah.

Therapist: Yet the other direction is equally challenging: If you agree that I didn't mean to hurt you, what happens to your pain?

Client: I can't have it.

Therapist: Right. So that doesn't work either. But there is a way through this. We can both acknowledge that I didn't mean to hurt you and that you were hurt—both at the same time. It's hard, because we want it to be one or the other. But I can hold all of this: that even if I didn't intend to, I said or did something hurtful, *and* that I'm not an intrinsically cruel person. You can have pain, and I'm responsible for responding to your pain. So as we work together, if I misstep, can we try that kind of approach? Can we try to hold both: that how I behaved was painful to you, and that I didn't intend harm? That way you don't have to protect me from feeling shame, and I can show up 100 percent regarding how my behavior impacted you.

Plummer (2012) emphasizes that FAP is not to be practiced any differently with GSM clients: the rules are consistently followed, focusing on the functions of behaviors rather than their topography; the clinician develops a thorough case conceptualization; and the clinician attempts to evoke CRB2, just as with any other client. However, we do recommend that therapists, especially straight therapists, directly discuss microaggressions when working with GSM clients.

The radical behavioral foundations of FAP and ACT bring the focus of therapy to psychological flexibility. In FAP, the focus is on interpersonal flexibility, and in ACT it is on intrapersonal flexibility. When the two approaches are combined, the scope of treatment is complete (Kohlenberg & Callaghan, 2012). Ultimately, psychological flexibility doesn't consist of a defined set of healthy behaviors; rather, it involves responding to one's life in an open, accepting, and values-consistent way.

Using FAP to Deliver ACT

Barbara Kohlenberg and Glenn Callaghan (2012) suggest four ways to blend FAP and ACT:

- using the five rules of FAP and defining CRB1s as ACT inflexibility processes

- using in vivo reinforcement within the therapeutic relationship to shape psychological flexibility

- using ACT to help clients respond to their emotions, thoughts, and sensations differently so they can engage in new behaviors within the therapeutic relationship

- adding ACT to FAP to help therapists respond openly and in a nondefended manner when faced with their own difficult and painful experiences during therapy

Regarding the fourth point, because therapists' responses are such a powerful part of the therapeutic relationship, it's crucial to have principles to follow in regard self-disclosure. Although many therapists are given scant training in disclosing their own experiences, using ACT and FAP together offers clear guidelines for addressing difficult emotional interactions (Kohlenberg & Callaghan, 2012).

Case Example: Working with Therapist Microaggressions

In this case example focusing on therapist heteronormative microaggressions, the clients are Ray and Carl. Ray is a twenty-eight-year-old Caucasian transgender man (designated female at birth). He has had top surgery (breast reduction) but has no interest in bottom surgery (phalloplasty). Ray is a working artist and musician. He's short and slender, and although he takes testosterone, he doesn't have heavy facial hair or a deep voice. He has been physically attacked several times by men, including his father, for not being a "man," and by other men for not being a "woman."

Carl is a Caucasian man who is cisgender, meaning that he is living a gender role concordant with the sex assigned to him at birth. He has been openly bisexual for about ten years. He is thirty-two, has a graduate degree, and holds a professional position. Ray and Carl have been together for five years, and although they complain about distress in their relationship, they say they're committed to each other. They are considering parenthood, and if they proceed, Ray will carry the baby.

The therapist is the first author, Joanne, referred to in the first person throughout this example. I am a Caucasian, middle-class, heterosexual married mother with one heterosexual daughter. I've seen many gay, lesbian, and bisexual clients, but only a few transgender clients. At the outset, I know that I equate "pregnancy" with "female" and that this may present challenges. I accept that my struggle will be to see where I impose a gender narrative that doesn't fit. I also accept that I will feel confused and disoriented as I try to remain present with my clients and that I will experience that as aversive. I commit to asking difficult questions and really listening to my clients' answers, and to encouraging Ray and Carl to do the same. I realize that it's inevitable that I will commit microaggressions, and I can hold the duality wherein my intent is not to cause pain but sometimes the effects of my behavior may be hurtful to my clients. In the intake session, I begin to address these issues. In this first transcript, I will focus on T1s and T2s, along with the relevant ACT processes.

Joanne: Before you both decide whether I'm the right person to work with, I'd like to discuss some issues that might impact our work. [Defusion, committed action toward my value of being of service to my clients, leading to the T2 of directly addressing this issue.]

Ray: (Looks at Carl, and both appear to be uncomfortable.) Like?

Joanne: Well, it's obvious I'm not male. What's not as obvious is that I'm straight and you are both members of a gender or sexual minority. [T2: speaking about something that is difficult; committed action and acceptance of and defusion from anxiety about how this will be experienced by the couple.] It's scary for me to bring this up when we don't really know each other, but I value being of service to you. I've worked a lot with gay and lesbian people and a few bisexual and transgender people. But the transgender people I've worked with have been male to female. I've never worked with a couple like you, wanting to have a child. I'm going to be clumsy, like that comment I just made: "a couple like you." [T2: self-disclosure; acceptance, defusion, values, committed action, and flexible perspective taking.]

Carl:	And you want us to educate you? [This brings up shame and anxiety for me, leading to an urge to abandon the conversation, but reconnecting with my values leads to T2: committed action in going forward.]
Joanne:	I suppose we'll all educate each other. My life experience has taught me to see things in binary terms: male, female, gay, straight… [T2: risking being very honest; defusion, present-moment awareness, values, and committed action.]
Carl:	So you can't wrap your head around us? [This brings up fears of being seen as narrow-minded and bigoted for me, initially leading to fusion, rigid perspective taking, and another T1: an urge to change the subject.]
Joanne:	I'll need to be able to check my assumptions out with you regularly, and I'll also need to collaborate. I'm a fast learner. In any case, these issues seem important to address from the beginning. [T2: continuing the conversation; defusion and flexible perspective taking.]
Ray:	It's not fair that we have to do this, you know. [Again, this brings up shame and anxiety for me.]
Joanne:	That's true. [T2: not justifying or arguing; acceptance and present-moment awareness.]
Carl:	(*Speaks to Ray.*) Maybe we should look for a different therapist—someone who doesn't have to be taught. [This brings up more shame and anxiety for me, as well as relief. I have a strong urge to engage in a T1: agreeing, which I am able to resist via acceptance and committed action.]
Joanne:	I can respect that choice if it's your decision. If we do work together, you don't need to take care of me, but I will need to check in with both of you more carefully,

. especially as we're getting to know each other. [My shame and anxiety could have evoked a T1: trying to convince Ray and Carl that I'm a good person, rather than just letting them decide. However, I draw upon flexible perspective-taking, acceptance, and committed action to engage in T2: being quiet and waiting for them to reach a decision.]

Ray: *(After pausing and looking at Carl.)* I'm willing to give it a go.

Carl: Me too. [This offers me relief from shame, but I still feel anxious and wonder whether I can do this.]

We continued to work together, and soon Ray and Carl decided to proceed with having a baby. Six months into his pregnancy, Ray came into therapy very distraught by the way people were reacting and by his sense that Carl didn't support him. I coached Ray to take Carl's perspective, and in doing so I committed a microaggression. By looking at Ray through the lens of heteronormativity, I missed the possibility that Ray was genuinely unsafe in some contexts. Ray became angry and tearful and eventually stopped speaking altogether. Because the idea of microaggression was an open topic with this couple and we'd revisited it often during our work together, Carl was the first to notice my microaggression.

In the following transcript, I'll focus on how I blended ACT and FAP, with detailed notes on CRBs, Ts, and the five rules of FAP. The transcript is somewhat complex because it reflects the struggles in the room, the challenges of applying the rules of FAP, and how I assessed for CRBs and Ts. The references to the FAP rules refer to my own intentions. Throughout the interaction, I used rule 1, watching for CRBs and Ts by paying attention to the functions of behavior in the room. A great deal of the interaction involves a combination of rules 2 and 3, evoking CRB and reinforcing CRB2 that demonstrates psychological flexibility.

Carl: Joanne, I think neither you nor I are showing up right now. [CRB2: Carl seems to be demonstrating acceptance, values, committed action, and present-moment awareness.]

Joanne: How do you mean? [Rules 2: evoking further CRB2.]

Carl: *(Puts his hand on Ray's leg.)* This is really hard for me to say, but when I see you with your pregnant tummy, it sometimes feels really weird. [Could be CRB1 or CRB2, depending on whether Carl is being genuinely vulnerable. Carl is struggling with his own heteronormative history in this moment. Perhaps his mind tells him that only women are supposed to be pregnant, and this is an intractable thought for him.]

Ray: *(Pushes Carl's hand off.)* Fuck you both. I'll do this by myself. [Mostly CRB2: clearly voicing distress and responding directly to the microaggressive content.]

Joanne: No, Ray, please wait. Your reaction is sensible. We're the ones with the weirdness. I think I know what you mean, Carl. Seeing a man pregnant is… [Rule 3: reinforcing Ray's CRB2. T2: acceptance, flexible perspective taking, and present-moment awareness in noticing that my attempt to guide Ray in perspective taking had constituted a microaggression. But notice also my struggle with the strong relation of "pregnancy" with "female" and how that relation impacts Ray, as well as a new microaggression in starting to speak about Ray, not to him.]

Carl: You have to work to twist your head around it. [CRB1 and CRB2: speaking about the issue, but in a manner that excludes Ray. In addition, Carl and I are reinforcing our relational network with each other, and this has an invalidating impact on Ray.]

Ray: I'm right here, you know. [CRB2: speaking up in the present moment.]

Joanne: I know. I'm sorry, Ray. Right now the pattern is happening. We're in this shared reality club without you. [T2: acceptance, present-moment awareness, defusion from intense feelings of shame about the harm being done in the moment. Also T1: rather than disclosing my shame and pain, taking a more distancing stance and describing the situation. Rule 3: reinforcing Ray's CRB2.]

Carl: (*Begins to cry.*) Oh god. [This could be CRB1 or CRB2, depending on whether his distress is mostly about shame for himself or grief for the impact on Ray.]

Ray: That's exactly right. You two are the "right" ones and I'm the "wrong" one. That's the story of my fucking life. [CRB2, morphing quickly into CRB1: fusion, rigid perspective taking, unworkable persistence, and preoccupation with the past.]

Joanne: If I were you, I'd feel completely unsafe. Is that how it is for you right now? [Rule 3: reinforcing Ray's CRB 2; and attempting rule 4: assessing the effects of my behavior by checking in with Ray about his experience.]

This was a complex moment in the interaction, so I'll pause here to go into it more deeply. My response was complex. I engaged in T2 by attempting perspective taking, but without displaying much personal vulnerability. And I fell into T1 by taking the "therapist stance" and by not acknowledging the intense vulnerability that this client, a survivor of physical abuse, had revealed in our intake meeting. When Ray said, "You two are the 'right' ones and I'm the 'wrong one,'" he was speaking about the "shared reality club" Carl and I were forming and expressing that this is a dangerous and familiar pattern for him. This was a vital CRB2, and I missed an opportunity to evoke further disclosure in the moment. My response arose from my history of experiencing pregnancy as a safe condition around men. Importantly, language as a system has inevitable impacts on people's learning history. Because I related "pregnant" with "safe," I overlooked the terrifying possibility of being a pregnant man who might be aggressed upon by other men. Fortunately, my questions about whether Ray felt unsafe in the room opened the door to an ongoing, albeit limited, discussion of safety.

Ray: Yes. [CRB2: committed action in being open and vulnerable.]

Joanne: I'm so sorry. My story about what's "normal" completely prevented me from seeing you. This happening in here with us is so harmful—it's really big. [T2: beginning to open up and offer self-disclosure. Rule 3: reinforcing Ray's CRB2, but still focusing only on Ray's sense of safety in the present interaction.]

Carl: But you didn't mean to do anything. Neither did I. [Possible CRB1: avoiding and minimizing.]

Joanne: Whether we meant to or not, it's harmful. Ray's sense that he's alone in the room is valid. [T2: acceptance, present-moment awareness, and defusion. Rule 2: evoking both Ray and Carl's openness. Rule 3: reinforcing that openness and validating Ray's experience.]

Carl: I'm just afraid this is going to spin out and I'm never going to be forgiven. [CRB1: avoidance, preoccupation with the future, and fusion.]

Ray: (*Speaks to Carl.*) How come she can own her shit and you can't? [This could be CRB1 if Ray is fused with a rigid perspective of Carl, or CRB2 if he's specifically addressing Carl's previous response.]

Joanne: Maybe because I have a different relationship with you than he does? [Mostly T1: taking a very intellectual stance and attempting to rescue Carl.]

Ray: Exactly. He should be able to do it. [CRB1: rigidity about what's "right," which seems to be a very fused stance in regard to his partner, and rigid perspective taking in his perceptions of Carl.]

Carl: (*Puts his head in his hands.*) I know. I'm really a shit. [CRB1: fused and inflexible self-perspective.]

Joanne: That's not going to work. We need to own both our intent and our effect. I'm not a shit, and my reactions to this are painful for Ray, and I take responsibility for them. I'm not a bad person, *and* I've got my own internal rules here that are completely unworkable. It's my job to accept that they're here and own them. [Mostly T2: defusion, but with a distancing quality and still not being fully emotionally vulnerable. Rules 2 and 3: evoking and reinforcing everyone's engagement with painful content in the moment.]

Importantly, my T1s consisted not so much of committing microaggressions but of attempting to avoid awareness and acceptance of them. T2 would have involved open awareness and undefended acceptance of both my behaviors and their impacts on Ray. In the subsequent session, I worked to stay open to the probability of heteronormative microaggression and to address it directly, encouraging both Ray and Carl to see Ray's experience of being physically unsafe as a couple issue, and to work together to ensure that he was safe and protected.

Conclusion

Microaggressions can be described as incidents wherein previously learned and reinforced verbal categories override the direct experience of the person committing them. For humans, coherence is a strong reinforcer (Roche, Barnes-Holmes, Barnes-Holmes, Stewart, & O'Hora, 2002). Therefore, acceptance, defusion from rigid self-categorizations, and interacting with others from a place of not knowing (rather than assumptions) is unlikely to happen without a commitment to values-based action. It's crucial that clinicians consistently contact their values and attend to their own avoidance and control behaviors, while also accepting that their initial, less workable reactions are likely to be persistent. The challenge is to commit to continually engaging in second, third, and fourth responses that are firmly rooted in values. This approach will be more effective than scrutinizing your every response for stigmatization and attempting to avoid or control such reactions.

Given that problematic language processes are a natural and sometimes painful part of being human, we recommend approaching difficult interactions and microaggressions from a self-compassionate perspective. From a defused stance—one informed by holding both the intent of one's behavior and the effects of that behavior—therapists and clients alike can bring more flexibility into interactions. Ultimately, therapists can promote generalization of flexible and courageous interpersonal behavior via foundational FAP practices of functional analysis and reinforcement in the present moment. Integrating ACT with FAP casts CRB1 and T1 as normative processes of human language and provides a means for targeting these processes precisely. Blending these tools with the proposed view that microaggression is inevitable allows therapists to attend to, notice, and consciously work with microaggression while promoting greater generalization of flexible and courageous interpersonal behavior.

References

Callaghan, G. M. (2006). Functional analytic psychotherapy and supervision. *International Journal of Behavioral Consultation and Therapy, 2,* 416–431.

Hayes, S. C., Brownstein, A. J., Zettle, R. D., Rosenfarb, I., & Korn, Z. (1986.). Rule-governed behavior and sensitivity to changing consequences of responding. *Journal of the Experimental Analysis of Behavior, 45,* 237–256.

Hayes, S. C., Strosahl, K. D., & Wilson, K. G. (1999). *Acceptance and commitment therapy: An experiential approach to behavior change.* New York: Guilford.

Jacobson, N. S., Follette, W. C., Revenstorf, D., Baucom, D. H., Hahlweg, K., & Margolin, G. (1984). Variability in outcome and clinical significance of behavioral marital therapy: A reanalysis of outcome data. *Journal of Consulting and Clinical Psychology, 52,* 497–504.

Kanter, J. W., Weeks, C. E., Bonow, J. T., Landes, S. J., Callaghan, G. M., & Follette, W. C. (2009). Assessment and case conceptualization. In M. Tsai, R. J. Kohlenberg, J. Kanter, B. Kohlenberg, W. C. Follette, & G. M. Callaghan (Eds.), *A guide to functional analytic psychotherapy: Awareness, courage, love and behaviorism*. New York: Springer.

Kohlenberg, B., & Callaghan, G. M. (2012). FAP and acceptance commitment therapy (ACT): Similarities, divergence, and integration. In J. Kanter, M. Tsai, & R. J. Kohlenberg (Eds.), *The practice of functional analytic psychotherapy*. New York: Springer.

Kohlenberg, R. J., & Tsai, M. (1991). *Functional analytic psychotherapy: Creating intense and curative therapeutic relationships*. New York: Plenum.

Lillis, J., & Levin, M. (2014). Acceptance and mindfulness for undermining prejudice. In A. Masuda (Ed.), *Mindfulness and acceptance in multicultural competency: A contextual approach to sociocultural diversity in theory and practice*. Oakland, CA: New Harbinger Publications.

Luoma, J. (2014). Acceptance and mindfulness for undermining stigma. In A. Masuda (Ed.), *Mindfulness and acceptance in multicultural competency: A contextual approach to sociocultural diversity in theory and practice*. Oakland, CA: New Harbinger Publications.

MacDonald, K. (2013). Sexual orientation microaggressions in psychotherapy. *ProQuest Dissertations and Theses* publication number 3598433.

Matthews, B. A., Shimoff, E., Catania, A. C., & Sagvolden, T. (1977). Uninstructed human responding: Sensitivity to ratio and interval contingencies. *Journal of the Experimental Analysis of Behavior, 27*, 453–467.

McGeorge, C., & Carlson, T. S. (2011). Deconstructing heterosexism: Becoming an LGB affirmative heterosexual couple and family therapist. *Journal of Marital and Family Therapy, 37*, 14–26.

Moon, L. (2011). The gentle violence of therapists: Misrecognition and dis-location of the other. *Psychotherapy and Politics International, 9*, 194–205.

Plummer, M. D. (2012). FAP with sexual minorities. In J. W. Kanter, M. Tsai, & R. J. Kohlenberg (Eds.), *The practice of functional analytic psychotherapy*. New York: Springer.

Rait, D. S. (2000). The therapeutic alliance in couples and family therapy. *Journal of Clinical Psychology, 56*, 211–224.

Roche, B., Barnes-Holmes, Y., Barnes-Holmes, D., Stewart, I., & O'Hora, D. (2002). Relational frame theory: A new paradigm for the analysis of social behavior. *Behavior Analyst, 25*, 75–91.

Shelton, K., & Delgado-Romero, E. A. (2011). Sexual orientation microaggressions: The experience of lesbian, gay, bisexual, and queer clients in psychotherapy. *Journal of Counseling Psychology, 58*, 210–221.

Shimoff, E., Catania, A. C., & Matthews, B. A. (1981). Uninstructed human responding: Sensitivity of low-rate performance to schedule contingencies. *Journal of the Experimental Analysis of Behavior, 36*, 207–220.

Spitalnick, J. S., & McNair, L. D. (2005). Couples therapy with gay and lesbian clients: An analysis of important clinical issues. *Journal of Sex and Marital Therapy, 31,* 43–56.

Strosahl, K. D., Hayes, S. C., Wilson, K. G., & Gifford, E. V. (2004). An ACT primer: Core therapy processes, intervention strategies, and therapist competencies. In S. C. Hayes & K. D. Strosahl (Eds.), *A practical guide to acceptance and commitment therapy.* New York: Springer.

Tsai, M., Kohlenberg, R. J., Kanter, J. W., Kohlenberg, B., Follette, W. C., & Callaghan, G. M. (Eds.). (2009). *A guide to functional analytic psychotherapy: Awareness, courage, love, and behaviorism.* New York: Springer.

Vandenburghe, L., Tsai, M., Valero, L., Ferro, R., Kerbauy, R., et al. (2012). Transcultural FAP. In J. W. Kanter, M. Tsai, & R. J. Kohlenberg (Eds.), *The practice of functional analytic psychotherapy.* New York: Springer.

Weeks, C. E., Kanter, J. W., Bonow, J. T., Landes, S. J., & Busch, A. M. (2011). Translating the theoretical into practical: A logical framework of functional analytic psychotherapy interactions for research, training, and clinical purposes. *Behavior Modification, 36,* 87–119.

CHAPTER 9

Starting a Family: Same-Sex Parenting

Amy Murrell, *University of North Texas*; Fredrik Livheim, *Karolinska Institute*; and Danielle Moyer, Melissa Connally, and Kinsie Dunham, *University of North Texas*

Raising a child is no simple task. Parents in same-sex relationships may face additional difficulties, including legal and financial disadvantages and social stigma. This chapter will bring awareness to potential challenges and suggest acceptance and mindfulness strategies to address them. Clinical and personal perspectives are included. Although a thorough exploration of gender and sexual minority (GSM) issues that occur in the family context is beyond our scope, we hope our focus on same-sex parenting will serve as a useful example of how to view identity and sexual orientation in fluid ways, and how to work with these concepts in a flexible manner, including when they intersect with other contextual variables.

The Same-Sex Parent Household

Diverse family composition is increasing across the globe. In 2001, the Netherlands became the first country to make joint adoption by same-sex couples legal (Itaborahy & Zhu, 2013). As of September 2015, twenty-one countries were following this policy at the national level ("LGBT adoption," 2015). In some states or provinces, children of same-sex parents may only have one legal guardian. This can occur because one parent is given legal parent status due to a biological connection to the child, or because state or provincial laws allow for an unrelated child to be adopted by a person (but not a couple) who identifies as being in a same-sex relationship.

Second-parent adoption rights allow for the coparent to gain legal status. Currently, second-parent rights are granted in Finland, Germany, Slovenia, and some parts of Australia (Itaborahy & Zhu, 2013). Without second-parent adoption rights, guardianship becomes complicated if the sole legal parent falls ill or the couple decides to separate. In these cases, one parent may lose visitation rights or the child may be moved into foster care (Human Rights Campaign, 2015). These figures are important, given that same-sex couples are four times more likely to be raising adoptive children and six times more likely to be raising foster children, as compared to their different-sex (heterosexual) counterparts (Gates, 2013).

In the United States, it is estimated that more than 125,000 same-sex couples are raising children under the age of eighteen (Gates, 2013). On average, income in different-sex parents' households is $11,100 more than that of same-sex parents. Furthermore, same-sex parents have a higher prevalence of conditions associated with poverty (e.g., female, young, racial minority status), including being less likely than different-sex parents to be employed (Gates, 2013). As such, it is important to consider the implications of poverty and different minority statuses, and the effects of stereotypes, discrimination, and micro-aggressions. In addition, the intersectionality of different identity statuses calls for discussing these roles and evaluating them in context.

Mental Health and Well-Being of Children of Same-Sex Parents

In school settings, same-sex parents and their children are often treated differently by school personnel. At times, the children of same-sex parents are bullied by their peers. One American study found that 40 percent of these students are verbally harassed (Kosciw & Diaz, 2008). According to those same authors, approximately 50 percent of children of same-sex parents reported feeling unsafe at school, with 23 percent citing their parents' same-sex relationship as the reason they feel unsafe. By contrast, racial status was cited by only 6 percent of students as a reason for feeling unsafe (Kosciw & Diaz, 2008). Stigma within the educational system has a negative influence on same-sex parents' involvement with teachers and administrators. Furthermore, school satisfaction is directly related to perceived stigma (Goldberg & Smith, 2014).

While children of same-sex parents do face daily stressors, such as stigma and discrimination, those who are adolescents and report good relationships with their parents and peers don't experience decreases in well-being (van Gelderen, Gartrell, Bos, & Hermanns, 2013). Furthermore, peer and romantic relationships, which are closely related to the strength of parent-child relationships, are no different among children of same-sex versus different-sex parents (Wainright & Patterson, 2008; Wainright, Russell, & Patterson, 2004). Research has consistently found that children with same-sex parents don't experience adverse outcomes relative to children of different-sex parents (Anderssen, Amlie, & Ytteroy, 2002; Patterson, 2013). In fact, no differences have been found in regard to any major indicators of well-being, including academic achievement (Potter, 2012), substance abuse, or delinquency (Wainright & Patterson, 2008).

Mental Health and Well-Being of Same-Sex Parents

GSM individuals regularly face stigma and discrimination (Meyer, 2003). This can manifest as intolerant and negative attitudes held by others or oneself (Herek, Gillis, & Cogan, 2009), which can contribute to an increased prevalence of emotional distress (Meyer, 2003) and decreased relationship quality (Frost & Meyer, 2009). These factors are probably compounded when same-sex couples decide to enter parenthood.

Same-sex couples face many obstacles related to planning to have a family, navigating social systems, and transitioning into parenthood. For many, in vitro and surrogacy options are too expensive to be viable. Yet adoption and foster care also present difficulties for both parents and children (Brodzinsky, 2011). Social stigma and scrutiny create substantial unjustified barriers to adoption for same-sex couples (Brooks & Goldberg, 2001), and same-sex foster parents also report decreased support from social workers and the social system in general (Downs & James, 2006). Same-sex parents must often work harder to convince social workers that they are fit to be parents, despite the lack of evidence to the contrary (Goldberg, 2010).

Same-sex families receive less social support than their opposite-sex counterparts (Kurdek, 2004). For example, community centers and social clubs often don't allow same-sex parents to join along with their children; or, if they do admit the family, the parents are charged full cost for two single adults, whereas different-sex parents are given a family discount. In addition to facing this kind of stigma from society at large, these families also sometimes experience stigma even within their extended families and among friends (Gianino, 2008).

Despite these challenges, same-sex parents are not impervious to benefits of parenting. Becoming a father, for example, is associated with positive outcomes, including feeling closer to family members (Power et al., 2012). There are even some benefits specific to same-sex parenting, such as a more even division of labor resulting from decreased gender stereotypes (Perlesz et al., 2010). Nevertheless, the body of research suggests that same-sex parents and their children face many challenges due to a context of stigma and discrimination.

Supporting Families Across Contexts

One way to support families with same-sex parents is to reduce stigma across contexts. An example is that some librarians are already hosting programs or services inclusive of or even catered to same-sex caregivers and their children (Naidoo, 2013). In schools, implementing flexibly enforced nondiscrimination policies could help communicate a sense of safety for students and involved adults (Kosciw & Diaz, 2008; Lamme & Lamme, 2003). In addition, schools could make a concerted effort to ensure that all staff members receive diversity training, that current research on LGBT matters is accessible, and that they use inclusive language in all written materials (for example, using "caregiver" rather than "mother" or "father," and "partner" rather than "husband" or "wife"). For children, school counseling offers an opportunity to process concerns in a space free of judgment (Lamme & Lamme, 2003). Support groups and online communities (e.g., http://www.colage.org) can also provide a context within which both same-sex parents and their children can acknowledge their experiences and counter feelings of isolation.

Although the discussion of religion as it relates to GSM individuals is ongoing (see chapter 10), faith communities can be a source of support for same-sex parents and provide an opportunity to bring families together (Lamme & Lamme, 2003). Health care staff can become informed about changing laws within their state, identify and explore existing biases, and create a space where disclosure is safe (Burkholder & Burbank, 2012; Perrin & Kulkin, 1996).

Finally, parent and child well-being can be addressed within individual and family therapy. Research can inform advice, including considerations regarding the current social and political atmosphere and clients' comfort with their sexuality (Goldberg & Smith, 2011). More research is needed, but certain treatment modalities are well suited to working with this population. In particular, acceptance and commitment therapy (ACT; Hayes, Strosahl, & Wilson, 1999), which focuses specifically on the contextual factors influencing well-being, may provide useful strategies for working with same-sex parents and their children.

Using ACT with Same-Sex Parents and Their Children

Given that ACT has been addressed in previous chapters, in this chapter we will discuss it only insofar as is relevant to same-sex parenting. The overall goal of ACT—increasing psychological flexibility—is clearly applicable in same-sex parenting, just as it is for parenting in general. Parenting can be simultaneously the most rewarding and most difficult job a person does. For example, the joy of witnessing a child's first steps can be accompanied by fear due to the exponential increase in danger once the child is mobile. These kinds of complex emotions make parenting particularly vulnerable to rigid behavior patterns and psychological inflexibility (Murrell, Wilson, LaBorde, Drake, & Rogers, 2008).

Inflexibility leads to and maintains ineffective parenting strategies when parents become overly attached to thoughts and feelings about their children or their parenting abilities (Coyne & Wilson, 2004), and this tendency may be heightened in same-sex parents.

Consider the following interaction: Two mothers are watching their young children play at a park. One of the kids asks the other, "Where is your daddy?" The child who is asked gets red in the face and tenses up. His mom is also visibly distraught and begins packing up their things to leave, avoiding eye contact with the other mother and her child. Then the mother of the inquisitive child calmly says with a smile, "I'm a single mom myself. Are you too, or two mommies?" The other mom replies, "Two mommies," puts down her things, and tells her son to keep playing. Then she explains that her family is so used to being negatively judged that they avoid potentially hurtful interactions on a regular basis. She acknowledges that her child has lost friends because of this.

Inflexibility in parent-child contexts correlates with parent and child distress. For example, inflexibility around parenting can maintain parents' stress and depression (Shea & Coyne, 2011). Even parents who typically respond flexibly to distressing thoughts and feelings may engage in avoidant strategies in response to their children's distress (Tiwari et al., 2008). For example, a mother may notice the thought *I'm a bad parent* while acting consistently with her personal values. However, if she sees her child crying, she may become preoccupied with eliminating her child's distress—an approach that can be quite counterproductive, maintaining or increasing the child's distress (Cheron, Ehrenreich, & Pincus, 2009). Although using ACT with parents and families is progressing, research remains limited, and to date, no research has examined ACT specifically for families with same-sex parents. However, evidence suggests that ACT can facilitate positive changes in relation to stigma among sexual minorities (Yadavaia & Hayes, 2012); perhaps it can similarly facilitate psychological health and well-being within families.

In the remainder of this chapter, we'll turn to three case examples—two short and one more extended. But first, to sum up, we want to emphasize that flexibility around parenting can facilitate effective parenting strategies and improve well-being for both parents and children (Coyne & Murrell, 2009).

Case Example: Using ACT to Fight the System Without Battling Each Other or Thoughts

One of the authors worked with a gay couple, Jordan and Dan, in a Southern US state, where they had been allowed to adopt one of their two children together before state laws reverted and joint adoption by a same-sex couple became illegal again. A large part of the couple's treatment revolved around fostering an active willingness to experience sadness, and to go to places, like the local courthouse, that made them angry. This therapeutic work was necessary because Dan was shutting down and not taking the steps necessary for a second-parent adoption. This was causing a rift in Jordan and Dan's intimate relationship, and also placing their child's custody decision in jeopardy.

The clinician helped Dan defuse from thoughts of losing his child, which were paralyzing him with fear. She accomplished this through use of the Floating Leaves on a Moving Stream exercise (Hayes, 2005), which helped Dan be more in contact with the present moment in session. The clinician pointed out Dan's bodily changes before and after the exercise and asked Jordan to do the same. She also asked Jordan to help Dan notice both internal and external experiences as they occurred outside of session. Finally, because overt behaviors are often linked to a busy mind, she asked both partners to identify a discrete but detectable cue they might point out when the other person's mind was working hard and taking him away from the family.

Case Example: "You're Not the Boss of Me!"

To illustrate self-as-context work, we'll turn to an example involving a lesbian couple experiencing difficulties in parenting their teenage son. The mothers (Amanda and Stacey) had been together since the boy (Chris) was a toddler. Amanda was his biological mother. His father had been absent since before his birth. Although Stacey hadn't legally adopted him, Chris considered her his parent. Only in recent months, at age fifteen, had Chris started expressing anger about not having a male parental figure. He had been arrested for shoplifting and vandalism, and he physically attacked both of his parents when they tried to discipline him.

Amanda and Stacey came to one of the authors for treatment feeling that they had failed as parents and that they should have found a father figure for Chris years earlier. Clinical interventions included using the chessboard metaphor (Hayes et al., 1999) and having both mothers write stories with varied endings, such as one ending based on their son having a father figure and another based on not having one, and what might have turned out differently if their son hadn't gotten in trouble.

The clinician also did a great deal of values and committed action work with these parents. One powerful intervention was having each of the mothers write a letter to their son stating four things: what her greatest hopes for him were; what she feared might get in the way of those dreams; what her role in his ups and downs thus far had been; and a firm statement that she was committed to helping him reach his dreams, no matter what, and that she loved him unconditionally. Given that he had recently been arrested and had attacked them, this was a rich experience. And although both did include some statements specific to same-sex parenting, such as wanting their son to be a voice for young men being raised by women, most goals they listed were generalizable to most parents. For example, they said they wanted him to be happy and to find love, and Stacey wanted him to be able to forgive himself and to see himself as greater than his mistakes.

This case history brings up an important point: Just as children make mistakes, all parents do, as well. As clinicians, one of the most powerful things we can do is appropriately disclose our parenting successes and difficulties to clients who are struggling as parents.

A Personal Account of Acceptance and Mindfulness in Same-Sex Parenting

My name is Fredrik Livheim. I live in Sweden, and I'm a licensed psychologist, a peer-reviewed ACT trainer, and the proud father of two beautiful children. The reason I'm offering a glimpse from my perspective in this chapter is to share a hopefully inspirational example of how same-sex parenting can be experienced. My hope is that, for ACT therapists, my story elucidates where core ACT processes intersect with the day-to-day parenting experience. Luckily, I live in a part of the world where society is opening up and actively acknowledging same-sex relationships and parenting, and brave same-sex parents have paved the way and served as important role models for me and others. So today, I can sit here writing as my two beloved children (six months and nine months old) are happily giggling and having lunch in the next room.

I had been working with children as a teacher for many years before becoming a psychologist. As a psychologist, for several years I worked on developing and implementing parent training in Sweden and gave advice on parenting in magazines and newspapers and on national TV. Still, I couldn't adopt a child simply because I was married to a man. This was frustrating. In Sweden it's legal to adopt a child as a same-sex couple, but in practice this seldom, if ever, happens. When it comes to adoptions from abroad, many foreign countries don't allow same-sex parents to be adoptive parents. There are, of course, multiple ways to have children in a same-sex couple, as alluded to earlier in the chapter. However, surrogacy is not allowed in many European nations and is often cost prohibitive, so same-sex male couples sometimes use surrogate mothers from other parts of the world where costs and laws ease the process. Likewise, same-sex female couples sometimes travel to countries with fewer restrictions and greater access to in vitro techniques.

In sheer frustration, my husband and I researched same-sex parenting on the Internet, where we found a site for Swedish "rainbow-families." There, we posted a note that we were two men longing to spoil our future children with love and asked if any women were interested in becoming a mother. To our surprise, we got some answers—then quickly encountered one of the common differences between having a child in a same-sex relationship versus in a different-sex relationship: having to choose a parent outside the relationship. Eventually, we found a lesbian couple who had the idea that children could benefit from having four loving parents.

Our situation is unique compared to common practices among same-sex couples in other parts of the world. In order to accommodate both breastfeeding and two active fathers who wanted to bond early with the children, we decided to rent a house and all move in together for the first two years of the children's lives, and then to live in separate households with the children sharing their time between us. Today, however, none of us can imagine living away from the children, so we are actively looking for a large house with two flats where we can all live together and still have physical space to live as two separate couples.

I give thanks almost daily to the lucky circumstances that allow me to access ACT strategies to help our family constellation navigate the challenges of same-sex parenthood. ACT clearly makes both my life and parenthood easier, more vital, and more fulfilling. I believe it can do the same for any parent, regardless of GSM status. Becoming a parent is usually described as life changing and a time of turmoil for all parents, and strategies around attachment and child rearing are quite universal. Therefore, as a therapist, you may find the points I outline here useful in your work with any parent.

One way to describe ACT is through the six core ACT processes as modeled on the hexaflex (Hayes, Strosahl, & Wilson, 2012), as set forth in chapter 5 of this book. These six core processes are partially overlapping, but for clarity's sake, I'll address each separately. I'll also give a few examples of how each process facilitates psychological flexibility in parenting.

Acceptance. It can be challenging to open up to what we experience as parents—to contact and make room for emotions, thoughts, memories, worries, frustrations, joy, and everything life and parenthood offer. Acceptance is a core competency that I constantly choose to practice. All major life changes, including becoming a parent, will produce stress. It can be immensely helpful to know this and open up to our experience. The alternative—trying not to be in contact with what our nervous system is giving us in the moment—can be quite strenuous and consume a lot of energy. In my family's case, we took on several major life changes at the same time, chiefly becoming parents and moving in together as two couples. My aim is to open up again and again and again, allowing space for everything to be experienced.

Values. Being clear about what is important in life and what kind of parent I want to be is helpful for organizing what I do and how I do it. It has also been especially helpful in building cooperation between two couples who didn't know each other before we decided to create our family together. We've all found that actively focusing discussions on what we believe to be best for our children helps us cooperate. We might not always agree on the exact details, but our active focus on what's best for the children helps us see goodwill in each other and understand each other as parents.

Present-moment awareness. Infants and children are absolute experts at being in the here and now. It is a joy to see the world afresh through a child's curious exploration of sight, hearing, touch, and taste. I love having children as mindfulness teachers, whether the orientation is toward exploring new things or just enjoying moments of body contact as one of my children is sleeping in my arms.

Committed action. When I know what I value in parenting, when I'm actively accepting what I'm experiencing, and when I'm present in the here and now, I find plenty of opportunities to engage in committed action. A common example these days is waking up at 3 a.m. to the sound of a crying baby and, drop-dead tired and feeling mixed emotions like irritation, love, and frustration, dragging my resisting body out of bed to change a diaper or give the baby a bottle, and then singing the little one to sleep.

Defusion. Seeing my thoughts as thoughts and choosing to act according to what I value is an interesting practice. My mind is good at nagging and telling me that I'm not good enough. I find the little ACT exercise "I'm having the thought…" surprisingly effective in giving me a healthy perspective on my thinking process (Hayes et al., 1999). I silently think to myself (or sometimes say out loud) things like this: *I'm having the thought that I'm a bad parent, I'm having the thought that I will never stop being tired, I'm having the thought that I'm doing this right, and the other parents are doing it wrong,* or *I'm having the thought that I'm going crazy.* These kinds of exercises give me a little distance from my thinking process, allowing me to open up to what I'm experiencing in the moment, connect to what I value, and act effectively.

Self-as-context. Life is constantly changing, yet most of us usually have an experience of a stable, constant sense of self. I find it useful to keep this sense of self fluid and to actively practice taking different perspectives. Yes, I'm a father, and I'm also a partner in a relationship and a psychologist. I'm an expert in some areas and a novice in others. Actively working on taking the perspective of my coparents and the perspective of our children helps me gain new understandings and fuels empathy.

I am still a rookie when it comes to being a parent, I am far from perfect, and I'm bound to make many mistakes. Also, my heart is overflowing with love for the little ones. So far, I've been surprised at how uncomplicated being same-sex parents has turned out to be for all of us. Our contacts with different social institutions have worked well. And when I tell people about how we are four parents, the most common responses I hear are along the lines of "What a splendid solution! To be four parents must be an ideal arrangement." Right now I have another seven months at home with our beloved little ones and my husband, who is also home on parental leave. I'm using the time to deep dive into love and practicing psychological flexibility.

Conclusion

Fredrik's situation is ideal. Even so, his mind tells him that he isn't good enough. Parenting is hard for anyone and can be even harder for same-sex couples, who face legal, financial, and social discrimination all too often. However, the negative consequences of stigma can be eased in many ways: through political reform, as well as education and social and clinical support. ACT's emphasis on behavior in context, values, defusion, and psychological flexibility in general makes it an ideal clinical approach for helping same-sex parents navigate the challenges.

There's an old saying that raising a child is like shooting an arrow. Parents, and particularly those in same-sex relationships, will face both internal and external challenges. If they can stay grounded in present-moment awareness—with a solid yet flexible stance, shifting as needed to withstand wind and storms—while letting their uncontrollable thoughts, feelings, and negative circumstances pass by like leaves on the wind, their children will be aimed as precise rays of lights down valued paths. As children grow, their parents need to let go, just as with arrows. Psychological flexibility is perhaps never more important than in the role of parenting. With ACT in their quiver, parents will have exactly what they need.

References

Anderssen, N., Amlie, C., & Ytteroy, E. A. (2002). Outcomes for children with lesbian or gay parents: A review of studies from 1978 to 2000. *Scandinavian Journal of Psychology, 43*, 335–351.

Brodzinsky, D. M. (2011). Children's understanding of adoption: Developmental and clinical implications. *Professional Psychology: Research and Practice, 42,* 200–207.

Brooks, D., & Goldberg, A. (2001). Gay and lesbian adoptive and foster care placements: Can they meet the needs of waiting children? *Social Work, 46*, 147–158.

Burkholder, G. J., & Burbank, P. (2012). Caring for lesbian, gay, bisexual, and transsexual parents and their children. *International Journal of Childbirth Education, 27*, 12–18.

Cheron, D. M., Ehrenreich, J. T., & Pincus, D. B. (2009). Assessment of parental experiential avoidance in a clinical sample of children with anxiety disorders. *Child Psychiatry and Human Development, 40*, 383–403.

Coyne, L. W., & Murrell, A. R. (2009). *The joy of parenting: An acceptance and commitment therapy guide to effective parenting in the early years.* Oakland, CA: New Harbinger Publications.

Coyne, L. W., & Wilson, K. G. (2004). The role of cognitive fusion in impaired parenting: An RFT analysis. *International Journal of Psychology and Psychological Therapy, 4*, 469–486.

Downs, A. C., & James, S. E. (2006). Gay, lesbian, and bisexual foster parents: Strengths and challenges for the child welfare system. *Child Welfare: Journal of Policy, Practice, and Program, 85*, 281–298.

Frost, D. M., & Meyer, I. H. (2009). Internalized homophobia and relationship quality among lesbians, gay men, and bisexuals. *Journal of Counseling Psychology, 56,* 97–109.

Gates, G. J. (2013). LGBT parenting in the United States: Executive summary of a report of the Williams Institute. Retrieved December 14, 2015, from http://williamsinstitute.law.ucla.edu/wp-content/uploads/LGBT-Parenting.pdf.

Gianino, M. (2008). Adaptation and transformation: The transition to adoptive parenthood for gay male couples. *Journal of GLBT Family Studies, 4,* 205–243.

Goldberg, A. E. (2010). *Lesbian and gay parents and their children: Research on the family life cycle.* Washington, DC: American Psychological Association.

Goldberg, A. E., & Smith, J. Z. (2011). Stigma, social context, and mental health: Lesbian and gay couples across the transition to adoptive parenthood. *Journal of Counseling Psychology, 58,* 139–150.

Goldberg, A. E., & Smith, J. Z. (2014). Perceptions of stigma and self-reported school engagement in same-sex couples with young children. *Psychology of Sexual Orientation and Gender Diversity, 1,* 202–212.

Hayes, S. C. (with Smith, S.). (2005). *Get out of your mind and into your life: The new acceptance and commitment therapy.* Oakland, CA: New Harbinger Publications.

Hayes, S. C., Strosahl, K. D., & Wilson, K. G. (1999). *Acceptance and commitment therapy: An experiential approach to behavior change.* New York: Guilford.

Hayes, S. C., Strosahl, K. D., & Wilson, K. G. (2012). *Acceptance and commitment therapy: The process and practice of mindful change,* 2nd edition. New York: Guilford.

Herek, G. M., Gillis, J. R., & Cogan, J. C. (2009). Internalized stigma among sexual minority adults: Insights from a social psychological perspective. *Journal of Counseling Psychology, 56,* 32.

Human Rights Campaign. (2015). Second parent adoption. Retrieved December 22, 2015, from http://www.hrc.org/resources/entry/second-parent-adoption.

Itaborahy, L. P., & Zhu, J. (2013). A world survey of laws: Criminalization, recognition, and protection of same-sex love. *International Lesbian, Gay, Bisexual, Trans, and Intersex Association.* Retrieved March 17, 2015, from http://old.ilga.org/Statehomophobia/ILGA_State_Sponsored_Homophobia_2013.pdf.

Kosciw, J. G., & Diaz, E. M. (2008). *Involved, invisible, ignored: The experiences of lesbian, gay, bisexual, and transgender parents and their children in our nation's K-12 schools.* New York: Gay, Lesbian, and Straight Education Network (GLSEN).

Kurdek, L. A. (2004). Are gay and lesbian cohabiting couples *really* different from heterosexual married couples? *Journal of Marriage and Family Therapy, 66,* 880–900.

Lamme, L. L., & Lamme, L. A. (2003). Welcoming children from sexual-minority families into our schools. Bloomington, IN: Phi Delta Kappa Educational Foundation.

LGBT adoption. (2015, December 19). In *Wikipedia*. Retrieved December 22, 2015, from https://en.wikipedia.org/wiki/LGBT_adoption.

Meyer, I. H. (2003). Prejudice, social stress, and mental health in lesbian, gay, and bisexual populations: Conceptual issues and research evidence. *Psychological Bulletin, 129*, 674–697.

Murrell, A. R., Wilson, K. G., LaBorde, C. T., Drake, C. E., & Rogers, L. J. (2008). Relational responding in parents. *Behavior Analyst Today, 9*, 196–214.

Naidoo, C. J. (2013). Over the rainbow and under the radar. *Children and Libraries, 11*, 34–40.

Patterson, C. J. (2013). Children of lesbian and gay parents: Psychology, law, and policy. *Psychology of sexual orientation and gender diversity, 1*, 27–44.

Perlesz, A., Power, J., Brown, R., McNair, R., Schofield, M., Pitts, M., et al. (2010). Organising work and home in same-sex parented families: Findings from the Work, Love, Play study. *Australian and New Zealand Journal of Family Therapy, 31*, 374–391.

Perrin, E. C., & Kulkin, H. (1996). Pediatric care for children whose parents are gay or lesbian. *Pediatrics, 97*, 629–635.

Potter, D. (2012). Same-sex parent families and children's academic achievement. *Journal of Marriage and Family, 74*, 556–571.

Power, J., Perlesz, A., McNair, R., Schofield, M., Pitts, M., Brown, R., et al. (2012). Gay and bisexual dads and diversity: Fathers in the Work, Love, Play study. *Australian Journal of Marriage and Family, 18*, 143–154.

Shea, S. E., & Coyne, L. W. (2011). Maternal dysphoric mood, stress, and parenting practices in mothers of Head Start preschoolers: The role of experiential avoidance. *Child and Family Behavior Therapy, 33*, 231–247.

Tiwari, S., Podell, J. C., Martin, E. D., Mychailyszyn, M. P., Furr, J. M., & Dendall, P. C. (2008). Experiential avoidance in the parenting of anxious youth: Theory, research, and future directions. *Cognition and Emotion, 22*, 480–496.

Van Gelderen, L., Gartrell, N. N., Bos, H. M. W., & Hermanns, J. M. A. (2013). Stigmatization and promotive factors in relation to psychological health and life satisfaction of adolescents in planned lesbian families. *Journal of Family Issues, 34*, 809–827.

Wainright, J. L., & Patterson, C. J. (2008). Peer relations among adolescents with female same-sex parents. *Developmental Psychology, 44*, 117–126.

Wainright, J. L., Russell, S. T., & Patterson, C. J. (2004). Psychosocial adjustment, school outcomes, and romantic relationships of adolescents with same-sex parents. *Child Development, 75*, 1886–1898.

Yadavaia, J. E., & Hayes, S. C. (2012). Acceptance and commitment therapy for self-stigma around sexual orientation: A multiple baseline evaluation. *Cognitive and Behavioral Practice, 19*, 545–559.

CHAPTER 10

Religion, Spirituality, and Gender and Sexual Minorities: What Clinicians Need to Know

Finn Reygan, *Wits Centre for Diversity Studies (WiCDS), University of the Witwatersrand*; Aisling Curtin, *ACT Now Ireland*; and Geraldine Moane, *University College Dublin*

When working on issues of religion and spirituality with gender and sexual minority (GSM) clients, clinicians could benefit from a greater evidence base and more informed guidelines. For example, one of the gaps in knowledge relates to the multiplicity and diversity of GSM religious and spiritual pathways. A small but growing body of international research in this area is beginning to elucidate these multiple pathways. A stronger evidence base will assist clinicians in avoiding common myths in relation to GSM clients' religious and spiritual lives so they can be more informed and sensitive in their approach.

In this chapter, we will explore the relevance of GSM clients' spiritual diversity in relation to clinical work, look at how religious identity can be just as important for GSM individuals as gender or sexual identity, and consider why some GSM individuals may be motivated to remain affiliated with what could be considered a homophobic or transphobic religious community. We are aware that the research and writing in the area, including in this chapter, has a bias toward sexual orientation at the expense of gender identity.

Findings from the first author's research, as well from as the broader literature we cite in this chapter, indicate that homophobia is common in religious denominations, and that a similar attitude prevails toward other GSM populations. (For simplicity's sake, in this chapter we'll generally use the term "religious homophobia" to refer to the broader dynamic.) This can create challenges for individuals in integrating their religious and GSM identities. And while it is apparent that GSM individuals follow multiple spiritual, religious, and atheist pathways, for these populations there are clear differences between religion and spirituality. As we explore these themes, we will provide examples of how to integrate the existing research with evidence-based practices grounded in acceptance and commitment therapy (ACT; Hayes, Strosahl, & Wilson, 1999), with a focus on case conceptualization.

GSM Spiritual Pathways

Research to date reveals a gradual opening of some (mainly Protestant) denominations to GSM, and the creation of denominations specifically for GSM populations, such as the Metropolitan Community Church (e.g., Yip, 2005). More recent studies (e.g., Smith & Horne, 2007) indicate that nature-based traditions, such as Wicca, paganism, and shamanism, may be more welcoming of GSM. It also appears that GSM individuals are reclaiming religious space within otherwise hostile religious denominations. Furthermore, contemporary research (e.g., Lease, Horne, & Noffsinger-Frazier, 2005) suggests that GSM individuals are increasingly drawn to more personal and GSM-affirming forms of spirituality. And as noted, the literature indicates that GSM individuals follow multiple pathways in terms of their spiritual and religious lives, with atheism being one of the pathways. Yip (2005) describes the multiple ways in which GSM individuals develop strategies to deal with rejection from religious communities.

The prevalence of religious homophobia is a common theme in the literature. Lease and colleagues (2005) argue that pervasive homophobia within many mainstream religious traditions leads to the general presumption that GSM individuals will reject religion. There is a common perception that a nonheterosexual sexual orientation and religious identity are mutually exclusive. Schuck and Liddle (2001) found that lesbian, gay, and bisexual (LGB) individuals report internal conflict concerning their religious faith. This might be characterized by depression, shame, suicidal ideation, or blocks to accepting their sexual identity. Other researchers (Gage Davidson, 2000; Mahaffy, 1996; Ritter & Terndrup, 2002; Rodriguez & Ouellette, 2000) found that organized religion can have a negative impact on the psychological health of LGB people and that several factors may be responsible for this: negative religious teachings about homosexuality, strictures against openly gay religious officials, and the isolation of LGB people within communities of faith.

The literature also illuminates the ways in which GSM individuals may experience religion and spirituality differently. Gage Davidson (2000) suggests that because spirituality can be understood as distinct from religion, the development of spiritual practices away from formal religious contexts may reduce some of the effects of negative religious histories among LGB individuals. Lease and colleagues (2005) argue that the distinction between formal religion and personal spirituality could be particularly salient for LGB people. Ritter and Terndrup (2002) point to the development of alternative spiritual practices among GSM individuals, and Shallenberger (1998) indicates that new spiritual practices may involve a reworking of traditional religious observances. Smith and Horne (2007) cast light on new forms of spirituality, such as Earth-based worship and shamanism, among GSM populations and suggest that these faiths generally provide a healthy alternative to mainstream religious denominations; they also argue that these faiths may be attractive to GSM individuals because they entail a belief in a connection to a higher power, often in the form of a god or goddess and revolving around personal experiences of spiritual connectedness in which nature is central. Earth-spirited faiths may offer GSM individuals an opportunity for spiritual connection while still maintaining their sexual and gender identities (Smith & Horne, 2007).

In short, recent years have seen increased international research into the spiritual lives of GSM populations. While GSM religious experiences may continue to be challenging, recent research in theology, the social sciences, and religious studies has begun to elucidate the complexity and nuance of that experience. And in tandem with the expanding worldwide GSM rights movement, GSM individuals have begun to create safe religious spaces for themselves, both within existing religions and by establishing new denominations. Similarly, the limited research in this area indicates that GSM populations have begun to embrace numerous spiritual traditions that enable them to incorporate their spiritual, sexual, and gendered selves. This eclectic and multicolored spiritual landscape indicates that the previous understanding of GSM religious and spiritual life as one of pain and struggle may not accurately reflect the contemporary situation. While many religions and some spiritual traditions continue to be limited by heterosexism and genderism, GSM individuals who are so inclined have begun to create their own sense of religious and spiritual belonging.

Themes and Clinical Applications

Clarke, Ellis, Peel, and Riggs (2010) suggest that psychologists need to be cognizant of a number of issues regarding the intersection of religion, spirituality, and sexuality. They call for a recognition that GSM clients can be committed to organized religions or to spiritual experiences and that there are numerous ways in which these clients experience faith. Further, they advise psychologists to be aware that religions have wide-ranging views on homosexuality and that different branches of the same religion may hold different views, as is often the case with orthodox versus liberal wings of the same tradition. In this sense, there is no one correct interpretation of the ways in which GSM people are viewed in sacred texts. Clarke and colleagues also point to diversity within religious GSM populations and argue that individuals may have different experiences of the same religious or spiritual tradition.

In the following sections, we describe findings from the first author's interpretative phenomenological analysis study of eighteen GSM clients in Dublin who were divided into three categories: religious, spiritually identified, and atheist. The four core themes that emerged that are most relevant for clinicians are negative impacts of religious homophobia, positive aspects of spirituality for GSM, an understanding that religion and GSM status are not mutually exclusive, and spirituality as a pathway to gender balance. The quotations we use to illustrate these themes are based on participants' responses.

Theme 1: Negative Impacts of Religious Homophobia

Both the literature and GSM participants in the first author's research clearly speak to the negative impacts of religious homophobia on the psychological, emotional, physical, and spiritual health of GSM individuals. Clinicians need to be aware of the intrapsychic distress caused by internalization of such messages and by extended exposure to homophobia in religious contexts. This led many of the participants in the first author's study to experience a dark night of the soul as they attempted to reconcile themselves with the teachings of their church on GSM. For example, Frank found his experiences of the Catholic Church to be detrimental to his health and well-being when he was growing up. He came to believe that there was no place for him as a gay person within the church, and as a result, he abandoned religion, rebelled against the institution and its homophobia, and was deeply hurt by the experience:

Not surprisingly, the Catholic Church was very detrimental. I lost respect for it when I discovered my sexuality and realized that there was no place for me in the church anymore. My faith was no longer valid, and I wasn't prepared for that. On one hand, I was strong and kind of gave the finger to the church, but on the other, it got in very deep and really hurt.

Peter was also aware of how detrimental the Catholic Church's stance on homosexuality was for him:

The church's teaching was that homosexuality was intrinsically disordered and represented a propensity for intrinsic moral evil. That was very clear, and the personal cost was huge. It was devastating to be painted in those kinds of terms.

As a result of religious teaching on GSM, participants in the study generally agreed that most GSM individuals would have to leave organized religion. For example, Ciara believed that many lesbians and gay men reject religion because it becomes intolerable for them:

I don't know the extent to which other lesbians and gays have a spiritual practice. I think that for many of us, at some point religious practice and institutionalized religion became completely intolerable and had to be abandoned.

There was a palpable sense of anger among participants at the abusive stance of many of churches in relation to GSM. For example, Barbara felt that religion didn't abuse straight people as it did gay people, and she didn't understand why gay people would want to associate with an organization that rejected them:

Religion never tells straight people that they're an abomination against God because of their sexual orientation. People can't pick out passages in the Bible to support hatred against straight people. Why would you want to be a member of any club that doesn't want you as a member? Go fuck yourself—that's how I feel about religion. I think all gay people should feel the same.

Theme 2: Positive Aspects of Spirituality for GSM Clients

Clinicians can benefit from understanding the multiple ways in which spirituality can enhance the health and well-being of GSM clients. In the first author's research, some participants reported that spirituality fostered or sustained their well-being. For example, Frank believed that the gay community as a whole would benefit if even a small proportion of members were to explore their spirituality:

I think it would make a massive change if even just 10 percent of the gay community decided to explore their spirituality a bit. I think it could have immense positive effects on our community and really help younger gay men. It would be great if there were more spiritual people within the gay community—people to look out for younger gay men coming out and give them a hand. What I've noticed is that most of the men that I've dated have had a drinking problem, and I feel that in the majority of cases the reason they drink so much is because they're self-loathing and can't accept their sexuality. Any tools we can arm ourselves with to help us accept ourselves would be a good thing.

Some participants also reported that spirituality provided them with much-needed support in very difficult times. For example, Emer's spirituality helped her when she was coming out because it increased her self-esteem and allowed her to move forward. She believed that, while spirituality was an important tool more generally, it was particularly useful for gay men and lesbians in fostering personal integrity and self-acceptance:

A lot of spirituality is about letting go of negative stuff. For me, that negative stuff would have largely been self-hatred. Well, maybe "self-hatred" is too strong a word...I guess I mean not liking yourself, wasting energy giving yourself a hard time, and overanalyzing stuff in the past.

Theme 3: Religion and GSM Identity Aren't Mutually Exclusive

Although the detrimental impact of religious homophobia on the health and well-being of GSM individuals is apparent, clinicians need to also be aware that religion can provide succor and support for GSM clients. In the first author's research, religious participants were disappointed by what they saw as a lack of religiousness or spirituality among GSM populations because they felt that religion could be a life-affirming experience. In short, the presumption that religion is always anathema to GSM individuals wasn't borne out in the experience of some of the participants in the study.

For example, Peter felt that participation in a gay religious group provided experiences that were missing from other aspects of gay culture. He found that the group allowed members to be more relaxed and open and less sexualized and competitive than was otherwise the case. In this sense, religious worship and its social aspects provided a venue for gay people to be more truly themselves:

Religious participation deconstructs all of the aspects of gay culture that I can't stand—namely, that the sole purpose of being there isn't trying to get off with each other. People are actually relating as people, rather than as objects of erotic release exploiting one another. There's something refreshingly unguarded about relating in a religious group. I suppose by implication I'm saying that I find commercial gay culture to be excessively about facade and pretense.

The sense of spiritual belonging and community experienced by participants in mainstream religious congregations was apparent. For example, Rory had directly experienced the potentially affirming and welcoming nature of a mainstream congregation:

> *The parish newsletter that I get every Sunday has a statement that specifically says they welcome people who are lesbian and gay, people who are single and married, and people who are divorced. It specifically listed many different groups of people in different states of life. It was beautiful to see that written down.*

Mary and her partner, Linda, had reinterpreted their religion to be welcoming and affirming, viewing Jesus as a man of the people who wouldn't have a problem with affirming same-sex love:

> *If Jesus was here with us today—man of the people! Texts that were written two thousand years ago are a different story. It was a different world back then. We think Jesus would be fine with today's diversity. He'd be saying, "You know what? Love one another! It's all fine! Why not let everyone worship together?"*

Theme 4: Spirituality as a Pathway to Gender Balance

Given that gender identity and expression are key facets of life for many GSM individuals, finding a sense of wholeness, completeness, and balance in terms of gender could be a therapeutic milestone in working with GSM clients. The interplay between gender identity, gender expression, and spirituality was key for many participants in the first author's research, with spirituality providing an opportunity to balance the male and female aspects within themselves and find a sense of wholeness and completeness.

Janet was troubled by gender constraints in society and the way these constraints manifested in religious practice. She had difficulty with the binary notion of gender and had developed a sense of spirituality in which she saw herself as complete, whole, and the simultaneous embodiment of both genders:

I was always troubled by the male/female, priest/priestess duality, embodying two opposing aspects, like the yin and yang of nature, that had to be fused. While I understood the theory behind that, it made me uncomfortable, and I started to think, Male energy, female energy—why do they even have to be fused? Aren't we okay as we are? And why do I have to embody just one kind of energy? Why does a man have to embody just one sort of energy? Don't we all embody all energy?

Frank believed that one of the challenges of being human was balancing male and female energies, and that in this regard, gay people had an advantage:

I feel that as humans we are here to achieve balance, and one of the things we are here for is to achieve balance in our lives. By balance I mean balancing the masculine and the feminine within ourselves. And as gay men and women we have the most amazing opportunity to achieve that very quickly—a much better opportunity than our straight counterparts have. I think we're in a privileged and lucky position, and I think it's important to achieve this balance.

ACT Case Conceptualization for Religious and Spiritual GSM Clients

ACT provides a flexible, evidence-based therapeutic approach for working with GSM clients who have diverse spiritual pathways. ACT aims to instill psychological flexibility by increasing clients' willingness to connect more fully and compassionately with the present moment, while also finding some meaning and purpose in their lives and actively living in line with those values. In this section, the second author, Aisling, will outline how the four themes just discussed relate to relevant ACT processes. She also shares a case study and describes several experiential exercises that she has developed for working with spirituality within the GSM community.

Theme 1: Negative Impacts of Homophobia

When clients have experienced the negative impacts of what they may term "religious homophobia," it is of paramount importance to explore this from the vantage point of the present moment in a manner that facilitates compassion, getting unhooked from previous messages, and flexible perspective taking. The following exercise, "Building Compassion Toward Experiences of Religious Homophobia," was developed by the second and third authors to assist clients in healing past wounds related to religion. This exercise is along the lines of a guided visualization. (For a downloadable audio recording of the guided exercise, please visit http://www.newharbinger.com/34282.) For illustrative purposes, in the written script we've included references to the various ACT processes engaged by the exercise.

BUILDING COMPASSION TOWARD EXPERIENCES OF RELIGIOUS HOMOPHOBIA

To conduct this exercise, ask clients to sit in a comfortable position, close their eyes or fix their gaze at a fixed point on the floor, and tune in to their body and breath as they attend to your words:

Take some time to ground yourself in the present moment through attention to your breath and body. Take three mindful, connected breaths from a stance of mindfulness: open, connected, and alert. [Present-moment awareness.]

Once you're connected to your breath and body, imagine that you're looking at a filing cabinet. [Perspective taking.] *This filing cabinet contains various moments when you felt the effects of religious homophobia. Focus on the first time you realized that the church in which you grew up had a negative view of non-heterosexuality.* [Willingness.] *What messages did you get from your church at that time?* [Defusion, perspective taking.] *What feelings did you have about this?* [Willingness.]

Now move on to another time—a time when you were older and were reminded of negative religious views about non-heterosexuality. [Perspective taking, willingness.] *Take some time to look at various such moments... Notice what themes or patterns arise throughout these experiences.* [Perspective taking, defusion.] *Also notice the feelings that arise as you consider these themes.* [Willingness.] *Acknowledge that these various experiences have affected how you experience the world in this present moment.* [Compassion, perspective taking.]

Now I'd like to invite you to imagine taking a step back to look at the "you" that is right here, right now. [Perspective taking.] *With awareness that you've had these various experiences of religious homophobia, imagine looking into the eyes of the you that has had these experiences and asking, "What is it that you need?" Imagine extending a compassionate hand to yourself in this present moment.*

Theme 2: Positive Aspects of Spirituality for GSM

For many GSM individuals, spirituality offers a context for exploring values—those things that matter most. It can also provide a medium for unhooking from limiting thoughts about what GSM individuals should and should not be. To tap into that potential, the second author has adapted Wilson's "Sweet Spot" exercise (2009), which involves a dialogue around deeply connecting with values in a moment of sweetness, to create the "Spiritual Sweet Spot" exercise. It's a two-part exercise that involves first guiding clients to identify and reexperience a spiritual high point in their life, and then debriefing the visualization through a dialogue exploring that sweet spot, the values it might illuminate, and any vulnerabilities it reveals. The exercise offers an avenue for exploring clients' underlying values and how they can more fully integrate their values into their lives. You can find an audio recording of the guided exercise, as well as a written transcript with instructions, with the downloadable accessories for this book at http://www.newharbinger.com/34282. We will explore this concept further in a case example at the end of this chapter.

Theme 3: Religion and GSM Status Aren't Mutually Exclusive

ACT attends to the potentially negative impacts of therapists being fused with, or hooked by, their thoughts about particular clients or particular topics, and few topics incite opinion as much as religion. Those who believe in organized religion often consider this part of their self-identity to be essential to their sense of who they are. In contrast, those who don't support organized religion often view it as a vehicle of oppression and for exerting misguided power. Just as it will serve GSM clients to work with a clinician who affirms their GSM status, so too will GSM clients with religious beliefs benefit from working with a clinician who is both open-minded and openhearted in regard to GSM clients who maintain an active religious conviction.

The following defusion exercise, which the second author has extended from Russ Harris's exercise "Naming the Story" (2007), may be helpful for you, as a clinician, to do in order to disentangle yourself from your own stories about religion. (Visit http://www.newharbinger .com/34282 for a downloadable supplementary worksheet.)

RECOGNIZING OUR STORIES ABOUT GSM CLIENTS AND RELIGION

Take some time to reflect on the following questions and write your responses on a single sheet of paper or on the downloadable worksheet:

1. What is your learning history in regard to religion? Did you have positive or negative experiences?

2. Please describe religion in three words.

3. How do you believe religions treat GSM?

4. What is your gut response when individuals tell you that they're religious?

5. Do you hold more negative connotations about some religious traditions than others? If so, which ones?

Now review what you wrote. As best you can, take a nonjudgmental stance toward your responses. Absolutely all of us have judgments and evaluations about religion.

Now experiment with what you've written. Hold the piece of paper really close. How would this perspective affect your view of clients? How might it blind you to individual clients and their beliefs? Is there a chance that you could shame clients, who have probably already endured many shame-inducing reactions to their gender or sexual orientation, their religious beliefs, or both?

Now experiment with actively trying to suppress your thoughts. You can do this physically by pushing the piece of paper away from you. How would it be to work with clients from this stance? How much time and energy would you have to connect with clients and their current struggles if you're actively attempting to suppress or avoid having these thoughts?

Now consider a third way: Take a look at what you've written again. Now fold the piece of paper in half so that the contents of your thoughts are inside, like the words in a book. On the front "cover," write "Ah, there's the _____ _____ story again," using just two words to encapsulate the theme. It's crucial to name the theme or pattern in just two words, as anything longer may increase fusion, rather than decreasing it. Examples of story names could be "religious oppression story," "need God story," or "antigay God story." The aim is to sum up your views, whether favorable or unfavorable, about religion and GSM.

Next, turn the piece of paper over and on the back "cover," draw a horizontal line to divide it into two parts. On the top half, write your responses to these questions:

How do I want to respond to my client's religious or spiritual beliefs?

How would I like my client to describe me in three words?

Then, on the bottom half of the back "cover," answer this question:

What can I do in session to help me move closer toward being the affirming therapist I want to be for my client?

Be sure to list a number of small actions that might make a big difference for a given client.

Having completed this exercise, you can probably see that it's also useful in contexts other than religion.

Theme 4: Spirituality as a Pathway to Gender Balance

The first author's study of eighteen GSM clients in Dublin revealed that balancing their internal masculine and feminine aspects was very important to participants. For many GSM individuals, and many non-GSM individuals, for that matter, typical cultural expectations in regard to gender and how people should and should not be in the world are oppressive, to say the least. ACT defusion strategies, which are aimed at loosening the grip of self-limiting content, can be an ally to spirituality, or an alternative if need be, in helping GSM clients achieve gender balance.

One way to promote such defusion is to preface judgments about gender (e.g., "Boys shouldn't show it when they're upset") with the phrase "I'm having the thought that…" (e.g., "I'm having the thought that boys shouldn't show it when they're upset"). Alternatively, you might ask clients to preface such statements with a phrase like "My gendered mind is telling me that…" Through these kinds of subtle distinctions, GSM clients can gradually come to distinguish the difference between what the mind is dictating in regard to gender norms and how they would choose to genuinely and authentically express themselves in the world.

Case Example: Working with GSM Clients Who Identify as Spiritual

This case example illustrates some of the experiential exercises that the second author has found most beneficial when working with GSM clients who have active religious or spiritual beliefs. The client is Jamie, a forty-eight-year old Caucasian gay man who has found great solace in spirituality outside of religion. Throughout their therapeutic interactions, they looked deeply at the pain Jamie had experienced in relation to an abundance of harsh messages and experiences within religious contexts. Jamie learned to acknowledge how his past pain was arising in the here and now, and to see when he was getting hooked by these past messages. Through experiential exercises, including those outlined earlier in this chapter, Jamie learned to extend kindness toward himself, something that was exceedingly difficult for him when he entered therapy. The following dialogue took place during the fifth of ten sessions.

Jamie: I'm starting to see more clearly where my past is tripping me up, but it's hard. I really want to connect with people in a deep way, yet sometimes it feels like gay culture is so superficial.

Aisling: I'd like to explore this a little more deeply with you to really get a sense of what's important to you and what seems to be missing in your life. Would you be open to doing an exercise with me? It's called the "Spiritual Sweet Spot" exercise.

Jamie: Okay.

Aisling then led the exercise. What follows is the debriefing dialogue about Jamie's spiritual sweet moment. You may notice that in this debriefing Aisling also brings in elements of the ACT matrix (Polk & Schoendorff, 2014) and functional analytic psychotherapy (FAP; Kohlenberg & Tsai, 1991), which she had previously introduced to Jamie. (For more on the matrix, see chapter 2. For more on FAP, see chapters 3 and 7.)

Jamie: I was in a group and we had done this really beautiful loving-kindness exercise. I didn't even know half the people there, yet I felt so connected. It's weird, but I kind of felt like I could hug them all. I felt like they understood me and accepted me just as I was. I didn't think they cared that I'm almost fifty and don't look as good as I did ten years ago.

Aisling: Wow! It sounds like you touched some kind of experience where you felt as though you were enough, just as you are. I'm guessing that felt great, given how many messages you've received in the past that told you quite the opposite. I'm really glad that you have a place where you can go and experience this kind of connection. I'm curious: If we were to look at a video of your interactions with others in that meditation group and then at your interactions with others in a gay bar, would we see anything different in your actions?

Jamie: I've never thought about it that way. I just assumed that because others were kinder to me, the moment was sweeter. But, yeah...I was different too. In the meditation group, my shoulders were relaxed, I had an open stance toward everyone else, and I was smiling. In the bar, my expression looks different. I look judgmental. It's almost like I just hang out in the background waiting to be rejected.

Aisling: And do those actions bring you closer toward who and how you want to be, or further away?

Jamie: Toward in the spiritual group, but definitely further away in the gay community.

Aisling: Okay. Well, the great thing is that we both know that you can engage in a way that's a toward move. You did it with your spiritual group. You've also connected at that deep level here with me many times, and for that I'm really grateful. So, next time you're in a situation outside your spiritual community, would you be willing to open up to the discomfort that you might get rejected and still engage even just a bit more fully than you currently do?

Jamie: It feels scary, but yes, I'll do it.

This exercise allowed Jamie to identify key areas he wished to work on and consciously move toward, primarily a sense of connection, belonging, and authenticity. Gradually, he started to consciously bring these qualities into his intimate relationships and interactions with friends who weren't spiritual. This led to a major increase in his overall quality of life and relationships.

Conclusion

The religious and spiritual lives of GSM individuals are multifaceted and defy neat categorization. Although the GSM rights movement has begun to shift the thinking of some religious denominations in regard to GSM, many religions continue to perpetuate homophobia and transphobia. Clinicians must be prepared to work on the negative effects of these attitudes on the health and well-being of GSM individuals.

Further, the general presumption that religion and a GSM identity are mutually exclusive is incorrect and further marginalizes GSM individuals who lead religious lives. Yet spirituality can have profoundly beneficial effects on the health and well-being of GSM individuals, including in terms of mental health. It can help build resilience and aid in finding a workable gender balance. To this end, ACT is a powerful tool for honoring the spiritual stance of GSM clients and amplifying the positive impacts of engaging in a life imbued with meaning, purpose, and values.

References

Clarke, V., Ellis, S. J., Peel, E., & Riggs, D. W. (2010). *Lesbian, gay, bisexual, trans, and queer psychology: An introduction.* Cambridge, UK: Cambridge University Press.

Gage Davidson, M. (2000). Religion and spirituality. In R. M. Perez, K. A. DeBord, & K. J. Bieschke (Eds.), *Handbook of counseling and psychotherapy with lesbian, gay, and bisexual clients.* Washington, DC: American Psychological Association.

Harris, R. (2007). *ACT with love: Stop struggling, reconcile differences, and strengthen your relationship with acceptance and commitment therapy.* Oakland, CA: New Harbinger Publications.

Hayes, S. C., Strosahl, K. D., & Wilson, K. G. (1999). *Acceptance and commitment therapy: An experiential approach to behavior change.* New York: Guilford.

Kohlenberg, R. J., & Tsai, M. (1991). *Functional analytic psychotherapy: A guide for creating intense and curative therapeutic relationships.* New York: Plenum.

Lease, S., Horne, S., & Noffsinger-Frazier, N. (2005). Affirming faith experiences and psychological health for Caucasian lesbian, gay, and bisexual individuals. *Journal of Counseling Psychology, 52,* 378–388.

Mahaffy, K. A. (1996). Cognitive dissonance and its resolution: A study of lesbian Christians. *Journal for the Scientific Study of Religion, 35,* 392–402.

Polk, K. L., & Schoendorff, B. (Eds.). (2014). *The ACT matrix: A new approach to building psychological flexibility across settings and populations.* Oakland, CA: New Harbinger Publications.

Ritter, K. Y., & Terndrup, A. I. (2002). *Handbook of affirmative psychotherapy with lesbians and gay men.* New York: Guilford.

Rodriguez, E. M., & Ouellette, S. C. (2000). Gay and lesbian Christians: Homosexual and religious identity integration in the members and participants of a gay-positive church. *Journal for the Scientific Study of Religion, 39,* 333–347.

Schuck, K. D., & Liddle, B. J. (2001). Religious conflicts experienced by lesbian, gay, and bisexual individuals. *Journal of Gay and Lesbian Psychotherapy, 5,* 63–82.

Shallenberger, D. (1998). *Reclaiming the spirit: Gay men and lesbians come to terms with religion.* New Brunswick, NJ: Rutgers University Press.

Smith, B., & Horne, S. (2007). Gay, lesbian, bisexual, and transgendered (GLBT) experiences with Earth-spirited faith. *Journal of Homosexuality, 52,* 235–248.

Wilson, K. G. (with DuFrene, T.). (2009). *Mindfulness for two: An acceptance and commitment therapy approach to mindfulness in psychotherapy.* Oakland, CA: New Harbinger Publications.

Yip, A. K. T. (2005). Queering religious texts: An exploration of British nonheterosexual Christians' and Muslims' strategy of constructing sexuality-affirming hermeneutics. *Sociology, 39,* 47–65.

CHAPTER 11

Minority Stress and Resilience

Brian A. Feinstein, *Northwestern University*; and
Brian P. Marx, *National Center for PTSD*

I t is well documented that gender and sexual minorities (GSM) experience mental health problems at higher rates than the general population. "Gender minorities" refers to a diverse group of people who don't conform to culturally defined gender categories. This includes people whose gender identity is different from the sex they were assigned at birth, those who endorse a gender-variant identity (e.g., transgender, gender nonconforming, genderqueer), and those who express themselves in a manner that is considered atypical for their gender. "Sexual minorities" refers to a similarly diverse group of people who endorse nonheterosexual attractions, behaviors, or identities (e.g., gay, lesbian, bisexual, queer).

Minority stress theory (Meyer, 2003) provides a framework for understanding why mental health disparities exist for these populations, positing that this is due to the unique stressors that GSM populations experience as a result of their stigmatized social status. Although many GSM individuals demonstrate considerable resilience, many others experience stress and mental health problems. Thus, there is a need for effective interventions to reduce psychological difficulties and promote resilience in these populations. Given the chronic and unavoidable nature of many of the unique stressors that GSM individuals experience, mindfulness- and acceptance-based strategies may be particularly helpful. This chapter will briefly review the literature on GSM stress and resilience and then describe the application of mindfulness- and acceptance-based strategies among these populations, illustrating this approach with an extended case example.

Mental Health Problems Among GSM

Lifetime rates of mood, anxiety, and substance use disorders are approximately 2.5 times higher among sexual minorities than heterosexuals (Meyer, 2003). This has been demonstrated across diverse conceptualizations of sexual orientation, such as attraction, behavior, and identity (Bostwick, Boyd, Hughes, & McCabe, 2010; McCabe, Hughes, Bostwick, West, & Boyd, 2009), underscoring the robustness of these findings. Although less is known about the prevalence of mental disorders among gender minorities, high rates of mental health problems have been documented in samples of transgender individuals, such as 55 to 62 percent endorsing depression symptoms (Clements-Nolle, Marx, Guzman, & Katz, 2001; Díaz, Ayala, Bein, Henne, & Marin, 2001); 40 to 48 percent endorsing anxiety symptoms (Budge, Adelson, & Howard, 2013); and 20 to 40 percent endorsing substance use (Benotsch et al., 2013; Operario & Nemoto, 2005; Sevelius, Reznick, Hart, & Schwarcz, 2009). Rates of suicidal ideation and suicide attempts are also substantially higher among GSM populations (Clements-Nolle et al., 2001; Fergusson, Horwood, & Beautrais, 1999; Garofalo, Wolf, Kessel, Palfrey, & DuRant, 1998; Testa et al., 2012).

Minority Stress

As noted, the unique stressors that GSM individuals experience related to their stigmatized social status, referred to as minority stress, help explain why these populations are at increased risk for mental health problems relative to heterosexual and cisgender individuals (Meyer, 2003). Various minority stressors have been identified (e.g., discrimination, victimization, and internalization of negative societal attitudes), and experiencing such stressors appears to be common among GSM individuals. In a meta-analysis of 138 studies, Katz-Wise and Hyde (2012) found that 41 percent of sexual minorities had experienced discrimination related to their sexual orientation. They also found that sexual minorities endorsed high rates of other types of victimization, such as verbal harassment (55 percent), sexual harassment (45 percent), abuse from family members (28 to 40 percent), physical assault (28 percent), and sexual assault (27 percent).

High rates of minority stress have also been documented among gender minorities. Grant and colleagues (2011) found that 78 percent of transgender individuals reported being harassed, 35 percent reported being physically assaulted, and 12 percent reported being sexually assaulted at school. Testa and colleagues (2012) found high rates of physical violence (38 percent) and sexual violence (27 percent) against transgender individuals, with the majority reporting that at least one incident was due to their gender identity or expression. Transgender individuals also have higher rates of unemployment and economic discrimination (e.g., being denied a job or being fired from a job) relative to the general population (Grant et al., 2011; Lombardi, Wilchins, Priesing, & Malouf, 2001).

Research has consistently supported the notion that minority stress is associated with mental health problems. For instance, sexual minorities who were victims of hate crimes based on their sexual orientation had more anxiety, depression, and post-traumatic stress symptoms than those who hadn't experienced any crimes or who had experienced crimes not based on their sexual orientation (Herek, Gillis, & Cogan, 1999). Additionally, Mays and Cochran (2001) found that sexual minorities were significantly more likely than heterosexuals to report that discrimination had made their life harder and interfered with having a full and productive life. They also found that perceived discrimination was associated with poorer mental health, including increased likelihood of being diagnosed with a psychiatric disorder. Similarly, several studies of transgender and gender-nonconforming individuals have demonstrated associations between minority stress and mental health problems. Specifically, among transgender individuals, discrimination and victimization are associated with higher levels of psychological distress (Bockting, Miner, Swinburne Romine, Hamilton, & Coleman, 2013), as well as increased suicidal ideation and suicide attempts (Clements-Nolle, Marx, & Katz, 2006; Testa et al. 2012).

It is also important to note that there are unique types of minority stress that specific GSM groups experience. For instance, sexual minority women may be sexually objectified by heterosexual men, such as being propositioned to have sex with them and another female (Hequembourg & Brallier, 2009). In contrast, it has been suggested that sexual minority men are most likely to anticipate HIV-related stigma because of the disproportionately high prevalence of HIV among gay men (Starks, Rendina, Breslow, Parsons, & Golub, 2013).

Bisexuals also experience unique stressors, such as being discriminated against by both heterosexual and gay or lesbian individuals due to negative attitudes toward bisexuality and stereotypes about the illegitimacy and instability of bisexuality (e.g., Brewster & Moradi, 2010; Mohr & Rochlen, 1999). Gender minorities experience unique stressors that sexual minorities do not, such as challenges around marking sex designations on official documents (Currah & Moore, 2009) and accessing public restrooms (Hines, 2007). Finally, the intersection between GSM status and other minority statuses, such as race or ethnicity, can contribute to unique types of minority stress. (For a detailed discussion of the intersectionality, see chapter 13.)

Resilience

Most of the existing literature on GSM populations has focused on stress and pathology, with only limited attention devoted to resilience. Despite the challenges associated with identifying as GSM, many GSM individuals exhibit considerable resilience in the face of adversity. Several factors related to resilience have been implicated in the health and well-being of GSM individuals, including family acceptance and support, connection to the GSM community, and having a positive GSM identity. Among sexual minorities, research has demonstrated that parental acceptance of one's sexual orientation is associated with improved well-being and buffers against the negative consequences of minority stress (Feinstein, Wadsworth, Davila, & Goldfried, 2014). Family support, in general, is associated with reduced depression and increased self-esteem (Detrie & Lease, 2007). Participation in the sexual minority community has also been proposed as a protective factor against minority stress and its consequences (Meyer, 2003), and research has supported a link between community connectedness and improved well-being (Detrie & Lease, 2007).

Similar findings have been demonstrated among transgender individuals, including social support being associated with reduced depression and anxiety (Budge et al., 2013), and connection with other transgender people being associated with improved well-being (Mizock & Lewis, 2008; Singh, Hays, & Watson, 2011). Further, exposure to other transgender people early in the process of an individual's identity development is associated with reduced anxiety and suicidality and feeling more comfortable about acknowledging one's transgender identity (Testa, Jimenez, & Rankin, 2014).

Positive aspects of identifying as GSM have also been documented (Riggle & Mohr, 2015; Riggle, Mohr, Rostosky, Fingerhut, & Balsam, 2014). First, many GSM individuals report that this identity helped them create social support systems, including a broad community of similar individuals, as well as smaller "families of choice" or groups of individuals considered to be family regardless of birthright. Second, many report that their minority identity has contributed to increasing their capacity for insight, self-awareness, and empathy, allowing them to lead more authentic lives and relate better to others. Third, many GSM individuals noted that their minority identity freed them from feeling like they had to adhere to societal norms related to sex and gender. Finally, identifying as GSM increased their concerns about all forms of oppression and their involvement in social activism. Higher endorsements of these aspects of positive GSM identity have been associated with greater life satisfaction and reduced depression symptoms (Riggle et al., 2014). Thus, although many GSM individuals experience considerable stress related to their minority identity, there are also benefits to belonging to these social groups that can enhance well-being.

Promoting Resilience via Mindfulness- and Acceptance-Based Approaches

For treating psychological difficulties among GSM populations, cognitive behavioral therapies have received the most attention in the literature (e.g., Martell, Safren, & Prince, 2004). These approaches focus on teaching clients skills to reduce symptoms, such as challenging distorted thoughts and engaging in pleasurable activities. In contrast, third-wave behavioral therapies, such as mindfulness- and acceptance-based approaches, focus on reducing attempts to change internal experiences and instead engaging in behaviors that are consistent with one's values even in the face of distress. Several specific treatment approaches are rooted in principles related to mindfulness and acceptance, such as acceptance and commitment therapy (ACT; Hayes, Strosahl, & Wilson, 1999) and dialectical behavior therapy (DBT; Linehan, 1993); however, the techniques included in these approaches can also be applied as part of an eclectic evidence-based approach. The remainder of this chapter will briefly review mindfulness- and acceptance-based approaches, describe why they might be particularly useful with GSM clients, and conclude with a case example to demonstrate their application.

"Mindfulness" refers to nonjudgmental awareness of the present moment and includes the abilities to sustain attention to the present moment, switch attention between aspects of one's experience, and adopt a curious, open, and accepting attitude toward all experience (Bishop et al., 2004). As such, mindfulness techniques can be used to help clients increase their awareness of thoughts, feelings, and behaviors and their effectiveness in responding to them (Keng, Smoski, & Robins, 2011). Similarly, acceptance-based approaches emphasize the importance of being willing to experience thoughts and feelings without attempting to alter them (Hayes, 2005). Thus, these strategies aim to reduce tendencies to avoid, suppress, or excessively engage distressing thoughts and emotions. They also seek to help clients identify their core values and increase behaviors that are in line with those values even in the face of distress (Hayes, 2005). These approaches contrast with more traditional cognitive and behavioral methods that focus instead on altering the form or frequency of thoughts and emotions.

Mindfulness- and acceptance-based strategies may be particularly helpful for GSM clients for several reasons. The first is that experiences of discrimination, rejection, and victimization are largely outside of one's control. Furthermore, many of the social stressors that GSM populations experience are unlikely to disappear in the near future, including structural-level stressors (e.g., lack of federal protection against discrimination) and individual-level stressors (e.g., nonaffirmative family members). And even if there are steps an individual can take to reduce the likelihood of experiencing these stressors to some extent (e.g., seeking out people and environments that are affirmative of GSM groups), it is impossible to completely avoid them. Therefore, maintaining well-being in the face of these stressors requires some degree of acceptance. In addition, it can be tempting to avoid certain people and places due to concern about the possibility of being rejected or discriminated against. Although a certain degree of caution may be necessary for safety, it is important that people not let their fears dictate their behavior or impede pursuit of their goals.

A second factor is that experiences of discrimination and rejection are likely to lead to negative thoughts and feelings about oneself, others, or the world. Even in the absence of explicit discrimination, GSM individuals receive constant messages, often in the form of subtle or even unintentional behaviors, that there is something wrong with them. Being on the receiving end of these messages can produce distress that may lead to attempts to get rid of the negative thoughts and feelings that arise. However, attempting to suppress thoughts or feelings has a paradoxical, opposite effect, making them more persistent (Wenzlaff & Wegner, 2000). Being able to acknowledge these experiences with a nonjudgmental attitude, rather than fighting with them and attempting to change them, has the potential to reduce the extent to which they cause suffering. It is common for GSM individuals to experience negative thoughts and feelings related to their sexual orientation or gender identity at some point in life. As such, having the ability to experience these thoughts and feelings without excessively engaging with them is critical to fostering healthy psychological adjustment.

Finally, third-wave behavioral therapies' emphasis on engaging in behavior that is consistent with one's values may be particularly relevant for GSM individuals whose values differ from those that are prevalent in mainstream society. For instance, although many GSM individuals prefer monogamy and there is considerable variability in the types of relationships preferred by sexual minorities and heterosexuals alike, nonmonogamy appears to be more common among sexual minorities, particularly gay men. Research has found that gay men are more likely to engage in nonmonogamous relationships (Gotta et al., 2011), and that bisexual individuals have more positive attitudes toward nonmonogamy than those with other sexual orientations (Mark, Rosenkrantz, & Kerner, 2014). For those who do not prefer monogamy, it can be challenging to maintain a sense of authenticity in a society that largely values monogamy. Thus, it is important to have a clear understanding of one's values and how to engage in values-based action when confronted with such challenges.

Further, other traditional values, such as those surrounding marriage and parenting, may be less valued by some GSM individuals. While many may want to get married and have children, there is some evidence that gay men are less interested in getting married than lesbian women (Baiocco, Argalia, & Laghi, 2014), and that gay or lesbian individuals are less interested in being parents than heterosexual individuals (Riskind & Patterson, 2010). Mindfulness- and acceptance-based approaches are well suited to addressing these challenges, given that they encourage people to embrace their individual values, which can counter social pressures placed on stigmatized social groups. Clinically, this may involve helping GSM clients understand how stigma and discrimination can lead to problematic behaviors and that behaving in ways that are consistent with their values, regardless of negative thoughts and feelings, may counteract this tendency.

Very few studies have specifically examined the efficacy of mindfulness- and acceptance-based treatment approaches for psychological difficulties among GSM clients. Among the few studies that have, ACT delivered in a group format reduced self-stigma and depression and increased quality of life and social support in a small sample of gay and lesbian individuals experiencing conflict over their sexual orientation (Yadavaia & Hayes, 2012), and mindfulness-based stress reduction reduced avoidance symptoms and increased positive affect among HIV-positive gay men (Gayner et al., 2012). Skinta (2014) has noted that ACT principles are well suited for addressing various aspects of minority stress, such as targeting self-stigma with cognitive defusion,

targeting expectations of stigma with acceptance, targeting conceal‑
ment with values‑based action, and targeting discrimination with
contact with the present moment.

Case Example: Using ACT to Promote Resilience in GSM Clients

The following is an example of how the first author used ACT prin‑
ciples to reduce suffering and promote resilience when working clini‑
cally with Neil, a twenty‑one‑year‑old gay Indian‑American college
student who presented with symptoms consistent with major depres‑
sive disorder. His struggle with these symptoms began in early adoles‑
cence when he first realized he was gay. He developed a negative
attitude toward his sexual orientation because he felt different from
his peers and struggled to fit in. Although he didn't experience overt
victimization, his social interactions were limited, and he was afraid
people would reject him if they found out he was gay. He didn't dis‑
close his sexual orientation at the time but sought help for his depres‑
sion and received cognitive behavioral therapy. He learned skills to
manage his symptoms but continued to struggle with accepting his
sexuality.

Neil decided to seek treatment again at the age of twenty‑one
because his symptoms had become increasingly difficult to manage
after he finally disclosed his sexual orientation to his parents. His
parents weren't supportive, as being gay conflicted with their tradi‑
tional and religious values. They encouraged him to pray for absolu‑
tion and commit to academic and professional pursuits until he met a
woman with whom he could settle down. Their frequent attempts to
change his sexual orientation caused him a great deal of distress and
exacerbated the shame he already struggled with. He responded by
avoiding situations that might raise questions about his sexual orien‑
tation and engaging in substance use to avoid his pain.

Several ACT principles and exercises were particularly helpful in
this case (all described in Hayes, 2005), including clarifying values
and engaging in values‑based action; cognitive defusion; and reducing

experiential avoidance. A major focus of ACT is identifying one's values and living a life that is consistent with them. Neil had lost sight of his values because he was so focused on the fact that his parents didn't accept him for being gay. In session, we had several discussions about what values are, how they're different from goals, and how to engage in behaviors that are consistent with values in an effort to lead a satisfying life.

One exercise Neil found particularly helpful was Attending Your Own Funeral, which involves writing two versions of a eulogy to be read at one's own funeral: one focused on what might be said if the person continues to live life in the same way, and one focused on what might be said if the person lives in a way more consistent with individual values. This exercise resonated with him, because the first version of the eulogy that he wrote described the life his parents wanted for him, rather than the life he wanted for himself. He imagined someone recounting a version of his life in which he'd told his parents that he was wrong about being gay and had married and had children, despite his lack of interest in doing so. In this version, he imagined being described as an unhappy man who lost himself in work and kept to himself. His parents were happy with his choices, but he lived a lie and his depression never lifted.

The second version of the eulogy described the life Neil wanted for himself. He imagined someone recounting a version of his life that involved living in a big city and exploring his passions for art and entertainment. He was remembered for having a vibrant personality, being able to make people laugh, and having a long-lasting romantic relationship that endured the challenges of life. When he considered these two versions of his eulogy, it became apparent to him that he valued close relationships, personal growth, and leisure more than he valued education, career, and his relationship with his parents. Although he acknowledged that this might change over time, he realized that he wanted to take some time to develop his relationships with people, explore his interests in arts and culture, and become more independent.

After this exercise, we engaged in a more structured exercise that focused on clarifying what Neil valued in various life domains, such as intimate relationships, family relationships, friendships, career, and leisure pursuits. For each domain, he wrote about what he valued and identified one key value. Then he rated how important each value was to him and how closely he had been living in alignment with each value on a scale of 1 to 10. By examining the differences between these ratings for each domain, Neil could see how much his life needed to change in each area in order to be in line with what really mattered to him. Then we identified goals he might pursue relevant to each value, along with actions he could take to accomplish each goal, potential barriers, and strategies for overcoming those barriers.

For Neil, a major barrier to engaging in values-based action was fusion—being hooked by negative attitudes toward being gay that he had internalized. He was plagued by negative self-evaluations in the form of thoughts like *There is something wrong with me because I'm gay* and *No one will accept me because I'm gay*. Getting hooked by these thoughts caused him a great deal of distress and led him to avoid situations that might draw attention to his sexual orientation, such as situations where he would meet new people who might ask him personal questions.

From the ACT perspective, suffering occurs when people firmly believe and become fused with the content of their thoughts (Hayes, 2005). This certainly applied to Neil. How could he possibly pursue his goal of developing relationships with people if he was constantly fighting his negative self-evaluations, avoiding meeting new people, and trying not to disclose personal information to others? As such, an important aspect of Neil's treatment was using cognitive defusion and mindfulness techniques to help him acknowledge his thoughts without engaging with them. We discussed the fact that just because he had a thought, that didn't mean it was true, and he worked on labeling thoughts rather than just thinking them. For instance, when he had the thought *There is something wrong with me because I'm gay*, he would label it as "I am having the thought that there is something wrong with me because I'm gay." By labeling his thoughts rather than just thinking them, he was able to gain some distance from them and reduce their influence on his emotions and behaviors. We also used mindfulness exercises to help him practice acknowledging and labeling his thoughts without engaging with them and to increase his ability to focus on the present moment with a nonjudgmental attitude.

Finally, as noted, Neil had been turning to substance abuse, drinking and smoking marijuana in an attempt to cope with painful thoughts and feelings about himself, and also to cope with the stress he was experiencing in his relationship with his parents. Although he perceived these habits as helpful in the short term, he recognized that they had long-term consequences and didn't solve his problems. ACT posits that experiential avoidance—the attempt to control or alter the form or frequency of internal experiences even when doing so results in harm (Hayes, Wilson, Gifford, Follette, & Strosahl, 1996)—is at the root of psychopathology. By struggling to avoid negative thoughts and feelings, the experiences actually become more salient (Wenzlaff & Wegner, 2000). In session, we discussed how attempts to control or avoid negative internal states kept Neil from engaging in values-based action and reinforced the strength of the thoughts and feelings he was trying to avoid. Together, we reflected on the costs of his efforts to avoid thoughts and feelings related to being gay, and Neil realized he needed to find more functional solutions. Although he was reluctant to reduce his substance use, he gradually developed a greater willingness to experience negative thoughts and feelings as he came to accept that what he had been doing (avoiding them) was actually maintaining and increasing his suffering.

Ultimately, Neil was able to reduce his suffering and become more resilient by identifying his true values, committing to engaging in values-based action, disengaging from his thoughts using cognitive defusion and mindfulness techniques, and accepting negative internal states without engaging in experiential avoidance. These ACT processes have the potential to be powerful agents of change for GSM individuals, given the chronic stress so many of them experience throughout their lives. In the face of such stress, it can be challenging for people to remain mindful of what's really important to them and the extent to which they're actively working toward accomplishing goals that are in line with their values.

Conclusion

Given that GSM individuals are at increased risk for stress, largely due to stigma, which heightens their risk of mental health problems, effective interventions to address these concerns are critical to reducing the health disparities these populations experience. Although a range of cognitive behavioral techniques are likely to be helpful for GSM individuals, mindfulness and acceptance may be particularly well suited to the challenges they face. These approaches distinguish between what is within one's control (e.g., how individuals respond to their thoughts and feelings) versus what isn't within one's control (e.g., stigma and discrimination, and whether or not a negative thought or feeling arises in the first place). Further, these approaches emphasize the importance of identifying one's core values and behaving in ways that are consistent with them even while experiencing distress. Whether clinicians utilize a specific mindfulness- or acceptance-based intervention (e.g., ACT or DBT) or integrate mindfulness- or acceptance-based techniques into an eclectic evidence-based treatment approach, they have the potential to teach GSM clients a new way of relating to their internal experiences that can promote well-being and enhance quality of life.

References

Baiocco, R., Argalia, M., & Laghi, F. (2014). The desire to marry and attitudes toward same-sex family legalization in a sample of Italian lesbians and gay men. *Journal of Family Issues, 35,* 181–200.

Benotsch, E. G., Zimmerman, R., Cathers, L., McNulty, S., Pierce, J., Heck, T., et al. (2013). Non-medical use of prescription drugs, polysubstance use, and mental health in transgender adults. *Drug and Alcohol Dependence, 132,* 391–394.

Bishop, S. R., Lau, M., Shapiro, S., Carlson, L., Anderson, N. D., Carmody, J., et al. (2004). Mindfulness: A proposed operational definition. *Clinical Psychology: Science and Practice, 11,* 230–241.

Bockting, W. O., Miner, M. H., Swinburne Romine, R. E., Hamilton, A., & Coleman, E. (2013). Stigma, mental health, and resilience in an online sample of the US transgender population. *American Journal of Public Health, 103,* 943–951.

Bostwick, W. B., Boyd, C. J., Hughes, T. L., & McCabe, S. (2010). Dimensions of sexual orientation and the prevalence of mood and anxiety disorders in the United States. *American Journal of Public Health, 100*, 468–475.

Brewster, M. E., & Moradi, B. (2010). Perceived experiences of anti-bisexual prejudice: Instrument development and evaluation. *Journal of Counseling Psychology, 57*, 451–468.

Budge, S. L., Adelson, J. L., & Howard, K. A. S. (2013). Anxiety and depression in transgender individuals: The roles of transition status, loss, social support, and coping. *Journal of Consulting and Clinical Psychology, 81*, 545–557.

Clements-Nolle, K., Marx, R., Guzman, R., & Katz, M. (2001). HIV prevalence, risk behaviors, health care use, and mental health status of transgender persons: Implications for public health intervention. *American Journal of Public Health, 91*, 915–921.

Clements-Nolle, K., Marx, R., & Katz, M. (2006). Attempted suicide among transgender persons: The influence of gender-based discrimination and victimization. *Journal of Homosexuality, 51*, 53–69.

Currah, P., & Moore, L. J. (2009). "We won't know who you are": Contesting sex designations in New York City birth certificates. *Hypatia, 24*, 113–135.

Detrie, P. M., & Lease, S. H. (2007). The relation of social support, connectedness, and collective self-esteem to the psychological well-being of lesbian, gay, and bisexual youth. *Journal of Homosexuality, 53*, 173–199.

Díaz, R. M., Ayala, G., Bein, E., Henne, J., & Marin, B. V. (2001). The impact of homophobia, poverty, and racism on the mental health of gay and bisexual Latino men: Findings from 3 US cities. *American Journal of Public Health, 91*, 927–932.

Feinstein, B. A., Wadsworth, L. P., Davila, J., & Goldfried, M. R. (2014). Do parental acceptance and family support moderate associations between dimensions of minority stress and depressive symptoms among lesbians and gay men? *Professional Psychology: Research and Practice, 45*, 239–246.

Fergusson, D. M., Horwood, L. J., & Beautrais, A. L. (1999). Is sexual orientation related to mental health problems and suicidality in young people? *Archives of General Psychiatry, 56*, 876–880.

Garofalo, R., Wolf R. C., Kessel S., Palfrey J., & DuRant R. H. (1998). The association between health risk behaviors and sexual orientation among a school-based sample of adolescents. *Pediatrics, 101*, 895–902.

Gayner, B., Esplen, M. J., DeRoche, P., Wong, J., Bishop, S., Kavanagh, L., et al. (2012). A randomized controlled trial of mindfulness-based stress reduction to manage affective symptoms and improve quality of life in gay men living with HIV. *Journal of Behavioral Medicine, 35*, 272–285.

Gotta, G., Green, R., Rothblum, E., Solomon, S., Balsam, K., & Schwartz, P. (2011). Heterosexual, lesbian, and gay male relationships: A comparison of couples in 1975 and 2000. *Family Process, 50*, 353–376.

Grant, J. M., Mottet, L. A., Tanis, J., Harrison, J., Herman, J. L., & Keisling, M. (2011). Injustice at every turn: A report of the National Transgender

Discrimination Survey. Washington, DC: National Center for Transgender Equality and National Gay and Lesbian Task Force.

Hayes, S. (with Smith, S.). (2005). *Get out of your mind and into your life: The new acceptance and commitment therapy.* Oakland, CA: New Harbinger Publications.

Hayes, S. C., Strosahl, K. D., & Wilson, K. G. (1999). *Acceptance and commitment therapy: An experiential approach to behavior change.* New York: Guilford.

Hayes, S. C., Wilson, K. G., Gifford, E. V., Follette, V. M., & Strosahl, K. D. (1996). Experiential avoidance and behavioral disorders: A functional dimensional approach to diagnosis and treatment. *Journal of Consulting and Clinical Psychology, 64,* 1152–1168.

Hequembourg, A. L., & Brallier, S. A. (2009). An exploration of sexual minority stress across the lines of gender and sexual identity. *Journal of Homosexuality, 56,* 273–298.

Herek, G., Gillis, J., & Cogan, J. (1999). Psychological sequelae of hate crime victimization among LGB adults. *Journal of Consulting and Clinical Psychology, 67,* 945–951.

Hines, S. (2007). Transforming gender: Transgender practices of identity, intimacy, and care. Bristol, UK: Policy Press.

Katz-Wise, S. L., & Hyde, J. S. (2012). Victimization experiences of lesbian, gay, and bisexual individuals: A meta-analysis. *Journal of Sex Research, 49,* 142–167.

Keng, S. L., Smoski, M. J., & Robins, C. J. (2011). Effects of mindfulness on psychological health: A review of empirical studies. *Clinical Psychology Review, 31,* 1041–1056.

Linehan, M. M. (1993). *Cognitive-behavioral treatment of borderline personality disorder.* New York: Guilford.

Lombardi, E. L., Wilchins, R. A., Priesing, D., & Malouf, D. (2001). Gender violence: Transgender experiences with violence and discrimination. *Journal of Homosexuality, 42,* 89–101.

Mark, K., Rosenkrantz, D., & Kerner, I. (2014). "Bi"ing into monogamy: Attitudes toward monogamy in a sample of bisexual-identified adults. *Psychology of Sexual Orientation and Gender Diversity, 1,* 263–269.

Martell, C. R., Safren, S. A., & Prince, S. E. (2004). *Cognitive-behavioral therapies with lesbian, gay, and bisexual clients.* New York: Guilford.

Mays, V. M., & Cochran, S. D. (2001). Mental health correlates of perceived discrimination among lesbian, gay, and bisexual adults in the United States. *American Journal of Public Health, 91,* 1869–1876.

McCabe, S. E., Hughes, T. L., Bostwick, W. B., West, B. T., & Boyd, C. J. (2009). Sexual orientation, substance use behaviors, and substance dependence in the United States. *Addiction, 104,* 1333–1345.

Meyer, I. (2003). Prejudice, social stress, and mental health in lesbian, gay, and bisexual populations: Conceptual issues and research evidence. *Psychological Bulletin, 129,* 674–697.

Mizock, L., & Lewis, T. K. (2008). Trauma in transgender populations: Risk, resilience, and clinical care. *Journal of Emotional Abuse, 8,* 335–354.

Mohr, J. J., & Rochlen, A. B. (1999). Measuring attitudes regarding bisexuality in lesbian, gay male, and heterosexual populations. *Journal of Counseling Psychology, 46,* 353–369.

Operario, D., & Nemoto, T. (2005). Sexual risk behavior and substance use among a sample of Asian Pacific Islander transgendered women. *AIDS Education and Prevention, 17,* 430–443.

Riggle, E. B., & Mohr, J. J. (2015). A proposed multi factor measure of positive identity for transgender identified individuals. *Psychology of Sexual Orientation and Gender Diversity, 2,* 78–85.

Riggle, E. B., Mohr, J. J., Rostosky, S. S., Fingerhut, A. W., & Balsam, K. F. (2014). A multifactor Lesbian, Gay, and Bisexual Positive Identity Measure (LGB-PIM). *Psychology of Sexual Orientation and Gender Diversity, 1,* 398–411.

Riskind, R. G., & Patterson, C. J. (2010). Parenting intentions and desires among childless lesbian, gay, and heterosexual individuals. *Journal of Family Psychology, 24,* 78–81.

Sevelius, J. M., Reznick, O. G., Hart, S. L., & Schwarcz, S. (2009). Informing interventions: The importance of contextual factors in the prediction of sexual risk behaviors among transgender women. *AIDS Education and Prevention, 21,* 113–127.

Singh, A. A., Hays, D. G., & Watson, L. (2011). Strategies in the face of adversity: Resilience strategies of transgender individuals. *Journal of Counseling and Development, 89,* 20–27.

Skinta, M. D. (2014). Acceptance- and compassion-based approaches for invisible minorities: Working with shame among sexual minorities. In A. Masuda & A. Masuda (Eds.), *Mindfulness and acceptance in multicultural competency: A contextual approach to sociocultural diversity in theory and practice.* Oakland, CA: New Harbinger Publications.

Starks, T. J., Rendina, H. J., Breslow, A. S., Parsons, J. T., & Golub, S. A. (2013). The psychological cost of anticipating HIV stigma for HIV-negative gay and bisexual men. *AIDS and Behavior, 17,* 2732–2741.

Testa, R. J., Jimenez, C. L., & Rankin, S. (2014). Risk and resilience during transgender identity development: The effects of awareness and engagement with other transgender people on affect. *Journal of Gay and Lesbian Mental Health, 18,* 31–46.

Testa, R. J., Sciacca, L. M., Wang, F., Hendricks, M. L., Goldblum, P., Bradford, J., et al. (2012). Effects of violence on transgender people. *Professional Psychology: Research and Practice, 43,* 452–459.

Wenzlaff, R. M., & Wegner, D. M. (2000). Thought suppression. *Annual Review of Psychology, 51,* 59–91.

Yadavaia, J. E., & Hayes, S. C. (2012). Acceptance and commitment therapy for self-stigma around sexual orientation: A multiple baseline evaluation. *Cognitive and Behavioral Practice, 19,* 545–559.

PART III

Life in Context: Challenges in the World

CHAPTER 12

The Lasting Impact of HIV/AIDS

C. Virginia O'Hayer, David S. Bennett, and Jeffrey M. Jacobson, *Drexel University*

The AIDS disease is caused by a virus, but the AIDS epidemic is not. The AIDS epidemic is fueled by stigma, violence, and indifference.

—Sir Elton John

HIV/AIDS affects 1,250,000 Americans (Pennsylvania Department of Health, 2010). Nationally, the prevalence of people living with HIV (PLWH) is increasing, rising 7 percent from 2006 to 2012, with 50,000 Americans infected yearly (Centers for Disease Control and Prevention [CDC], 2015b). Men who have sex with men comprise 63 percent of new infections, and 57 percent of PLWH in America are gay or bisexual men (CDC, 2015b). Therefore, as a group, men who have sex with men are at elevated risk for HIV.

Transgender people, particularly trans women, are also at risk for HIV (CDC, 2011). Accurate data, however, are lacking for various reasons, including the failure of electronic medical records to correctly identify transgendered people, the failure of medical professionals to ask about gender, and the discomfort some transgendered people feel about self-identifying due to fear of being stigmatized. Among trans women newly diagnosed with HIV, 50 percent had histories of substance abuse, sex work, homelessness, incarceration, or sexual abuse, compared with only 31 percent of newly diagnosed cisgender people. These factors, along with negative experiences with health care professionals, contribute to an elevated risk for HIV and reduced likelihood of HIV testing among trans women (CDC, 2011).

HIV/AIDS is now a highly treatable disease due to advances in antiretroviral therapies (ARTs) and preventive medicine. With optimal medication adherence, a patient's viral load can be suppressed to undetectable levels, minimizing negative effects of the disease and its transmission. However, depression, shame, and stigma associated with HIV/AIDS may decrease medication adherence and routine health care use, increasing opportunistic infections, emergency care, and health care costs.

The Changing Nature of Treatment

During chronic HIV infection, HIV is actively replicating, often with an absence of symptoms. The end stage of HIV infection, AIDS, is marked by a CD4 cell count of fewer than 200 CD4+ T lymphocyte cells per cubic millimeter of blood. Normal CD4 counts are between 500 and 1,600 cells per cubic millimeter of blood. CD4 cell count reflects the degree of immune damage and estimates the immune system's ability to combat infection. AIDS can also be diagnosed by the occurrence of an opportunistic infection or neoplasm. Without treatment, people with AIDS typically survive about three years, or less if they encounter a dangerous opportunistic infection (CDC, 2015a).

Recently, HIV management and treatment has changed considerably. Previously, HIV was only treated via medication when CD4 cell count declined below a certain level. Current guidelines (CDC, 2015d), however, recommend treatment with ART regardless of CD4 count. This approach improves the health and longevity of PLWH and reduces HIV transmission.

Treatments themselves have also become less toxic and more tolerable and can now be administered in a one-pill-a-day regimen. If taken as prescribed, ARTs are highly effective at reducing viral load to the point that it is undetectable (less than 20 copies of the virus per milliliter of blood), significantly reducing HIV transmission.

Two recent approaches to reducing HIV transmission are post-exposure prophylaxis (PEP) and pre-exposure prophylaxis (PrEP). PEP involves administration of ART after a high-risk potential exposure to HIV (e.g., a condom breaking with an HIV+ partner, a sexual assault, or a needlestick injury at work). PrEP, in contrast, is a medication regimen initiated in combination with safer sex practices prior to potential exposure to HIV. PrEP is available by prescription for noninfected partners of PLWH. When taken daily, PrEP can result in a 92 percent reduction in HIV transmission (CDC, 2015c).

The Psychological Impact of HIV

Despite these promising treatment developments, societal change has proven slower than medical advancement, and HIV/AIDS remains one of the most stigmatized health conditions. Among PLWH, depression is much more common than among the general population (Bing et al., 2001) and is associated with poor adherence to ART (Mellins et al., 2009), leading to impaired immune function, including CD4 cell loss (Dowlati et al., 2010). Accordingly, depression is associated with increased health care costs, morbidity, and mortality among PLWH (Bouhnik et al., 2005; Ickovics et al., 2001).

The high rates of depression and treatment nonadherence among PLWH may be due in part to the high levels of shame among PLWH (Bennett, Traub, Mace, Juarascio, & O'Hayer, 2015). Shame, a painful state in which one perceives the self to be globally defective (Lewis, 2000), is perhaps more prevalent among PLWH than among people suffering from any other health condition. Despite shame being recognized as a significant problem for PLWH in qualitative studies, it is rarely examined in quantitative or prospective studies among PLWH. However, shame is a significant risk factor for depression, including among PLWH (Bennett, Hersh, Herres, & Foster, 2015; Bennett, Traub, et al., 2015; Kim, Thibodeau, & Jorgensen, 2011).

PLWH may attempt to temporarily avoid the discomfort of shame via distracting behaviors that increase the risk of HIV transmission, such as substance abuse and unprotected sex, further inducing shame and depression (Lewis, 1995). Avoidance of such emotional experiences can lead to a rebounding of the suppressed emotion, intensifying future shame and depression (Hayes, Luoma, Bond, Masuda, & Lillis, 2006). Similarly, shame can lead to avoidant coping, which further increases risk for depression (Aldao, Nolen-Hoeksema, & Schweizer, 2010), medication nonadherence, CD4 cell loss, and increased viral load (Ironson et al., 2005), hastening progression to AIDS (Leserman et al., 2000).

Shame predicts a pro-inflammatory state, leading to poor health outcomes among PLWH (Dickerson, Kemeny, Aziz, Kim, & Fahey, 2004). In addition, shame can prevent PLWH from seeking health care and adhering to their medication regimen (Blashill, Perry, & Safren, 2011), further challenging the immune system. Depression is also associated with low CD4 counts among PLWH (Olisah, Adekeye, & Sheikh, 2014), although the directionality of this effect is unclear. Collectively, these findings suggest that, among PLWH, shame and depression stress an already challenged immune system.

Cognitive behavioral therapy (CBT) can limit HIV disease progression and improve survival (DeLorenze, Satre, Queensberry, Tsai, & Weisner, 2010; Mkanta, Mejia, & Duncan, 2010). Moreover, CBT was recently associated with reductions in depression, greater treatment adherence, and higher CD4 counts among PLWH than treatment as usual (Safren et al., 2012). These gains from CBT, however, are generally modest and not consistently maintained at follow-up (Crepaz et al., 2008). This may be due to CBT's focus on cognitive restructuring, which may be better suited for depression related to distorted thinking patterns than that stemming from the reality of experiencing high levels of stigma, as PLWH do (Butler, Chapman, Forman, & Beck, 2006). Therefore, while CBT can help PLWH, more effective interventions are needed.

A Model of ACT with HIV

A potentially more effective treatment for improving the emotional and physical health of PLWH is acceptance-based behavior therapy (ABBT), a term that includes acceptance and commitment therapy (ACT; Hayes, Strosahl, & Wilson, 1999), dialectical behavior therapy (DBT; Linehan, 1993), and mindfulness-based stress reduction (MBSR; Kabat-Zinn, 1990). ABBT differs from CBT in that cognitions are not direct targets of change (Hayes et al., 2006; Herbert, Forman, & England, 2009). Rather, ABBT seeks to change one's relationship with distressing thoughts or feelings using acceptance-based strategies (Hayes et al., 1999).

A primary goal in ABBT is to increase experiential acceptance of difficult thoughts and feelings, such as shame and depression, through exercises that help develop a nonjudgmental stance. Accordingly, behaviors designed to temporarily reduce or avoid shame, such as substance use and risky sex, are no longer needed. ABBT also emphasizes identification of one's core values (e.g., "being a good parent") and engaging in committed action toward these values (e.g., taking medications to optimize health, in order to support good parenting), thereby fostering motivation.

A recent meta-analysis found ACT to be more effective than CBT in treating depression (Ruiz, 2012). We expect this difference to be amplified among PLWH due to ABBT's potential to decrease distress associated with shame, leading to improved medication adherence. In a pilot study of sixteen PLWH in our clinic, a promising trend was found in which ABBT improved medication adherence and led to increased CD4 count by 31 percent and decreased viral load by 89 percent after five group sessions (Moitra, Herbert, & Forman, 2011). Mindfulness meditation, a core component of ABBT, also has been shown to increase immune function (Jacobs et al., 2011).

Further support for the efficacy of ABBT comes from a study of shame associated with substance abuse, a common comorbid problem for PLWH (Bing et al., 2001). ABBT was associated with greater reductions of shame at four months post-treatment, better attendance, and reduced substance use compared to treatment as usual, or TAU (Luoma, Kohlenberg, Hayes, & Fletcher, 2012). Therefore, ABBT is a promising intervention among PLWH, although further research is needed, including studies directly examining its effects on shame, depressive symptoms, and treatment adherence. We are currently piloting such a study, described below.

ACT with HIV Study

Drexel University's Partnership Comprehensive Care Practice is one of the largest primary care practices in the nation for the treatment and management of PLWH. On an annual basis, it serves 1,750 patients and refers 200 clients to Drexel's Center City Clinic for Behavioral Medicine for outpatient mental health care.

In examining the efficacy of ABBT in our clinic, we hypothesize that ABBT will be better than TAU in decreasing shame and depressive symptoms post-treatment and at three-month follow-up; that ABBT will be better than TAU at improving treatment adherence at three-month follow-up; that improvement in treatment adherence in the ABBT group will be mediated by improvements in shame and depressive symptoms; and that ABBT will be associated with improved CD4 counts and reduced viral load.

Study Design

HIV+ participants with elevated depression scores (greater than 13 on the Beck Depression Inventory—II; Beck, Steer, & Brown, 1996) are randomly assigned to ABBT or TAU. ABBT follows our piloted treatment manual, *ACT with HIV* (Bennett, O'Hayer, Juarascio, & Winch, 2013), based on prior work in our clinic (Moitra et al., 2011) and existing ACT manuals, including one targeting shame among substance abusers (Luoma et al., 2012). TAU consists of supportive psychotherapy (Winston, Rosenthal, & Pinsker, 2004). ABBT and TAU are provided during six weekly, individual one-hour sessions. Our ABBT protocol is both feasible and well accepted by clients, with twenty-one of the twenty-two clients who received ABBT preferring to continue with ABBT following the intervention.

Measures

Shame, depressive symptoms, and treatment adherence are assessed at baseline, post-treatment (six weeks later), and three-month post-treatment follow-up. Shame is assessed using the HIV-Related Shame Scale (Sikkema, Hansen, Meade, Kochman, & Fox, 2009) and the Internalized Shame Scale (Cook, 1994) to examine the relative contributions of HIV-specific and general shame. Depressive symptoms are assessed using the Beck Depression Inventory—II (Beck et al., 1996). Treatment adherence is assessed using the Adherence to Refills and Medications Scale (Kripalani, Risser, Gatti, & Jacobson, 2009) and the Adult AIDS Clinical Trials Group adherence interview (Chesney et al., 2000), and by tracking attendance at routine medical appointments and the number of urgent appointments needed for acute crises, which often result from poor treatment adherence. CD4 and viral load are examined at baseline and for twelve months following treatment.

The Six-Week ACT with HIV Protocol

Our ACT condition involves six weekly sessions, each beginning with a mindfulness practice. The overall approach encourages participants to move toward their values with HIV, rather than struggling against having HIV, giving up, or waiting passively for a cure. In the sections that follow, we provide details on each session. (Our full treatment manual is available for download at http://www.newharbinger.com/34282.)

SESSION 1: IDENTIFYING VALUES AND OBSTACLES

In session 1, clients identify values they want their life to stand for by imagining an ideal speech at their ninetieth birthday party (adapted from Harris, 2009). Clients then sort through cards of possible values (e.g., "being a loving partner," "honest and accountable," and "strong religious faith") and choose the five that are most important to them. On the back of each card they write any perceived barriers to moving toward that value, including issues related to stigma in relationships with family, friends, or others and self-stigma (e.g., labeling oneself as "unlovable" or "toxic").

Home practice involves carrying these cards, with values on one side and barriers on the other, and looking at them daily.

SESSION 2: CREATIVE HOPELESSNESS AND ACCEPTANCE

In session 2, we turn to creative hopelessness: experiencing how past attempts to solve a problem have been ineffective and considering a radically different approach. In an approach inspired by Harris (2009), the therapist reviews past attempts to solve the problem of having HIV, saying something along these lines: "Let's examine ways you've become stuck in your life because of HIV and any shame or stigma you feel. What have you tried in the past to eliminate or deal with this feeling?" Clients list their strategies, such as avoiding medications and other reminders of HIV, isolating themselves socially, using drugs, trying not to think about the problem, and not disclosing their HIV status. The costs of these control strategies are then examined in terms of valued living, with the therapist asking, "What have you given up as a consequence of attempting to manage or avoid stigma or shame related to HIV? What would you do with your time if you weren't spending it trying to manage shame and stigma, unsettling thoughts and memories?"

The therapist introduces the idea that clients' prior attempts to control their unwanted experiences may be the problem, with acceptance being the alternative. This is illustrated using the Quicksand metaphor (Hayes et al., 1999), with the therapist explaining, "The more you struggle, the more you sink. The solution is to lie back, maximizing contact with the quicksand so that you float out." We then use the Tug-of-War with a Monster metaphor (Harris, 2009; Hayes et al., 1999) to emphasize the point, saying something along these lines: "The monster is life with an HIV diagnosis. It's huge, ugly, and very strong. Between you and the monster is a bottomless pit. You're pulling backward as hard as you can, but the monster keeps pulling you closer and closer to the pit. The harder you pull, the harder the monster pulls. You're stuck. The hardest thing to see is that our job is not to win the tug-of-war. Our job is to drop the rope. The monster is still there, but you're no longer in a struggle with it. Then you can go and do something more useful.

This metaphor demonstrates that letting go of a futile struggle is a viable option. It helps clients realize that struggling with the realities of living with HIV can be exhausting, frustrating, and distracting. Acceptance means experiencing whatever you are thinking or feeling; it's "dropping the rope."

Home practice involves having clients identify times when they are struggling to control their experience of having HIV, and then practicing dropping the rope and accepting their experiences at those times.

SESSION 3: COMMITTED ACTION

Session 3 focuses on committed action—doing what it takes to engage in actions guided by individual values. The Passengers on the Bus metaphor (Hayes et al., 1999) illustrates this well. To describe it, we say something like "We are all driving the bus of our life. We have a chosen direction we want to go. Unfortunately, we have a whole bunch of often unruly passengers in the back. The passengers are our thoughts and feelings. At times they can be a nuisance. Sometimes they shout out 'You're a useless driver,' 'You're going the wrong way,' 'You have the virus—there's no hope for you,' or 'You'll die alone!' It's easy to get derailed with passengers like this on the bus with us. We can attempt to placate them or stop the bus and give up. Or we can accept the presence of these passengers and drive on in our chosen direction anyway."

As home practice, the therapist asks clients to take a stand for their values and verbally commit to small steps in those directions. For example, a client might make the following commitment: "Promoting my health is really important to me. This week, I'll take my HIV meds every day."

SESSION 4: ACCEPTANCE AND CONTACT WITH THE PRESENT MOMENT

In session 4, the therapist focuses on openly addressing shame by encouraging contact with the present moment. To that end, we use a brief guided mindfulness practice, which we present like this: "Think about what you like least about yourself. It may or may not be related to having HIV. What is it about you that keeps getting in the way of what you want in life? See if you can get that in mind right now... Notice what it has cost you to be like that. Let yourself be with it... Notice if any stories come up that are connected with it. See what evidence your mind offers to support why you are like that."

A Chinese finger trap is presented as a physical metaphor illustrating the futility of attempting to eliminate distress related to HIV or other aspects of the client's life, bringing in the ACT process of creative hopelessness (Hayes et al., 1999). Instead of struggling to pull one's fingers out of the trap, pushing them into the trap allows them to be released. This is analogous to releasing oneself from the struggle against having HIV by choosing acceptance.

In this session, clients experience how struggling to avoid distress associated with HIV, such as medication side effects or fear of stigmatization, actually worsens the experience and exacerbates symptoms. We highlight this by saying, "So, you can see how trying to push back against something in our life, including beliefs related to HIV, such as "I'm tainted" or "People will reject me," doesn't really work. In fact, we may actually think even more about the thing that we're trying to avoid thinking about." We also explore how thoughts and feelings about disclosure, discovery, or avoidance of HIV lurk under the surface during many interactions in the client's daily life.

For home practice, clients are asked to track their thoughts about stigma or shame and HIV, and to track whether they avoided interacting with someone or doing something enjoyable because of having HIV. The goal is to increase mindfulness and acceptance while reducing avoidance.

SESSION 5: DEFUSION—AIDS AIDS AIDS

Cognitive fusion is the human tendency to get caught up in our thoughts, holding them tightly as Truth. As a result, a thought such as *I'm worthless* can lead to maladaptive behavior and depressive symptoms. Similarly, thoughts associated with a stigmatized word, such as "AIDS," can prompt shame and other painful emotions. To address this, we use a derivation of a classic defusion exercise (Titchener, 1916), in this case having clients repeat "AIDS, AIDS, AIDS" hundreds of times until it becomes meaningless and devoid of emotion (M. Skinta, personal communication, March 2013).

Clients next list whatever thoughts their mind churns out when trying to move toward their values; for example, *I won't live to see my kids graduate college, No one will want to date me,* and *I can't be a parent; I have AIDS.* The therapist writes each thought on an index card and, after alerting the client, tosses the cards at the client quickly, while the client tries to keep them from landing on him or her (Hayes et al., 1999). The client experiences the energy invested in keeping the cards away, the impossibility of keeping all the cards away, and the difficulty of moving toward values while also being fully invested in keeping the cards away. The therapist then models willingly holding the cards without trying to get rid of them, a physical metaphor for accepting the existence of such thoughts. The defusion exercises in session 5 help clients recognize that thoughts and feelings, including preconceived notions about HIV, are products of their minds and can be acknowledged without having to be "true." This frees them to move toward their chosen values.

Home practice involves carrying the index cards generated during the session—a physical metaphor for acceptance. It also includes practices that further encourage defusion, such as singing one's shame-inducing thoughts and voicing them in different accents (Hayes et al., 1999).

SESSION 6: SELF-AS-CONTEXT—PATTERN SMASHING

In session 6, we turn to perspective taking and developing a view of self-as-context, rather than self-as-content, or conceptualized self. To access a conceptualized self (our story of who we are), clients fill in "I am _____" badges (e.g., "I am a father"; "I am someone with HIV," "I am a student"; "I am gay"; "I am black"). The therapist then introduces self-as-context, pointing out that all of these statements have an "I" in common—the self who is the one here, now, noticing all of these labels—saying something along these lines: "So all of these are you in some sense, but there's another you, too: the one here having and noticing all of these experiences" (Harris, 2009).

We use a common metaphor to further illustrate this: "Imagine yourself as a mountain and your thoughts, feelings, and other experiences are the changing flora, fauna, and weather around the mountain. Notice that the one constant is the mountain; the one constant is you, observing your experiences. Notice that the mountain is not the plants and animals that inhabit it, or the weather, the storms, or the seasons." Self-as-context is particularly relevant for PLWH, who often have a fragmented sense of self, divided into "before HIV" and "with HIV."

For home practice, we encourage clients to practice pattern smashing (Hayes, 2005). This involves experiencing self-as-context by noticing that we are not defined by our habits and actions. Clients identify a common habit or pattern of behavior (e.g., "I am a person who never mentions that I have HIV"), and then intentionally break it to increase psychological flexibility (e.g., "I will tell a close friend that I have HIV").

Case Example: Applying the ACT with HIV Protocol

One attendee of our HIV support group was Michael, a forty-year-old bisexual African-American with severe depression and shame preventing him from disclosing his health status to family members. In his view, disclosing his HIV+ status would essentially be outing himself to his family as bisexual. He had witnessed family members discussing an HIV+ cousin, saying, "He has the virus. I guess he's gay." Since Michael was closeted about being bisexual, he could not imagine disclosing his HIV status. Further, because he hid his bisexual identity from almost everyone he was close to, his sex with men occurred solely in impersonal group settings, increasing his sense of shame and isolation.

Michael frequently referred to himself as "a walking, talking biohazard." He described himself using identical wording, every group session. He acknowledged repeating this statement mentally every few minutes. Whenever he made this statement aloud, his downcast eyes and slumped body posture suggested profound shame.

Michael agreed that viewing himself as "a walking, talking biohazard" was not helpful and probably contributed to his depression and near-total isolation. However, he could not let go of his attachment to this statement. It seemed to serve as his trump card when other group members offered advice about meeting prospective partners on HIV+ dating sites or shared success stories about disclosing their HIV status to supportive family members. Michael's fusion with being "a walking, talking biohazard" reflected not only deeply ingrained shame and self-stigma about his HIV diagnosis, but also his alienation from society in general and even from his HIV support group.

We tried various strategies to help Michael view himself differently. We challenged the utility of this thought (e.g., "How is that thought working for you?"). In keeping with traditional CBT, we encouraged him to weigh the evidence for and against the thought (e.g., "Your viral load is undetectable, so are you a high infection risk?"). We used the downward arrow technique to access his core beliefs (e.g., ". . . and therefore you feel fundamentally unlovable"). We ignored the comment in efforts to extinguish it. No luck—Michael persisted in referring to himself as "a walking, talking biohazard."

After attending an ACT Boot Camp, we employed an acceptance-based intervention (the "I am _____" exercise from session 6 of our protocol). When Michael next stated, "I'm a walking, talking biohazard," the therapist asked, "And what else are you?" This prompted Michael to generate other aspects of himself while also acknowledging the presence of "walking, talking biohazard" in his self-network. After a few moments of contemplative silence, he replied "I'm a father." As the therapist repeatedly asked, "And what else are you?" he replied, "I'm a son. I'm a brother. I'm a friend. I'm someone with diabetes. I'm someone who used to sell drugs to pregnant women."

We were then able to parse out justified versus unjustified shame and guilt, concepts commonly used in dialectical behavior therapy (Linehan, 1993). According to DBT, shame and guilt are justified when one's actions could result in exclusion from one's community. Otherwise, they are unjustified. Justified shame and guilt warrant a repair. In Michael's case, a repair for selling drugs to pregnant women could involve volunteering time or donating funds to a shelter for new mothers recovering from substance use.

While Michael's guilt about his prior drug-selling was justified (his community would exclude him for having sold drugs to pregnant women), his shame about having HIV was unjustified, as he would not be excluded from his community (his HIV support group) for having HIV. Unjustified shame and self-stigma can be targeted by engaging in the shame-inducing behavior repeatedly as an exposure practice, depleting its power through repetition. This goal can also be accomplished via defusion. Using the phone-based app Songify, by Smule, Michael recorded himself saying, "I'm a walking, talking biohazard," then set it to a rap beat. Group members encouraged him to play the song repeatedly, setting it to different beats. Michael listened to it over and over until it lost meaning and became a series of sounds devoid of emotional valence.

Traditional change strategies failed Michael, but by accepting his internal experience and recognizing other aspects of himself he could increase his psychological flexibility. Acceptance was furthered by defusion, as he observed his thoughts without becoming entangled with them. He had overidentified with his maladaptive thought and it had become a Truth to which his mind was very attached (Harris, 2009). Through defusion, Michael was able to see his label "walking, talking biohazard" as just a thought, freeing him to engage in committed action, including a repair for his prior transgressions (by making a donation to a women's shelter), to support his value of being an honorable man. Michael also chose to disclose his HIV+ status to his adult children, who, surprisingly to him, were accepting and supportive. His depressive symptoms mostly resolved, and he decided to pursue classes toward becoming an HIV peer counselor.

Conclusion

Both our pilot study and Michael's case study illustrate how ABBT techniques can be applied to PLWH with promising effectiveness. While shame and stigma remain among the largest obstacles to living with HIV today, acceptance-based interventions may decrease their negative impact, thereby decreasing depressive symptoms and increasing medical adherence and quality of life among PLWH.

References

Aldao, A., Nolen-Hoeksema, S., & Schweizer, S. (2010). Emotion-regulation strategies across psychopathology: A meta-analytic review. *Clinical Psychology Review, 30*, 217–237.

Beck, A. T., Steer, R. A., & Brown, G. K. (1996). *Manual for the Beck Depression Inventory—II.* San Antonio, TX: Psychological Corporation.

Bennett, D. S., Hersh, J., Herres, J., & Foster, J. (2015). HIV-related stigma, shame, and avoidant coping: Risk factors for internalizing symptoms among youth with HIV? *Child Psychiatry and Human Development*, epub ahead of print.

Bennett, D. S., O'Hayer, C. V., Juarascio, A., & Winch, E. (2013). ACT with HIV: Reducing shame and depression among HIV+ individuals through acceptance and commitment therapy: A treatment manual. Philadelphia, PA: Drexel University College of Medicine Department of Psychiatry.

Bennett, D. S., Traub, K., Mace, L., Juarascio, A., & O'Hayer, C. V. (2015). Shame among people living with HIV: A literature review. *AIDS Care, 28*, 87–91.

Bing, E. G., Burnam, M. A., Longshore, D., Fleishman, J. A., Sherbourne, C. D., London, A. S., et al. (2001). Psychiatric disorders and drug use among human immunodeficiency virus-infected adults in the United States. *Archives of General Psychiatry, 58*, 721–728.

Blashill, A. J., Perry, N., & Safren, S. A. (2011). Mental health: A focus on stress, coping, and mental illness as it relates to treatment retention, adherence, and other health outcomes. *Current HIV/AIDS Reports, 8*, 215–222.

Bouhnik, A. D., Preau, M., Vincent, E., Carrieri, M. P., Gallais, H., Lepeu, G., et al. (2005). Depression and clinical progression in HIV-infected drug users treated with highly active antiretroviral therapy. *Antiviral Therapy, 10*, 53–61.

Butler, A. C., Chapman, J. E., Forman, E. M., & Beck, A. T. (2006). The empirical status of cognitive-behavioral therapy: A review of meta-analyses. *Clinical Psychology Review, 26*, 17–31.

Centers for Disease Control and Prevention. (2011). HIV infection among transgender people. Retrieved January 23, 2016, from http://www.cdc.gov/hiv/transgender/pdf/transgender.pdf.

Centers for Disease Control and Prevention. (2015a). HIV/AIDS: About HIV/AIDS. Retrieved January 23, 2016, from http://www.cdc.gov/hiv/basics/whatishiv.html.

Centers for Disease Control and Prevention. (2015b). HIV/AIDS: Basic statistics. Retrieved January 23, 2016, from http://www.cdc.gov/hiv/basics/statistics.html.

Centers for Disease Control and Prevention. (2015c). HIV/AIDS: PrEP. Retrieved January 23, 2016, from http://www.cdc.gov/hiv/basics/prep.html.

Centers for Disease Control and Prevention. (2015d). HIV/AIDS: Recommended prevention services. Retrieved January 23, 2016, from http://www.cdc.gov/hiv/prevention/programs/pwp/art.html.

Chesney, M. A., Ickovics, J. R., Chambers, D. B., Gifford, A. L., Neidig, J., Zwcki, B., et al. (2000). Self-reported adherence to antiretroviral medications among participants in HIV clinical trials: The AACTG adherence instruments. *AIDS Care, 12*, 255–266.

Cook D. (1994). *Internalized Shame Scale: Professional manual.* Menomonie, WI: Channel Press.

Crepaz, N., Passin, W. F., Herbst, J. H., Rama, S. M., Malow, R. M., Purcell, D. W., et al. (2008). Meta-analysis of cognitive-behavioral interventions on HIV-positive persons' mental health and immune functioning. *Health Psychology, 27*, 4–14.

DeLorenze, G., Satre, D., Queensberry, C., Tsai, A. L., & Weisner, C. (2010). Mortality after diagnosis of psychiatric disorders and co-occurring substance use disorders among HIV-infected patients. *AIDS Patient Care and STDS, 24*, 705–712.

Dickerson, S. S, Kemeny, M. E., Aziz, N., Kim, K. H., & Fahey, J. L. (2004). Immunological effects of induced shame and guilt. *Psychosomatic Medicine, 66*, 124–131.

Dowlati, Y., Herrmann, N., Swardfager, W., Liu, H., Sham, L., Reim, E. K., et al. (2010). A meta-analysis of cytokines in major depression. *Biological Psychiatry, 67*, 446–457.

Harris, R. (2009). *ACT made simple: An easy-to-read primer on acceptance and commitment therapy.* Oakland, CA: New Harbinger Publications.

Hayes, S. C. (with Smith, S.). (2005). *Get out of your mind and into your life: The new acceptance and commitment therapy.* Oakland, CA: New Harbinger Publications.

Hayes, S. C., Luoma, J. B., Bond, F. W., Masuda, A., & Lillis, J. (2006). Acceptance and commitment therapy: Model, processes and outcomes. *Behaviour Research and Therapy, 44*, 1–25.

Hayes, S. C., Strosahl, K. D., & Wilson, K. G. (1999). *Acceptance and commitment therapy: An experiential approach to behavior change.* New York: Guilford.

Herbert, J. D., Forman, E. M., & England, E. L. (2009). Psychological acceptance. In W. O'Donohue & J. E. Fisher (Eds.), *Cognitive behavior therapy: Applying empirically supported treatments in your practice.* Hoboken, NJ: Wiley.

Ickovics, J. R., Hamburger, M. E., Vlahov, D., Schoenbaum, E. E., Schuman, P., Boland, R. J., et al. (2001). Mortality, CD4 cell count decline, and depressive symptoms among HIV-seropositive women: Longitudinal analysis from the HIV Epidemiology Research Study. *JAMA, 285*, 1466–1474.

Ironson, G., Balbin, E., Stuetzle, R., Fletcher, M. A., O'Cleirigh, C., Laurenceau, J. P., et al. (2005). Dispositional optimism and the mechanisms by which it predicts slower disease progression in HIV: Proactive behavior, avoidant coping, and depression. *International Journal of Behavioral Medicine, 12*, 86–97.

Jacobs, T. L., Epel, E. S., Lin, J., Blackburn, E. H., Wolkowitz, O. M., Bridwell, D. A., et al. (2011). Intensive meditation training, immune cell telomerase activity, and psychological mediators. *Psychoneuroendocrinology, 36*, 664–681.

Kabat-Zinn, J. (1990). *Full catastrophe living: Using the wisdom of your body and mind to face stress, pain, and illness.* New York: Random House.

Kim, S., Thibodeau, R., & Jorgensen, R. S. (2011). Shame, guilt, and depressive symptoms: A meta-analytic review. *Psychological Bulletin, 137*, 68–96.

Kripalani, S., Risser, J., Gatti, M. E., & Jacobson, T. A. (2009). Development and evaluation of the Adherence to Refills and Medications Scale (ARMS) among low-literacy patients with chronic disease. *Value in Health: The Journal of the International Society for Pharmacoeconomics and Outcomes Research, 12*, 118–123.

Leserman, J., Petitto, J. M., Golden, R. N., Gaynes, B. N., Gu, H., Perkins, D. O., et al. (2000). Impact of stressful life events, depression, social support, coping, and cortisol on progression to AIDS. *American Journal of Psychiatry, 157*, 1221–1228.

Lewis, M. (1995). *Shame: The exposed self.* New York: Simon and Schuster.

Lewis, M. (2000). Self-conscious emotions: Embarrassment, pride, shame, and guilt. In M. Lewis & J. Haviland-Jones (Eds.), *Handbook of emotions*, 2nd edition. New York: Guilford.

Linehan, M. M. (1993). *Cognitive-behavioral treatment of borderline personality disorder.* New York: Guilford.

Luoma, J. B., Kohlenberg, B. S., Hayes, S. C., & Fletcher, L. (2012). Slow and steady wins the race: A randomized clinical trial of acceptance and commitment therapy targeting shame in substance use disorders. *Journal of Consulting and Clinical Psychology, 80*, 43–53.

Mellins, C. A., Havens, J. F., McDonnell, C., Lichtenstein, C., Uldall, K., Chesney, M., et al. (2009). Adherence to antiretroviral medications and medical care in HIV-infected adults diagnosed with mental and substance abuse disorders. *AIDS Care, 21*, 168–177.

Mkanta, W. N., Mejia, M. C., & Duncan, R. P. (2010). Race, outpatient mental health service use, and survival after an AIDS diagnosis in the highly active antiretroviral therapy era. *AIDS Patient Care and STDS, 24*, 31–37.

Moitra, E., Herbert, J. D., & Forman, E. M. (2011). Acceptance-based behavior therapy to promote HIV medication adherence. *AIDS Care, 23*, 1660–1667.

Olisah, V. O., Adekeye, O., & Sheikh, T. L. (2014). Depression and CD4 cell count among patients with HIV in a Nigerian university teaching hospital. *International Journal of Psychiatry in Medicine, 48*, 253–261.

Pennsylvania Department of Health. (2010). *Integrated epidemiologic profile of HIV/AIDS in Pennsylvania: 2009–2010.* Harrisburg, PA: Pennsylvania Department of Health.

Ruiz, F. J. (2012). Acceptance and commitment therapy versus traditional cognitive behavioral therapy: A systematic review and meta-analysis of current empirical evidence. *International Journal of Psychology and Psychological Therapy, 12*, 334–357.

Safren, S. A., O'Cleirigh, C. M., Bullis, J. R., Otto, M. W., Stein, M. D., & Pollack, M. H. (2012). Cognitive behavioral therapy for adherence and depression (CBT-AD) in HIV-infected injection drug users: A randomized controlled trial. *Journal of Consulting and Clinical Psychology, 80*, 404–415.

Sikkema, K. J., Hansen, N. B., Meade, C. S., Kochman, A., & Fox, A. M. (2009). Psychosocial predictors of sexual HIV transmission risk behavior among HIV-positive adults with a sexual abuse history in childhood. *Archives of Sexual Behavior, 38,* 121–134.

Titchener, E. B. (1916). *A beginner's guide to psychology.* New York: Macmillan.

Winston, A., Rosenthal, R. N., & Pinsker, H. (2004). *Introduction to supportive psychotherapy.* Washington, DC: American Psychiatric Publishing.

CHAPTER 13

Doubly Disenfranchised: An Acceptance- and Compassion-Based Approach to Being a Minority Within GSM Communities

Khashayar Farhadi-Langroudi, *American School of Professional Psychology at Argosy University–San Francisco Bay Area*; and Kayla Sargent and Akihiko Masuda, *Georgia State University*

Your task is not to seek for love, but merely to seek and find all the barriers within yourself that you have built against it.

—Rumi

Across the globe, when individuals have any type of minority status, whether related to gender, ethnicity, sexual orientation, or other qualities, this can have significant negative impacts on health. Historically, health disparities have been used to justify discriminatory diagnostic and treatment practices toward minority individuals (Li, Jenkins, & Sundsmo, 2007), perpetuating stigmatization and negative medical and behavioral health outcomes for these individuals (Bailey, 1999). For example, in the United States, conversion therapies for sexual minorities persisted for decades after publication of the second edition of the *DSM*, which eliminated homosexuality as a diagnostic category in 1973. Furthermore, ethnic minorities in the United States are often misdiagnosed, or diagnoses are made based on mainstream cultural norms rather than the appropriate psychosocial criteria for a given client (Ridley, Li, & Hill, 1998).

While the field of behavioral health care has begun to pay greater attention to the impact of a minority status on health, behavioral health professionals may not adequately approach the subgroups of minorities and their health, particularly multiple-minority individuals, such as ethnic minorities within a gender and sexual minority (GSM) community. Multiple-minority status is found to be linked to greater emotional distress and hardship (Berdahl & Moore, 2006; Pak, Dion, & Dion, 1991), but professionals tend to focus exclusively on a single aspect of a person's identity, such as gender, and its impact on the person's health, while overlooking intersecting identities. One way to contribute to this field is to offer a potential working model that allows professionals to understand and promote the behavioral health of multiple-minority individuals. We think an acceptance- and compassion-based approach (Skinta, 2014; Skinta, Lezama, Wells, & Dilley, 2014; Tirch, Schoendorff, & Silberstein, 2014) serves as such a model.

Focusing on the individual level of analysis—the acts of a whole person in context—this chapter presents an acceptance- and compassion-based approach to the health of multiple-minority individuals, especially those in GSM communities. Our model has been drawn mainly from acceptance and commitment therapy (ACT;

Hayes, Strosahl, & Wilson, 1999), compassion-focused therapy (CFT; Gilbert, 2010), and the integration of the two (Skinta, 2014; Skinta et al., 2014; Tirch et al., 2014). We first review the extant literature addressing the behavioral health of individuals with multiple-minority identities and present a prominent guiding conceptual model: the minority stress model. Subsequently, we outline our acceptance- and compassion-based approach, which has a focus on understanding and promoting the wellness of individuals with multiple-minority status. Finally, the first author shares his experience as a minority within a minority community.

Models of Minority Distress

Minority physical and mental health outcomes are well documented. For example, Western population-based studies have shown that gender and sexual minorities have a higher prevalence of behavioral health concerns, including mood and anxiety disorders, suicide, and substance abuse disorders (Bostwick, Boyd, Hughes, & McCabe, 2010; Mustanski, Garofalo, & Emerson, 2010). Similarly, ethnic minority individuals in the United States experience greater hardships and distress than their white American counterparts (Mulia, Ye, Zemore, & Greenfield, 2008).

One prominent guiding model for understanding the behavioral health of minority individuals is Meyer's minority stress theory (Meyer, 2003; Meyer & Ouellette, 2009). According to this theory, the prevailing mechanism for these negative behavioral health outcomes is stress, as opposed to status. More specifically, a hostile social environment that involves stigma, prejudice, and discrimination associated with a socially constructed status (e.g., gay) causes distress in minority individuals, which ultimately leads to negative behavioral health outcomes (Mays & Cochran, 2001; Mays, Cochran, & Barnes, 2007; Meyer & Ouellette, 2009).

Regarding the health of GSM and multiple-minority individuals, several features of hostile social environments are worth noting. First, it is important to understand how socially constructed gender expectations play a role in minority stress. Adherence to gender roles remains a powerful force (Connell, 2005), with most contemporary societies continuing to operate within a patriarchal system that undervalues women and gender-nonconforming people (Yoshihama, 2005). Because patriarchy, by definition, values male dominance and female submissiveness, gender expressions that violate, challenge, or attenuate this hierarchy are subject to punishment. Consequently, "men behaving as women" or "women behaving as men" by engaging in homosexual or gender-nonconforming behaviors are viewed as a threat to the pervasive social hierarchy.

Second, it is also crucial to consider how cultural gender expectations intersect with other majority cultural norms (Johnson & Yarhouse, 2013). For example, in Western gay communities, white, affluent, and educated voices tend to be most loudly heard, while voices of ethnic minorities are marginalized (Giwa & Greensmith, 2012), further persecuting and stigmatizing multiple-minority individuals. In reality, a given identity of a person is just one dimension of that individual, and assessing clients from a single identity is likely to activate unhelpful stereotypes and assumptions. Therefore, it is of paramount importance to perceive each individual as a whole person.

Third, minority stress is particularly complex and dynamic because it is inherently social and verbal (Hayes, Niccolls, Masuda, & Rye, 2002; Masuda, 2014). And because the contingencies of isms (e.g., sexism, racism) that maintain minority distress are socially constructed, a person can experience such stress in virtually any context.

Fourth, while social progress has slowly created a safer arena for self-expression, we must pay close attention to the actual outcomes (workability) of any given "social justice" movement. Some such movements, while seemingly encouraging and celebrating the acceptance of diversity, actually conceal discrimination in certain sociocultural contexts. For example, in 1979 Iran became the first Islamic country to allow cosmetic and legal sex changes for individuals identifying as transsexuals. This decision, however, was not born of tolerance. The government, headed by fundamentalist Ayatollah Khomeini, perceived nontraditional gender expression as a medical condition that should be addressed by "corrective" surgery. Outcomes were further complicated by discriminatory practices regarding Iranian women: having completed the transition, Iranian trans women were stripped of rights reserved exclusively for men. In this way, the social construct of binary gender functions in part to maintain the cultural practice of male dominance. Because broad acceptance of nonconforming gender expression would attenuate the salience of male dominance, the Iranian government allowed sex change as a mechanism for maintaining a discriminatory hierarchy, pathologizing gender-nonconforming citizens. Thus, the context and function of this social behavior are what constitutes discrimination, rather than the social behavior itself.

ACT and CFT Case Conceptualization for Multiple-Minority Clients

ACT- and CFT-based approaches to the treatment of multiple-minority individuals aim to promote valued, vital living (Skinta, 2014; Skinta et al., 2014). Valued living, which is often termed "psychological flexibility" in ACT, is viewed as interacting with or relating to one's experiences, thoughts, feelings, and identities in a personally meaningful way without being confined, restricted, or burdened by rigid adherence to them. According to ACT, the extent to which clients interact with their external environment and internal experiences flexibly, as whole individuals, represents their overall functioning across diverse life domains. Similarly, dysfunction is also understood in terms of how people interact with their internal and external environments. It is important to note that in addition to hostile external factors (e.g., experienced and perceived environmental discrimination), in ACT- and CFT-based approaches, minority distress is seen as also manifesting internally in part due to fusion with self-stigmatizing thoughts (e.g., *My relationship is weird*) and emotions (e.g., *I am worthless*) that receive confirmation within a stigmatizing environment (Skinta, 2014). As such, when working with multiple-minority clients, clinicians must consider how these clients interact with the layers of their internal and external environments and how their patterns of interaction serve their overall function and flexibility.

Additionally, what is crucial in ACT- and CFT-based case conceptualization is the functional effectiveness, or workability, of a person's behavior in a given context, rather than mere symptom reduction (Hayes et al., 1999; Tirch et al., 2014). Such conceptualization focuses on the extent to which people engage in the three resiliency processes of change in their internal and external environments in the here and now (Harris, 2009; Hayes, Villatte, Levin, & Hildebrandt, 2011):

- Being centered

- Being open

- Being engaged

Deficits in any of these processes lead to diminished quality of life and impaired functioning.

Being Centered

One crucial factor to consider with multiple-minority clients is the degree to which they are centered in the present-moment context of their life events. From the perspective of minority stress theory, individuals with a multiple-minority status are likely to experience more layers of hardship, potentially keeping them from being centered fully in the here and now (Meyer, 2003; Meyer & Ouellette, 2009). For example, multiple-minority clients may struggle with issues around their ethnicity as "other" even if they are openly out and have celebrated their gender identity and sexuality. For them, in addition to hostile external environments, attachment to an internalized personal narrative of oppression (e.g., fixation on previous experiences of rejection and the fear of future discrimination) is likely to perpetuate avoidance and inflexibility, obscuring their here-and-now experience.

Being Open

The concept of openness applies broadly to thoughts, feelings, behaviors, and beliefs and stands in direct contrast to avoidance and inflexibility (Harris, 2009; Hayes et al., 2011). It is important to note that openness to different experiences, like the ACT process of acceptance, is a chosen behavior of a whole person, not a passive stance of surrender. Furthermore, openness involves active and intentional efforts to face the reality of one's experiences for the purpose of expressing and embodying one's deepest values (Wilson & Murrell, 2004).

Generally speaking, people's rigid adherence to avoidance and inflexibility stems from beliefs or narratives in which they are stuck. This kind of entanglement often evokes strong distress and pain and can result in efforts to avoid and downregulate these unpleasant reactions, often creating a vicious cycle that exacerbates the problem. One of the major costs of excessive adherence to avoidance is that it prevents people from recognizing that they are, in fact, responsible for the agency of their actions, and that they are also the locus where their chosen actions unfold (Hayes et al., 1999; Wilson & Murrell, 2004).

Being Engaged

For individuals with multiple-minority status, embodying their chosen values by engaging in committed action may be challenging, especially in the context of relationships. Personal connection and empowerment are important values for many GSM and multiple-minority individuals (Skinta, 2014). However, given the overarching sociocultural context, they are vulnerable to experiencing more exclusion, discrimination, and distress than majority-status individuals (Meyer, 2003). As noted above, GSM individuals who are also members of ethnic minority groups may feel even more alienated, especially if they perceive that some aspects of their GSM identity are inconsistent with their ethnic identity. If they then become attached to a narrative of further alienation, this can exacerbate lack of engagement in values-directed actions.

ACT and CFT Treatments for Multiple-Minority Clients

In parallel with the preceding perspective on case formulation, ACT- and CFT-based treatments for minority- and identity-related distress are aimed at three processes:

- Fostering present-moment awareness

- Improving contextual regulation of unhelpful language processes (e.g., narrative, categorization, association, evaluation)

- Promoting actions that differentially reinforce valued aspects of identity or character, such as self-care or activism, rather than stigmatized aspects—in other words, promoting values-based action

When integrated, these factors produce a present-moment process of improving contextual regulation while disempowering shame, stigma, and prejudice—a process that fosters broader psychological flexibility and enhances quality of life (Hayes et al., 2011; Masuda, Hill, Morgan, & Cohen, 2012). In the sections that follow, we'll briefly describe interventions that can promote these three intertwined processes.

Present-Moment Awareness

Present-moment awareness is a prerequisite for any behavioral change and is closely linked to the resiliency process of being centered. There are several treatment strategies that therapists can employ for promoting centered awareness. One simple yet often very powerful exercise is mindful breathing, in which clients are encouraged to notice the here-and-now experience of their breath. Once they become practiced in devoting present-moment attention to breathing, this type of attention can be gradually broadened to noticing feelings and thoughts in the same way, without judgment.

Improved Contextual Regulation

In ACT- and CFT-based treatments, improving contextual regulation involves the promotion of psychological openness. One way to accomplish this in the context of clients' avoidance and inflexibility is to elucidate experientially that they can choose to be open to activities or events that are incongruent with their preferences. To highlight this, the second author often uses a simple experiential exercise in which she asks clients to hypothetically choose between hot coffee or hot tea in the morning. They may say, for example, "I'd choose tea; I don't even like coffee," as if coffee is somehow an illegitimate choice, eliminated by their preference. When pressed with the question "Could you choose coffee instead, even if you don't want to?" they usually acknowledge that they can select it, despite not preferring it. This opens the door to illuminating that psychological openness is a choice they can make regardless of their preferences.

Values-Based Action

Finally, promoting values-based action involves activating the process of behavioral engagement (described above, in the section "Being Engaged"). Although values-consistent action is inherently intrinsically motivated, it's important to be aware that these activities can be extremely anxiety provoking, at least initially. For example, many GSM and multiple-minority individuals value developing their interpersonal relationships, such as intimate relationships and friendships (Skinta, 2014), yet they may also find reaching out to do so quite frightening due to previous experiences of social rejection and invalidation. As such, it is important for therapists to validate feelings of fear and ambivalence in regard to engaging in new, relationship-oriented values-consistent behaviors, and to empower clients in choosing values-consistent action even when they're afraid to do so.

To illustrate this point, therapists can revisit the "tea or coffee" exercise. For example, therapists can link this exercise to the possibility of reaching out to others despite rigid narratives, such as *When I reach out to people, I'm rejected, so I shouldn't reach out.* More specifically, through this exercise, therapists can gently help clients recognize that behaviors they assume are mandatory are actually choices: choices to not reach out to others and to not engage authentically as their true selves. When clients see their actions as choices, they can then evaluate whether their current choices move them toward vital living.

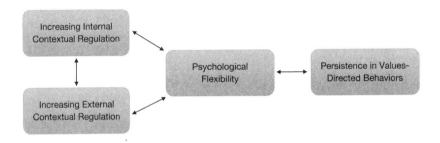

Figure 13.1. A model for psychological flexibility in treatment

Putting It All Together

In sum, as shown in figure 13.1, an ACT- and CFT-based intervention can emphasize increasing internal and external contextual regulation to promote greater functioning and quality of life. Clinicians may initially work with clients to increase their awareness of and openness to their internal contexts (e.g., automatic self-stigma) and external contexts (e.g., discriminatory experiences), increase self-compassion, and cultivate skills linked to valued living as defined by the individual client. Increasing internal contextual regulation facilitates openness, which also allows clients to take action in ways they otherwise would have avoided in their external environments. When clients are able to understand the context of their internal experiences and separate out unhelpful content from their evaluations of their abilities or character, they're more likely to engage in activities that enhance social support and active engagement in life. For other clients, experiencing contextual control by engaging in prosocial behaviors may serve as a helpful experiential tool, granting them access to present-moment awareness and reinforcing healthier internal regulation practices that they might otherwise avoid. Ultimately, targeting both internal and external processes in treatment increases persistence in values-directed behavior, promoting broader psychological flexibility.

Self-Compassion in an ACT- and CFT-Based Approach

When working with multiple-minority individuals, compassion and self-compassion are crucial for fostering vital living (Skinta, 2014; Skinta et al., 2014). Within an ACT- and CFT-based model, compassion can be viewed as a quality that flows organically from flexible and vital living. According to CFT, there are three types of emotion-regulation system: the threat and protection system, the drive (or incentive and resource-seeking) system, and the soothing, contentment, and safeness system. Balanced functioning of all three systems is required in order for people to function adaptively. Balance among these systems promotes psychological health, and imbalance can lead to mental health problems.

As an example of how these systems can become imbalanced, consider the stresses multiple-minority individuals face all too often. Their threat systems are likely to be overstimulated by the microaggression they probably face on a daily basis (for more on microaggression, see chapter 8). And, as noted above, they may have been dismissed by one or more of the minority groups to which they belong. In terms of the drive system, they may be working full time and responsible for providing financial security for a family. And at the same time, their sense of personal vulnerability might be exacerbated by an inability to activate the soothing system, which would otherwise help them cope with the difficulties of day-to-day life. In this way, challenges to healthy functioning are maintained. Additionally, as oppression is internalized, it begins to manifest as self-criticism. Thus, these complex dynamics and contingencies are all related, not separate, isolated factors.

As noted elsewhere (Tirch et al., 2014), ACT and CFT naturally overlap, in both treatment goals and interventions. Developing self-compassion helps clients access the internal suffering caused by unfair systems around them and also allows them to look at their journey from a positive and creative perspective. Furthermore, self-compassion has a comforting quality that promotes activation of the soothing system (Gilbert, 2010). It also liberates distressed clients from verbal processes that maintain their fusion with unhelpful thoughts, feelings, and beliefs. This allows clients to escape the limitations of a conceptual self to live directly in their here-and-now contextual experience. In addition, practicing self-compassion promotes courage. Empowered people, secure in the myriad of aspects of their identity, are more likely to advocate not only for themselves but for other individuals impacted by similar systemic and pervasive challenges.

Ultimately, people who belong to multiple minority groups have encountered choppier waters than most individuals coming from either a majority group or a single minority background. With such individuals, clinicians' goals must include connecting them with their internal resilience, assisting them in becoming aware of their identities in context, and fully engaging them with their values.

Case Example: Khashi's Lived Experience

I am Iranian by birth and came to live in the United States of America in January 2009. I mention the date because it is significant. Barack Obama was elected president in 2008, and I arrived in January of the following year, just in time for his inauguration. To me, the election of a minority president felt like a tangible reflection of how diversity is celebrated in the United States, and this world event changed my plans significantly. Prior to his election, I had embarked upon a program of study in Austria, but various complications with my student visa made it impossible for me to remain there. I was planning to move to Australia and had actually been given a visa to go, but

Obama's rise to power prompted me to reconsider my options. Suddenly, America felt like the only place for me to live and study. Admittedly, I have relatives in the United States, but this was a relatively minor consideration. Relocating to a country where a minority person could rise to the very peak of power was a major factor informing my decision.

However, moving to the United States wasn't easy. In fact, the opposite is true. To even apply for a visa to study in the United States, I had to visit the American embassy in Turkey. There is no American embassy in Iran, nor does Iran have an administrative presence in the United States. So I applied for a visa in Turkey and received it, and within a few months I was enrolled at a leading university in New York City.

America offered me more than a place in which to study. The United States was a safe space within which I could explore my sexuality. In Iran, as a homosexual man I had lived a life of secrecy and fear. I expected my experience in the States to be very different. I imagined that I would suddenly live a very connected life in a cohesive community that disregarded ethnicity and embraced all creeds under the umbrella of tolerance and mutual respect.

This was not the case.

There is a substantial Iranian population in the United States, but this community is far from welcoming to sexual minorities. In fact, coming out as gay is seen as evidence of being tainted by the West.

I soon came out to my cousins in New York City, thinking that because we were of a similar age they might be more receptive than their parents. Although they were understanding and accepting, they warned me that the community at large remained hostile. My cousins were genuinely worried for me, in addition to being supportive and nurturing. Other family members were not as receptive. I've faced ridicule and shame from other relatives in the States, and I continue to face hostility when dealing with my family in Iran, who have threatened to cut me off and discontinue their financial support of my studies unless I renounce my sexuality.

My experience is not unique. Even in the relatively enlightened West, gay people, regardless of their country of origin, often face aggression and ridicule from the majority population and, as a result, have created alternative family units and separate social spheres for themselves. This has led to a strong sense of community among GSM people. San Francisco is a city that prides itself on its gay community's visibility and power. It was only natural that I found myself drawn to this city, where I was sure I would find a home. But upon arriving in the city and visiting the bars so central to the gay scene, I quickly found that the culture wasn't nearly as welcoming as I thought it would be.

This manifested in several ways. For one thing, I was often one of only a few nonwhite people in a bar, and I was almost always the only Middle Eastern person. In addition, my Iranian nationality was the object of humor because a former president of Iran had recently told an audience at Columbia University that Iran didn't have homosexuals. I was also regarded as exotic—a "type"—which dehumanized and objectified me within a community in which I was seeking safety and understanding. All of these factors contributed to my increasing sense of isolation, leading to a heightened awareness that my values didn't match those of the community I had hoped would embrace me. This led to increased self-criticism and fear that I'd never find a place that could accept me and the diverse aspects of my identity, which worked against me in terms of community and acceptance.

At this critical juncture, a Jewish Iranian lawyer friend offered to assist me in applying for asylum status, presenting me with an incredibly difficult choice—a choice much bigger, heavier, and more complex than simply picking which country to reside in. I could resign myself to the continued struggle of feeling isolated in either country (the United States or Iran), or I could be willing to create a foundation for myself that included the possibility of genuine connection with others. This meant accepting and celebrating my own identity, in its many aspects, and questioning any tendencies I had to label any given aspect either "bad" or "good" when, in fact, all of them are part of who I am. I also became aware of the potential power of my inner voice, the importance of being cognizant of my inner critic, the value of not looking to any one community for validation, and the necessity of remaining open to true connection. Adopting this perspective was painful yet liberating, and ultimately gave me the strength to apply for asylum.

The application process required writing a detailed essay about myself and my experiences in Iran. In the process, I revisited painful past experiences of oppression and discrimination. One of the most difficult events in my life involved being arrested for attending a mixed gender party. I wasn't allowed to contact anyone for twenty-four hours, and I remained incarcerated for three days, endlessly and mercilessly humiliated the entire time. Processing this was painful, but being able to do so was a palpable demonstration of my resilience and strength. Psychologically, reflecting on this experience and expressing it in a nonnative language in order to stay in my adopted country meant reconsidering how I relate to my values; for example, my sense of what "home" and "community" meant underwent a transition.

I see this entire process as being directly informed by my own multiple-minority status and my gradual understanding and acceptance of this identity. I now understand home as a place that affords me the possibility of being in touch with my authentic self. In this place, the possibility of being harmed or threatened is not a part of my actual experience. I also accept that as a person of multiple-minority status, I may always carry with me a sense of isolation or difference. It's important for me to recognize that those feelings are rooted in a reality that has historical precedent and is real. And at the same time, I also know that if I'm willing, I can relate to this reality in a way that allows me to connect with others despite our differences. I can have compassion for myself when I struggle with difficult feelings. Rather than leaning in toward self-criticism, I can view my discomfort as an indication of the work left to do in creating a more socially conscious and culturally competent world.

My application for asylum was successful, so I can now live and work in the United States without fear of deportation. During my graduate training, I was awarded a generous scholarship on the strength of my academic abilities and my minority status, which enriched the diversity of the university. This vote of confidence in my scholarly abilities, coupled with a celebration of my status, gave me enormous confidence and validation and reframed the way I understood the important contributions of my unique, multiple identities within my community.

Over the course of my studies, I've discovered that advocacy for and celebration of diversity are defining aspects of my identity as a clinical psychologist. Participating in projects and groups that advocate for compassion, minority rights, and community building and doing this work alongside others who have faced common difficulties is an integral part of my work.

Reflecting on my journey reminds me of a meaningful interaction I had with my mother when I was in my late teens. She lost her temper and shouted, "Why do you have to come out? Why do you have to be the one to stand up for these rights? Why risk losing your status and privileges?"

My answer was simple: "It has to start somewhere."

Conclusion

Relieving human suffering is often cited as the underlying value associated with behavioral and mental health care. However, historical and current practices have illuminated the need for clinicians to utilize a more pragmatic and contextual approach to understanding suffering, rather than isolating suffering itself to content-based diagnoses, such as depression or anxiety, or statuses, such as motherhood or ethnic minority. In this chapter, we have presented a unique conceptualization of how multiple-minority statuses intersect, particularly with GSM and ethnic minorities. Most importantly, we have demonstrated that helping clients understand the complex, multifaceted aspects of their identities, and how these identities function in both private and public environments, is an integral component of the work of mental health professionals serving culturally diverse clients.

References

Bailey, J. M. (1999). Homosexuality and mental illness. *Archives of General Psychiatry, 56*, 883–884.

Berdahl, J. L., & Moore, C. (2006). Workplace harassment: Double jeopardy for minority women. *Journal of Applied Psychology, 91*, 426–436.

Bostwick, W. B., Boyd, C. J., Hughes, T. L., & McCabe, S. E. (2010). Dimensions of sexual orientation and the prevalence of mood and anxiety disorders in the United States. *American Journal of Public Health, 100*, 468–475.

Connell, R. W. (2005). Change among the gatekeepers: Men, masculinities, and gender equality in the global arena. *Signs: Journal of Women in Culture and Society, 30*, 1801–1825.

Gilbert, P. (2010). *Compassion focused therapy: Distinctive features.* New York: Routledge.

Giwa, S., & Greensmith, C. (2012). Race relations and racism in the LGBTQ community of Toronto: Perceptions of gay and queer social service providers of color. *Journal of Homosexuality, 59*, 149–185.

Harris, R. (2009). *ACT made simple: An easy-to-read primer on acceptance and commitment therapy.* Oakland, CA: New Harbinger Publications.

Hayes, S. C., Niccolls, R., Masuda, A., & Rye, A. K. (2002). Prejudice, terrorism and behavior therapy. *Cognitive and Behavioral Practice, 9*, 296–301.

Hayes, S. C., Strosahl, K. D., & Wilson, K. G. (1999). *Acceptance and commitment therapy: An experiential approach to behavior change.* New York: Guilford.

Hayes, S. C., Villatte, M., Levin, M., & Hildebrandt, M. (2011). Open, aware, and active: Contextual approaches as an emerging trend in the behavioral and cognitive therapies. *Annual Review of Clinical Psychology, 7*, 141–168.

Johnson, V. R. F., & Yarhouse, M. A. (2013). Shame in sexual minorities: Stigma, internal cognitions, and counseling considerations. *Counseling and Values, 58*, 85–103.

Li, S. T., Jenkins, S., & Sundsmo, A. (2007). Impact of race and ethnicity. In M. Hersen, S. M. Turner, D. C. Beidel, M. Hersen, S. M. Turner & D. C. Beidel (Eds.), *Adult psychopathology and diagnosis*, 5th edition. Hoboken, NJ: Wiley.

Masuda, A. (2014). *Mindfulness and acceptance in multicultural competency: A contextual approach to sociocultural diversity in theory and practice.* Oakland, CA: New Harbinger Publications.

Masuda, A., Hill, M. L., Morgan, J., & Cohen, L. L. (2012). A psychological flexibility–based intervention for modulating the impact of stigma and prejudice: A descriptive review of empirical evidence. *Psychology, Society, and Education, 4*, 211–223.

Mays, V. M., & Cochran, S. D. (2001). Mental health correlates of perceived discrimination among lesbian, gay, and bisexual adults in the United States. *American Journal of Public Health, 91*, 1869–1876.

Mays, V. M., Cochran, S. D., & Barnes, N. W. (2007). Race, race-based discrimination, and health outcomes among African Americans. *Annual Review of Psychology, 58*, 201–225.

Meyer, I. H. (2003). Prejudice, social stress, and mental health in lesbian, gay, and bisexual populations: Conceptual issues and research evidence. *Psychological Bulletin, 129*, 674–697.

Meyer, I. H., & Ouellette, S. C. (2009). Unity and purpose at the intersections of racial/ethnic and sexual identities. In P. L. Hammack & B. J. Cohler (Eds.), *The story of sexual identity: Narrative perspectives on the gay and lesbian life course*. New York: Oxford University Press.

Mulia, N., Ye, Y., Zemore, S. E., & Greenfield, T. K. (2008). Social disadvantage, stress, and alcohol use among black, Hispanic, and white Americans: Findings from the 2005 US National Alcohol Survey. *Journal of Studies on Alcohol and Drugs, 69*, 824–833.

Mustanski, B. S., Garofalo, R., & Emerson, E. M. (2010). Mental health disorders, psychological distress, and suicidality in a diverse sample of lesbian, gay, bisexual, and transgender youths. *American Journal of Public Health, 100*, 2426–2432.

Pak, A. W., Dion, K. L., & Dion, K. K. (1991). Social-psychological correlates of experienced discrimination: Test of the double jeopardy hypothesis. *International Journal of Intercultural Relations, 15*, 243–254.

Ridley, C. R., Li, L. C., & Hill, C. L. (1998). Multicultural assessment: Reexamination, reconceptualization, and practical application. *Counseling Psychologist, 26*, 827–910.

Skinta, M. D. (2014). Acceptance- and compassion-based approaches for invisible minorities: Working with shame among sexual minorities. In A. Masuda (Ed.), *Mindfulness and acceptance in multicultural competency: A contextual approach to sociocultural diversity in theory and practice*. Oakland, CA: New Harbinger Publications.

Skinta, M. D., Lezama, M., Wells, G., & Dilley, J. W. (2014). Acceptance and compassion-based group therapy to reduce HIV stigma. *Cognitive and Behavioral Practice, 22*, 481–490.

Tirch, D., Schoendorff, B., & Silberstein, L. (2014). *The ACT practitioner's guide to the science of compassion: Tools for fostering psychological flexibility*. Oakland, CA: New Harbinger Publications.

Wilson, K. G., & Murrell, A. R. (2004). Values work in acceptance and commitment therapy: Setting a course for behavioral treatment. In S. C. Hayes, V. M. Follette, & M. M. Linehan (Eds.), *Mindfulness and acceptance: Expanding the cognitive-behavioral tradition*. New York: Guilford.

Yoshihama, M. (2005). A web in the patriarchal clan system: Tactics of intimate partners in the Japanese sociocultural context. *Violence Against Women, 11*, 1236–1262.

CHAPTER 14

Flexible Organizations: Creating a Healthy and Productive Context for GSM Employees

Frank W. Bond and Joda Lloyd,
Goldsmiths, University of London

I t is fairly straightforward to imagine how mindfulness and acceptance skills can help gender and sexual minority (GSM) individuals live vital and effective lives, even when experiencing difficult circumstances. In an organizational setting, one can even imagine how individual or group training sessions can help promote mindfulness and acceptance. What about at the team and organizational levels of the workplace: Can we design teams and organizations that are "mindful" and that can promote mindfulness and acceptance in their employees?

We believe that this is possible and that it can be accomplished through the concepts and techniques associated with acceptance and commitment therapy (ACT; Hayes, Strosahl, & Wilson, 1999). ACT maintains that a process called psychological flexibility is at the core of helping people maintain good mental health and behavioral effectiveness. "Psychological flexibility" refers to people's ability to focus on their current situation and, based upon the opportunities afforded by that situation, take appropriate action toward pursuing their values-based goals, even in the presence of challenging or difficult psychological events in the form of thoughts, feelings, physiological sensations, images, and memories (Hayes, Luoma, Bond, Masuda, & Lillis, 2006). Later in this chapter, we will discuss how ACT can increase psychological flexibility in GSM employees. First, though, we will look at how the concept of psychological flexibility can be applied to creating an organizational environment in which these individuals can thrive, both emotionally and in terms of their productivity.

Psychological Flexibility

A key implication of psychological flexibility is that, in any given situation, people need to be flexible regarding the degree to which they base their actions on their internal events or the contingencies of reinforcement (or punishment) that are present in the situation. ACT maintains, and research suggests, that people are more psychologically healthy and perform more effectively when they base their actions on their own values and goals, regardless of the context in which they find themselves (Bond et al., 2011).

People will sometimes experience difficult and, often, unwanted psychological events (e.g., anxiety) while pursuing values-based goals. Thus, a great deal of the theory and practice of ACT emphasizes using mindfulness strategies when experiencing these events so they have less of a negative impact on individuals' psychological health and ability to pursue their values-based goals. When people are mindful of their psychological events, they deliberately observe them on a moment-to-moment basis in a non-elaborative, open, curious, and nonjudgmental manner (Kabat-Zinn, 1990). Thus, psychological flexibility emphasizes both committed action toward meaningful goals and mindfulness. It is this combination of mutually enhancing processes that probably accounts for the many mental health and performance benefits associated with psychological flexibility (see Bond et al., 2011, for a review).

Organizational Flexibility

We can design organizational characteristics that produce an organization that is both "mindful" and committed to pursuing its values, such as utilizing, supporting, and developing the talents of GSM employees. These characteristics, which can be combined in an organizational flexibility model (Bond, 2015), have been widely studied in the area of organizational behavior, a field of study that investigates the impacts that individual characteristics (e.g., personality, mental health), group characteristics (e.g., leadership, teams), and organizational characteristics (e.g., structure, processes) have on organizational effectiveness, including the health of individuals (Robbins & Judge, 2009). In the following sections, we will discuss how six key characteristics can combine to create a flexible environment in which GSM employees can thrive while the organization flourishes as well (Bond, 2015).

Purpose and Goals (Encourages Commitment to Values)

The purpose of an organization will guide its mission, vision, goals, and day-to-day actions. An organizational purpose has three characteristics (Marquis, Glynn, & Davis, 2007): it meets a need in the world that will function to make the world a better place (this could be anything from making machines for cancer treatment to promoting diversity); it meets a need in society (e.g., providing transport for city dwellers); and it needs to be constantly strived for—it cannot be achieved once and for all (e.g., providing first-rate customer service). Regarding mission, many organizations increasingly aim not only to promote equal treatment for GSM employees but also to provide a context in which they are actively valued (e.g., through organization-supported GSM groups whose meetings senior management occasionally attend and address).

Planned Action (Encourages Commitment to Values)

Organizations need to take planned action in order to further their purpose, mission, and goals. Planned action is facilitated by numerous project management techniques and strategies (see Martin, 2009) that clearly link the mission and values of the organization to specific actions necessary to realize the organization's values. Importantly, these techniques view problems as an inevitable aspect of working toward an organization's goals that should be expected and addressed (Martin, 2009). They are not seen as signs of trouble, undesirable, or blameworthy, or even as threatening to achieving goals; rather, they are to be revealed and addressed as quickly as possible. Planned action techniques can help organizations move toward their values or mission and create a nurturing environment for their GSM employees. And because these techniques assume some stumbling blocks will arise along the way, such hurdles are less demotivating when they occur, making it easier to identify strategies to overcome them.

Situational Responsiveness (Encourages Commitment to Values and a Mindful Organization)

Situationally responsive organizations keenly pursue and react to feedback from their environment (Leavitt, 1965): their customers, competitors, suppliers, government regulators, unions, market research, and so on. They make operational and strategic decisions based more on that feedback and less on their brand, culture, or history. Organizations that excessively base their actions on their brand or culture are likely to be less flexible and adaptable, and hence less effective in pursuing their purpose, values, and goals. As Leavitt (1965) noted, for organizations to remain effective in pursuing their purposes and goals, they have to adapt successfully to the changes in their task environment. Those that are overly entangled in their brand or culture find it hard to adjust as necessary.

Culturally bound organizations face many problems in terms of their effectiveness. These organizations may find it harder to move with the times and adopt progressive GSM policies, even if senior management is committed to progressive policies. To be responsive, organizations need to undergo nearly constant change, which is difficult and often anxiety provoking. It isn't surprising, therefore, that the organizational development literature is replete with strategies to overcome this psychological resistance to change (e.g., French & Bell, 1999).

Structures and processes born of unresponsive organizational cultures have the effect of limiting employees' capacity to seek out and respond to environmental feedback. One approach to ameliorate this situation is to design out, or at least minimize, organizational factors that restrict situational responsiveness. This is accomplished, in part, through effective work design.

Effective Work Design (Encourages a Mindful Organization)

Organizational researchers have long hypothesized that various forms of work design—that is, ways that people interact with their work tasks—can limit the negative impact that work demands have on people's physical and mental health. Karasek's demands-control model (1979) perhaps most explicitly makes this prediction. It maintains that highly demanding jobs will only have detrimental effects on workers, such as coronary heart disease and psychological distress, if people don't have sufficient job control. However, if organizations provide people with some influence over how they carry out their demanding tasks, they will not only experience fewer and less deleterious effects, but will also perform their work more effectively and be more motivated in carrying it out. A comprehensive review of the literature related to job control largely supports this hypothesis (Terry & Jimmieson, 1999).

Other well-established and empirically supported organizational behavior theories (e.g., the job characteristics model; Hackman & Lawler, 1971) hypothesize that other work design characteristics can also have advantageous impacts on the health, performance, and attitudes of workers. These include support in carrying out one's work, the opportunity to do a variety of tasks, and the ability to do a complete job, from start to finish. As for job control, long-standing and considerable research shows the health and performance benefits of these and other work design characteristics (Humphrey, Nahrgang, & Morgeson, 2007).

Many GSM employees face considerable demands that other employees don't have to deal with. For example, if they come out in the workplace, they may be (or feel like they could be) ostracized or given less support and less desirable work design characteristics than others (e.g., experiencing more monitoring and hence less control). And even if they don't come out, they may try to avoid unwelcome questions about their personal life, which may prevent them from obtaining the typical work support from colleagues that is so essential in promoting well-being and effectiveness. Thus, formally optimizing work design characteristics provides a far better context in which GSM employees can thrive.

Openness to Discomfort (Encourages a Mindful Organization)

Organizations can evoke challenging, difficult emotions in people. From the ACT perspective, it is useful for individuals to accept and be open to those emotions when pursuing their values. At the organizational and team levels, we suggest that this same open stance is crucial; indeed, the literature on organizational behavior champions many different structures, processes, strategies, and leadership approaches that require such openness to discomfort. Providing workers with job control is one such design principle that many managers find anxiety provoking. Others include allowing employees to participate in decision making; clearly, openly, and honestly communicating with employees in a timely manner; and taking a transformational approach to leadership, which requires a personal, open, and "lead by example" leadership style (Bass, 1998).

All of these beneficial organizational behavior characteristics (and many others) require that leaders, and the teams and organizations they design, be willing to be uncomfortable in the service of the organization's purpose and mission, and their own. Avoiding implementing these constructive characteristics in an effort to avoid discomfort compromises the effectiveness of an organization and the health of its employees. It is the role of leaders to implement these characteristics by modeling a willingness to experience disquiet, and by communicating this organizational need to employees.

GSM employees who are out at work may, at least at first, provoke discomfort in other employees, which can potentially lead to discrimination and damaging prejudices. If, however, the organization values inclusion, managers must be willing to implement policies, procedures, and a culture in which bullying and discrimination are not tolerated and in which GSM employees are seen as being equally valid, useful, and deserving of respect.

271

Awareness (Encourages Commitment to Values and a Mindful Organization)

ACT emphasizes the importance of being in the present moment and being aware of and open to one's internal events. We extend the same advice to teams and organizations. Indeed, this is consistent with an entire subfield within organizational behavior that focuses on maintaining system awareness: human resource management. Most organizations of any size have a human resources (HR) department that develops policies and practices that function either to aid in understanding what is happening within the organization (e.g., through performance evaluations and staff surveys), or to train employees to be aware of their actions (e.g., through diversity training and career development planning).

HR can be vital in monitoring patterns or pockets of GSM discrimination within an organization, whether it is flagrant (e.g., openly gay people never get promoted in a certain department) or insidious (e.g., the turnover rate is higher for GSM employees). If HR is properly monitoring these issues, the organization has the opportunity to take appropriate action to correct them, and where HR management sees best practices, they can then promote those practices in other departments.

Team Flexibility

In this section we highlight characteristics that serve to increase the flexibility of teams. For each, we discuss how the characteristic might be used to facilitate better working conditions for GSM employees.

Team Purpose

The organizational flexibility model previously discussed, highlights the importance of purpose in guiding an organization's goals and day-to-day actions (Bond, 2015). The concept of team purpose would appear to serve a similar function at the group level. Specifically, an effective team has a clear and precise purpose (aligned with the organization's) that provides direction and guidance for team members (Katzenbach & Smith, 1993). This purpose is an overall vision that helps teams stay on track under both stable and changing organizational conditions (Robbins & Judge, 2009). It can also be used to unite members of divided teams.

Team members may differ from each other in a number of ways, ranging from demographic characteristics (e.g., age, sexuality) to personal attributes (e.g., personality, work attitudes). If these differences become apparent, fault lines can develop—"hypothetical dividing lines that may split a group into subgroups based on one or more attributes" (Lau & Murnighan, 1998, p. 328). Such fault lines may lead to negative team outcomes, including poorer social integration (Rico, Molleman, Sánchez-Manzanares, & Van der Vegt, 2007), and emotional and task conflicts (Li & Hambrick, 2005). However, Rico, Sánchez-Manzanares, Antino, and Lau (2012) found that superordinate goals (goals aimed at establishing a common purpose) facilitated better decision making in teams with gender and education fault lines. Furthermore, van Knippenberg, Dawson, West, and Homan (2011) found that shared objectives (a shared focus consistent with team purpose) within senior management teams reduced the negative influence of gender and job history fault lines on performance. Finally, Homan, van Knippenberg, Van Kleef, and De Dreu (2007) examined whether the negative impact of diversity fault lines could be reduced by encouraging groups to value diversity. They found that informationally diverse groups (groups in which members differ in their knowledge bases and perspectives) performed better on a decision-making task when they held beliefs that favor diversity rather than similarity.

In sum, establishing a team purpose and integrating diversity as a central part of a team's purpose unified members of divided teams and allowed them to perform more effectively. Thus, team purpose represents a possible lever that could work to combat the unhelpful effects of divisiveness with a team. While the research just reviewed did not specifically involve GSM employees, increased disclosure of this aspect of identity in contemporary workplaces suggests that it could become a basis for divisiveness, in which case organizations would be wise to value employees' diversity in terms of gender and sexuality.

Effective Work Design for Teams

The organizational flexibility model draws attention to the importance of effective work design as a means of limiting the detrimental impacts of demanding work on employees' health and productivity (Bond, 2015). The concept of effective work design for teams could serve a similar function at the group level. In the present context, we focus on the design characteristic of team social support: the extent to which a team provides opportunities for support and assistance (e.g., task completion support, emotional support). Team social support is critical for effective team functioning (see Rosenfeld & Richman, 1997) and particularly important in identity-management decisions GSM employees face in the workplace (e.g., decisions around whether or not to come out at work).

In the workplace, GSM employees consistently have to decide whether to disclose or conceal their identity. This is not a straightforward decision, and outcomes of disclosure can be quite varied. For sexual minority employees, there is evidence that workplace disclosure can lead to negative outcomes such as discrimination (Waldo, 1999), as well as positive outcomes such as higher job satisfaction and lower job anxiety (Griffith & Hebl, 2002). For gender minority employees, there is evidence that workplace disclosure experiences are often difficult and traumatic (Budge, Tebbe, & Howard, 2010), but that they can also relate to higher job satisfaction, more organizational commitment, and lower job anxiety (Law, Martinez, Ruggs, Hebl, & Akers, 2011). These varied findings suggest that environmental characteristics of the context in which disclosure occurs may affect the consequences of that disclosure. In particular, research indicates that the characteristic of team social support may be important. Specifically, Ragins, Singh, and Cornwell (2007) found that sexual minority employees who worked in teams that were more supportive reported less fear and disclosed more than did employees who had lower levels of support. Furthermore, Ragins and Cornwell (2001) found that sexual minority employees were more likely to experience discrimination (based on self-reports) when they were in teams that were primarily heterosexual and when the organization lacked supportive policies. Finally, Dietert and Dentice (2009) found that workplace support was an important determinant of whether transgender individuals chose to disclose their gender identity or intent to transition (the process of aligning one's physical body with gender identity) at work.

In sum, higher levels of team social support appear to foster conditions in which GSM employees feel more comfortable to disclose their identity, and in which the outcomes of this disclosure are more positive for them. Thus, effective work design for teams represents a possible lever that could help GSM employees positively manage their identity at work.

Team Reflexivity

The organizational flexibility model highlights the importance of organizations maintaining awareness by consistently monitoring individuals, teams, and departments (Bond, 2015). This reflexivity characteristic seems to serve a similar function at the group level. Team reflexivity is the "extent to which group members overtly reflect upon the group's objectives, strategies and processes, and adapt them to current or anticipated endogenous or environmental circumstances" (West, 1996, p. 559). It involves actions such as questioning, planning, exploring, and analyzing (Hoegl & Parboteeah, 2006) and is based on the notion that there is a need for continual reflection within a team's constantly changing environment. Team reflexivity can foster conditions in which minority team members experience better-quality exchanges during task completion.

Evidence suggests that reflexivity may function as a context in which cooperative team behaviors are more likely to occur. De Dreu (2007) showed that when team reflexivity is high, perceived cooperative outcome interdependence (people in groups perceiving their own goals and those of others to be cooperatively linked) was related to more information sharing, more learning, and more effectiveness.

That is, the increased level of systematic and deliberate information processing afforded by higher reflexivity allowed a more constructive and open exchange of task-relevant information to take place. Evidence also suggests that, in a reflexive team, minority dissent is more likely to occur, meaning a minority within the group publicly opposes the beliefs, ideas, or procedures favored by the majority in the group (De Dreu & West, 2001). Research indicates that minority dissent promotes beneficial team performance outcomes because it improves the quality of decision making (Dooley & Fryxell, 1999). De Dreu (2002) showed that minority dissent was associated with more innovation and higher team effectiveness when there were higher levels of team reflexivity.

In sum, team reflexivity appears to both encourage team cooperation and provide a platform for dissenting views within a team. As such, it represents a possible lever by which to improve the quality of team member exchanges. While the research outlined above does not specifically involve GSM employees, more cooperative and open team climates may foster more equitable exchange conditions for these individuals. Specifically, GSM employees, by virtue of their different life experiences, may bring a unique set of ideas and expertise to a decision-making scenario. However, it may be hard to voice these ideas unless the environment fosters more open exchange and provides a receptive platform for individual voices.

The Individual

In this final section, we discuss the individual-level construct of psychological flexibility and explain how it can be used to facilitate better mental health and performance among GSM employees.

Psychological Flexibility and Identity Management in the Workplace

As previously discussed, GSM employees must continuously make decisions about whether to disclose their identity or conceal it. We suggest that psychological flexibility may be useful in helping GSM employees determine whether to disclose their identity, and in managing that process if they choose to disclose.

With regard to disclosure decisions, psychological flexibility may make people more aware of their working environment and how they can adapt their behavior according to the needs of that environment. While many countries' laws protect GSM people and their rights of expression, such laws are certainly not universal. Furthermore, even in countries where gender and sexual identity are protected by law, organizational policies and practices around equality, as well as general climates of acceptance, vary greatly. Therefore, GSM employees need to be aware of the conditions in which they are working and exercise care in their disclosure behaviors.

Psychological flexibility allows people to be more mindful of their internal experiences and, as a result of this awareness, more willing to let go of attempts to control these experiences. As a consequence, psychologically flexible people have more attentional resources for noticing and responding to their environments in effective ways (Bond & Hayes, 2002). While GSM employees may value being open about their identity, they must also consider their own psychological and physical safety. In some contexts it may be workable to behave in accordance with their values around disclosure, but in others it may be workable to behave in ways that preserve personal safety. Psychological flexibility can help GSM employees be flexible in the degree to which they base their behaviors on their own values or on the (sometimes punishing) contingencies within their current environment.

If GSM employees determine that a situation is safe for disclosure, psychological flexibility may further aid them in managing this process. As previously noted, within supportive contexts disclosure can have beneficial outcomes for GSM employees (Dietert & Dentice, 2009; Ragins et al., 2007). However, the emotional turmoil and fear of rejection associated with disclosing one's identity may be one of the most difficult challenges to overcome, even in a situation that is deemed as safe and supportive. In such a context, psychological flexibility can help GSM employees make contact with their values (e.g., being open about one's identity) and take steps toward achieving those values (e.g., disclosing to colleagues), even when difficult and challenging internal experiences (e.g., shame) show up. (For more on coming out, see chapter 3.)

Psychological Flexibility and Coping with Workplace Discrimination

As previously noted, GSM employees are sometimes subject to workplace discrimination. This may occur particularly in countries where gender and sexual identity are not protected by law, as well as in organizations with poor policies and practices around equality. GSM advocacy organizations are working toward legislation that will offer employees protection. However, it is unrealistic to believe that cultural change will be quick or straightforward. Therefore, increasing psychological flexibility may be useful as a complementary strategy for helping GSM employees cope with discrimination.

Early evidence indicates that higher levels of psychological flexibility may be an important personal resource for sexual minority employees, with one study finding that experiences of overt and covert workplace discrimination were associated with increased levels of strain, which in turn related to increased likelihood of quitting (Lloyd et al., 2015). However, the researchers found that this process was only significant for people with low levels of psychological flexibility. Furthermore, higher levels of psychological flexibility were associated with increased engagement, which in turn was related to reduced intentions to quit. Thus, psychological flexibility appears to offer sexual minority employees some protection from the harmful psychological effects of discrimination. In sum, psychological flexibility may represent an individual-level lever that has the potential to affect positive change for GSM employees.

While this is only one study, its findings are consistent with benefits proposed by psychological flexibility theory. In addition, the findings from this study suggest that further research may be warranted to examine the extent to which ACT can improve the well-being and behavioral effectiveness of GSM employees who choose to disclose.

Conclusion

Despite the importance of organizational behavior characteristics on the well-being and productivity of GSM employees, we are not familiar with any widely used interventions at the organizational or team level that have been empirically tested using this population, and individual-level interventions are just beginning to be empirically examined. This is unsurprising for at least two reasons. First, acknowledgment of GSM populations by society, let alone acceptance of them, is relatively new and still very incomplete. Thus, organizations and organizational behavior researchers have not yet felt the pressure, or pull, to examine the extent to which organizational, team, and individual characteristics affect outcomes for GSM employees. Second, methodologically rigorous studies are difficult to conduct at the organizational level and, to a lesser extent, at the team level. Thus, far more organizational behavior research is conducted at the individual level for all employee populations, including GSM employees, where at least one study has examined the relationship between GSM individuals and psychological flexibility. We hope that researchers will undertake more studies (and, in particular, intervention outcome research) at the individual, group, and organizational levels in order to identify effective ways to enhance the well-being and productivity of GSM employees and, hence, the organizations for which they work.

References

Bass, B. M. (1998). *Transformational leadership: Industrial, military, and educational impact*. Mahwah, NJ: Erlbaum.

Bond, F. W. (2015). *Organisational flexibility: Creating a mindful and purpose-driven organisation*. Manuscript in preparation.

Bond, F. W., & Hayes, S. C. (2002). ACT at work. In F. W. Bond & W. Dryden (Eds.), *Handbook of brief cognitive behaviour therapy*. Chichester, UK: Wiley.

Bond, F. W., Hayes, S. C., Baer, R. A., Carpenter, K. M., Guenole, N., Orcutt, H. K., et al. (2011). Preliminary psychometric properties of the Acceptance and Action Questionnaire—II: A revised measure of psychological inflexibility and experiential avoidance. *Behavior Therapy, 42*, 676–688.

Budge, S. L., Tebbe, E. N., & Howard, K. A. S. (2010). The work experiences of transgender individuals: Negotiating the transition and career decision-making processes. *Journal of Counseling Psychology, 57*, 377–393.

De Dreu, C. K. W. (2002). Team innovation and effectiveness: The importance of minority dissent and reflexivity. *European Journal of Work and Organizational Psychology, 11*, 285–298.

De Dreu, C. K. W. (2007). Cooperative outcome interdependence, task reflexivity, and team effectiveness: A motivated information processing perspective. *Journal of Applied Psychology, 92*, 628–638.

De Dreu, C. K. W., & West, M. A. (2001). Minority dissent and team innovation: The importance of participation in decision making. *Journal of Applied Psychology, 86*, 1191–1201.

Dietert, M., & Dentice, D. (2009). Gender identity issues and workplace discrimination: The transgender experience. *Journal of Workplace Rights, 14*, 121–140.

Dooley, R. S., & Fryxell, G. E. (1999). Attaining decision quality and commitment from dissent: The moderating effects of loyalty and competence in strategic decision-making teams. *Academy of Management Journal, 42*, 389–402.

French, W. L., & Bell, C. H. (1999). *Organization development: Behavioral science interventions for organization improvement*, 6th ed. Englewood Cliffs, NJ: Prentice Hall.

Griffith, K. H., & Hebl, M. R. (2002). The disclosure dilemma for gay men and lesbians: "Coming out" at work. *Journal of Applied Psychology, 87*, 1191–1199.

Hackman, J. R., & Lawler, E. E. (1971). Employee reactions to job characteristics. *Journal of Applied Psychology, 55*, 259–286.

Hayes, S. C., Luoma, J. B., Bond, F. W., Masuda, A., & Lillis, J. (2006). Acceptance and commitment therapy: Model, processes and outcomes. *Behaviour research and therapy, 44*, 1–25.

Hayes, S. C., Strosahl, K. D., & Wilson, K. G. (1999). *Acceptance and commitment therapy: An experiential approach to behavior change*. New York: Guilford.

Hoegl, M., & Parboteeah, K. P. (2006). Team reflexivity in innovative projects. *R & D Management, 36*, 113–125.

Homan, A. C., van Knippenberg, D., Van Kleef, G. A., & De Dreu, C. K. W. (2007). Bridging faultlines by valuing diversity: Diversity beliefs, information elaboration, and performance in diverse work groups. *Journal of Applied Psychology, 92*, 1189–1199.

Humphrey, S. E., Nahrgang, J. D., & Morgeson, F. P. (2007). Integrating motivational, social, and contextual work design features: A meta-analytic summary and theoretical extension of the work design literature. *Journal of Applied Psychology, 92*, 1332–1356.

Kabat-Zinn, J. (1990). *Full catastrophe living: Using the wisdom of your body and mind to face stress, pain, and illness*. New York: Random House.

Karasek, R. A. (1979). Job demands, job decision latitude, and mental strain: Implications for job redesign. *Administrative Science Quarterly, 24*, 285–308.

Katzenbach, J. R., & Smith, D. K. (1993). *The wisdom of teams: Creating the high-performance organization.* Boston: Harvard Business School Press.

Lau, D. C., & Murnighan, J. K. (1998). Demographic diversity and faultlines: The compositional dynamics of organizational groups. *Academy of Management Review, 23,* 325–340.

Law, C. L., Martinez, L. R., Ruggs, E. N., Hebl, M. R., & Akers, E. (2011). Transparency in the workplace: How the experiences of transsexual employees can be improved. *Journal of Vocational Behavior, 79,* 710–723.

Leavitt, H. J. (1965). Applied organizational change in industry: Structural, technical, and humanistic approaches. In J. G. March (Ed.), *Handbook of organizations.* Chicago: Rand McNally.

Li, J., & Hambrick, D. C. (2005). Factional groups: A new vantage on demographic faultlines, conflict, and disintegration in work teams. *Academy of Management Journal, 48,* 794–813.

Lloyd, J., Karlsson, D. C., Frasca, K., West, K., Thompson, M., & Bond, F. (2015). *Examining the job demands-resources (JD-R) model in sexual minority employees: A test of the model in a distinct socio-cultural population.* Manuscript in preparation.

Marquis, C., Glynn, M. A., & Davis, G. F. (2007). Community isomorphism and corporate social action. *Academy of Management Review, 32,* 925–945.

Martin, R. L. (2009). *The design of business: Why design thinking is the next competitive advantage.* Boston: Harvard Business Press.

Ragins, B. R., & Cornwell, J. M. (2001). Pink triangles: Antecedents and consequences of perceived workplace discrimination against gay and lesbian employees. *Journal of Applied Psychology, 86,* 1244–1261.

Ragins, B. R., Singh, R., & Cornwell, J., M. (2007). Making the invisible visible: Fear and disclosure of sexual orientation at work. *Journal of Applied Psychology, 92,* 1103–1118.

Rico, R., Molleman, E., Sánchez-Manzanares, M., & Van der Vegt, G. S. (2007). The effects of diversity faultlines and team task autonomy on decision quality and social integration. *Journal of Management, 33,* 111–132.

Rico, R., Sánchez-Manzanares, M., Antino, M., & Lau, D. (2012). Bridging team faultlines by combining task role assignment and goal structure strategies. *Journal of Applied Psychology, 97,* 407–420.

Robbins, S. P., & Judge, T. A. (2009). *Organizational behavior.* New Jersey: Pearson Education.

Rosenfeld, L. B., & Richman, J. M. (1997). Developing effective social support: Team building and the social support process. *Journal of Applied Sport Psychology, 9,* 133–153.

Terry, D. J., & Jimmieson, N. L. (1999). Work control and employee well-being: A decade review. In C. L. Cooper & I. T. Robertson (Eds.), *International review of industrial and organizational psychology,* vol. 14. Chichester, UK: Wiley.

Van Knippenberg, D., Dawson, J. F., West, M. A., & Homan, A. C. (2011). Diversity faultlines, shared objectives, and top management team performance. *Human Relations, 64,* 307–336.

Waldo, C. R. (1999). Working in a majority context: A structural model of heterosexism as minority stress in the workplace. *Journal of Counseling Psychology, 46,* 218–232.

West, M. A. (1996). Reflexivity and work group effectiveness: A conceptual integration. In M. A. West (Ed.), *Handbook of work group psychology.* Chichester, UK: Wiley.

CHAPTER 15

Queering the Globe: Promoting Equality, Connection, and Community

Matthew D. Skinta, *Palo Alto University*; and
Kip Williams, *Market Street Center
for Psychotherapy*

...when we speak we are afraid
our words will not be heard
nor welcomed
but when we are silent
we are still afraid.
So it is better to speak
remembering
we were never meant to survive.

—Audre Lorde

The twenty-first century has been a time of rapid change in the march toward equality for gender and sexual minority (GSM) individuals. Same-sex marriage wasn't legal in any country at the start of the century, but as of this writing, it is now legal in twenty countries. Trans rights have also advanced, with an increasing number of countries recognizing the rights of individuals to define their own gender, with the understanding that this recognition shouldn't be contingent upon surgical sterilization and that trans individuals should have the right to make their own decisions about their bodily integrity. Further, many of these changes have occurred as a result of social scientific findings that have influenced courts, legislative bodies, and the general public (e.g., *Obergefell v. Hodges*, 2015, a court decision that cites supporting research).

Not every trend is positive. Ten countries currently allow for sexual minorities to be put to death, and more than seventy-six countries criminalize GSM sexual intimacy (European Commission, 2015). Virtually no nation has completely eliminated violence against those perceived as gender nonconforming. It is incredibly difficult to know how much violence is directed toward transgender individuals, as such violence is probably underreported or inconsistently tracked, though we do know that trans women of color are currently murdered at an alarming rate (Teal, 2015).

In this chapter, we suggest some avenues toward creating the kind of nurturing societies that will allow GSM individuals to build fulfilling relationships, experience equality, and thrive. We explore how relational frame theory (RFT; Hayes, Barnes-Holmes, & Roche, 2001) and acceptance and commitment therapy (ACT; Hayes, Strosahl, & Wilson, 1999) can explain some of the recent advances and how they might help define a path forward. We also draw on our personal experiences with activism and social justice work to suggest concrete steps toward a more equitable future.

GSM Psychology: Inspirations and Nightmares

Magnus Hirschfeld founded what may have been the world's first sexual minority rights organization, the Scientific-Humanitarian Committee, in Berlin in 1897, less than a century after European nations began rescinding capital punishment for sodomy (Jordan, 1998). At his Institute for the Science of Sexuality, Hirschfeld documented the experiences, attractions, and lives of sexual and gender minorities, exploring questions that are being researched anew in contemporary science, such as patterns of successful relationships, the impacts of familial or societal stress, and the boundaries and separations of sexuality and gender diversity (Beachy, 2014). By the 1930s, however, Hirschfeld's institute had been shuttered and its archives destroyed by the Nazi Party.

In the decades following World War II, most European and North American medical providers promoted a disease model that required intervention for same-sex attraction or gender-nonconforming behavior. Numerous cases of lobotomy have been documented, as well as electroconvulsive therapy, both often in the context of involuntary hospitalization (Katz, 1992). Some faith-based programs in the United States still promote a belief that gay men are experiencing a failure of masculinity that can be overcome with extensive exercise (Williams, 2005), and acceptance and mindfulness techniques have even been proposed as means of reducing attractions to the same sex (Tan & Yarhouse, 2010). However, beginning in 2014 a number of US states and some European countries have banned or debated legislation to ban efforts aimed at changing people's sexual orientation, and in 2015 one prominent faith-based group that offered support for sexual orientation change efforts, Jews Offering New Alternatives for Healing (JONAH), was found guilty of consumer fraud in New Jersey (Khazan, 2015).

One Step Forward, Two Steps Back

In the latter half of the twentieth century, GSM visibility heralded a more rapid pace of change. Christine Jorgensen, who introduced the world to transgender lives in the early 1950s, was a powerful spokesperson for transgender causes and was closely followed by both the media and medical establishments (Rosario & Meyerowitz, 2004). In 1964, the Dutch designer Benno Premsela was one of the first public figures in the world to come out on public television with his face fully visible, in contrast to the previous practice of blurring the faces of those willing to discuss being gay or lesbian on television. Premsela was unwilling to remain closeted after having survived the Nazi era and concentration camps, and his bravery inspired the movement that led to the first marriage equality laws in the world (Shorto, 2013). Many global movements trace their beginning to the Stonewall riots, on June 28, 1969, when trans women, butch lesbians, gay men, and sex workers fought back against a police raid. However, this was just one uprising among many in the late 1960s (Chateauvert, 2014). Today, countries ranging from South Africa to Nepal have chosen to enshrine equality for all sexual orientations and gender identities in their constitutions.

Despite these developments, the general situation has often been bleak. During most of the twentieth century, prosecutors and police in the United States often specifically targeted GSM individuals in academic or government office. Prior to more contemporary economic entitlements, this condemned many people to poverty, homelessness, or even suicide out of desperation (e.g., Faderman, 2015; Werth, 2010). Furthermore, raids against GSM bars and clubs that cater to people of color have continued unabated in most of the United States (Mogul, Ritchie, & Whitlock, 2011). Many GSM communities fight to define themselves separately from the histories of the United States and Europe, as well as the postcolonial remnants of sexual racism and competing political agendas that shape contact between international GSM groups (e.g., Massad, 2008).

Meanwhile, US-based antigay organizations, frustrated by losses at home, have shifted their attention to Africa and Eastern Europe. They have been linked to the Ugandan "Kill the Gays" bill, which has been resubmitted or proposed repeatedly in the 2010s, and copycat bills that have been proposed in Nigeria, Kenya, and Zimbabwe. US spokespeople for antigay faith-based groups, such as Brian Brown and Scott Lively, have also testified before the Russian State Duma in support of increasingly oppressive antigay laws. Meanwhile, theocratic and sexually restrictive cultures continue to use state trials and public campaigns against GSM individuals to differentiate themselves from more secular societies (Weiss & Bosia, 2013). Similarly, in Europe, GSM asylum seekers sometimes have a decreased chance of being granted asylum if they are from so-called safe countries, even though some of the countries deemed "safe" criminalize homosexuality or have a history of violent bias (Jansen & Spijkerboer, 2011). A recent study comparing the sociological and legal battles across Italy, Slovenia, Hungary, and the UK found that social beliefs related to protecting children from exposure to homosexuality are common across a range of European cultures and are still strong barriers to effecting change (Trappolin, Gasparini, & Wintemute, 2012).

Nurturing a Vision for the Future with RFT

Contextual behavioral strategies have only recently been employed in the service of creating societal changes. Thus far, they have been proposed or implemented for smoking cessation (Vilardaga, Heffner, Mercer, & Bricker, 2014), improved parenting (Raftery-Helmer, Moore, Coyne, & Reed, 2015), and greater awareness of the impacts of global climate change (Biglan & Barnes-Holmes, 2015). The creation of nurturing, accepting environments that allow for connected, valued ways of living has been proposed as a powerful use of contextual behavioral science, with relational frame theory being particularly salient.

Now-Then Relations

One theme in the GSM resilience literature that has gained support is that resilience and the prevention of burnout in political engagement require a connection with values that are both personal and communal (Meyer, 2015), also sometime labeled a movement perspective (Russell & Richards, 2003). RFT conceptualizes this as an aspect of now-then deictic relations. This is one element of a core set of relational frames that we learn by being embodied, verbal organisms: I-you, here-there, and now-then (Barnes-Holmes et al., 2001). Gaining flexibility in now-then relations by considering the perspective of one's future self allows present behavior to be shaped, motivated, or reinforced by the future. Coming out to friends and family, speaking out against one's faith community, or walking in public in clothing that reflects a nontraditional gender identity for the first time—all confer the risk of immediate punishment from the environment yet may be intrinsically reinforcing if they reflect the type of life the individual wants to live.

If-Then Relations

This future orientation requires a certain type of learning about if-then, or causal, relations. Engaging in activism to create a world accepting of all gender and sexual identities requires both psychological contact with the future (temporal relations) and a sense that one's current behaviors will impact the future in a particular, predictable way. In some ways, contemporary GSM discourse is full of references to particular types of emotionally vulnerable behavior believed to have a causal link with future outcomes: "If I come out, my friendships will become more genuine." "If I speak to my neighbors about ballot measures that might harm me, they'll be less likely to vote for them." Specifically, GSM resilience research has stressed the value of successful witnessing—the experience of hearing a beloved family member or friend speak out against transphobic or heterocentric events in the popular media (Russell & Richards, 2003). For this to occur, however, GSM individuals must be willing to initiate such discussions in a vulnerable and genuine way, despite uncertainty about the outcome and despite the possibility of negative responses.

Rule-Governed Behavior

There are a variety of types of rules that behaviorists can explore when discussing rule-governed behavior (e.g., Hayes, Zettle, & Rosenfarb, 1989). In reference to GSM issues, it may be most meaningful to explore the role of pliance—following rules because of generally agreed upon social consequences that occur when we do or do not follow those rules—and tracking—"behavior under the control of the apparent correspondence between the rule and the way the world is arranged" (Hayes et al., 1989, p. 206). Marriage, or more specifically the word "marriage," illustrates this point beautifully. As Badgett (2009) describes, familial responses and societal mores regarding GSM populations shift quickly following the legalization of same-sex marriage. In part, this relates to the affective and verbal associations cultures attribute to the word "marriage," which include positive associations with thoughts of weddings, love, commitment, family, and joy and, even more broadly, with concepts such as faith, ritual, and God's will.

Although GSM identities have been associated with immorality, decadence, promiscuity, or gender nonconformity in many cultures, when this verbal network becomes linked with the network surrounding "marriage," behavioral repertoires broaden and negative rules regarding sexuality are defused (Wilson & Murrell, 2004). Further, once a conservative or traditional culture takes steps to ban or restrict gay rights, this creates justification for discussing gay rights in public forums, which raises the possibility of further reframing, increasing the likelihood that equality and greater acceptance of sexual minorities will follow (Badgett, 2009). In other words, when public debate about GSM rights no longer results in social consequences, pliance is no longer relevant, allowing views in support of GSM rights to be more readily accessed.

The Influence of the Past on Future Behavior

The processes described above, regarding how now-then relations provide perspective on the future, can also be applied to the past. Histories and coming out narratives of GSM activists, celebrities, and authors are incredibly popular and play a part in many GSM individuals' lives precisely because these narratives often bridge past and present and reflect the challenges and hurdles the GSM community has overcome (e.g., Feinberg, 1993; Forster, 1971; Mock, 2014; Winterson, 1994). However, the GSM community's history also contains episodes in which past freedoms are lost and in which persecution returns after a period of liberalization (e.g., Beachy, 2014; Isherwood, 1935; Somerville, 2000). So part of the attraction and meaning of these narratives may lie in the finding that the expectation of future losses appears to more greatly influence present behavior than the anticipation of future success (Baumeister, Bratslavsky, Finkenauer, & Vohs, 2001).

Bringing Theory to Action

From the preceding RFT analysis, we can begin to develop an ACT perspective of civic engagement and social action that can powerfully transform society and help individuals self-actualize through committed action and living their values. In the rest of this chapter, the second author will use personal stories from his time working in the lesbian, gay, bisexual, transgender, and queer (LGBTQ) movement in the United States to illustrate self-actualization through prosocial engagement and demonstrate how activism can actually be a form of experiential avoidance that reinforces psychological inflexibility. He will also describe his current work as an ACT group therapist and propose a model for therapeutic support that leads to greater health and flexibility for individuals working toward social change.

Self-Actualization and Social Change

In May of 2008, the California Supreme Court overturned the state's ban on same-sex marriage. As a young gay man who had immigrated from the rural South to San Francisco to find opportunity, respect, and community, I woke up that morning with a new legal right and with new possibilities for my future. I understood that state-sanctioned marriage isn't the defining right of LGBTQ equality or the cure for economic, social, and psychological suffering in our communities, but I couldn't deny that I felt different inside. This became clear to me—and to many others across the country—later that year when California voters approved Proposition 8 and rescinded the right to same-sex marriage through a process some legal scholars described as an abuse of the ballot system (e.g. Smith, 2010).

The grassroots uprising after Prop 8 was swift and astonishing. Young organizers formed an online network and called for a national day of coordinated action. A rich tapestry of personal stories and motivations inspired people to march in their communities that day. For me, the experience of losing a right I had been granted six months earlier shattered my rigid and unrecognized self-concept of inferiority. I no longer understood myself as "less than." I felt equal, and I was determined to reshape public policy at the state and federal levels. Many others across the country felt that same determination. Building on the decades of work and progress that came before, the grassroots movement for GSM equality in the United States leaped forward after a latency period characterized by professionalization and stagnation.

In the seven years following Prop 8, we achieved substantial changes in federal law and policy. The US Congress passed the Matthew Shepard and James Byrd, Jr., Hate Crimes Prevention Act in 2009, less than a month after 150,000 people marched on Washington, DC, with a unified demand for full federal equality. The "don't ask, don't tell" policy that required a profound degree of concealment from cisgender gays and lesbians during their military service was struck down in 2011, and same-sex couples gained the right to marry throughout the entire country in 2015. We have made headway on youth bullying and suicide, trans rights, homelessness, immigration, workplace protections, and federal policies such as the ban on blood donation by gay men. Public opinion on these issues has shifted dramatically. We have self-actualized through the process of committed action, and the world is a better place because of it. Perhaps the next generations of gender and sexual minorities will grow up with less stigma and more opportunity.

Activism and Experiential Avoidance

I want to acknowledge that activism can be a form of experiential avoidance—one in which we focus obsessively on campaigns and goals in order to avoid the challenges of our personal lives and the fear or anxiety we feel about facing those challenges. This ultimately leads to conflict and dissonance within movements that can be psychologically harmful and obstruct social change.

Anyone who has been actively involved in social movements will probably attest to the difficulty of collaborating with so many different egos, motivations, and personalities. Organizing both in California and nationally in the years following Prop 8, I had the strong impression that we were our own worst enemy. Many of us—myself included—put forth our critiques about strategy, message, and goals in the form of moral judgments. These moral judgments, in turn, were often the expression of underlying insecurity and a narcissistic search for validation at the expense of others. It was very unpleasant, and it may have threatened our progress more than the religious right or our political opponents. I saw the worst in many people, and many people saw the worst in me.

As for myself, I felt unresolved about the isolation and religious wounding I'd experienced due to my rural Southern Baptist childhood; about the rage, pain, and humiliation of my father's death in jail and my family's fruitless struggle for accountability and justice; and about my difficulty trusting and relating to other men. I suffered severe panic attacks in those days, but I never asked for help. A colleague of mine—a very charismatic organizer who stepped forward as a leader in those years as well—reflected on her own avoidance: "I knew there were problems in my marriage. I don't think I could have saved the relationship, but I could have been more present and the divorce could have been a better experience for us both. I was gone all the time, fighting for our families, until I realized I was spending more time away from my children than I was spending with them."

292

So which is it? Were we channeling our internal conflicts into dynamic leadership and self-actualizing through prosocial action that made an impact on society? Or were we avoiding our painful feelings and broken relationships by lashing out at each other and stewing in the agitation of a movement built by others who were also avoiding their problems, perpetuating our psychological suffering all the while?

Of course, each of those descriptions is a distortion—a simplified and incomplete snapshot of a complex situation. And this is crucial for therapists to understand when working with GSM clients who are engaged in social action. Activism can reflect both self-actualization and experiential avoidance at the same time. Clinicians, along with friends and family members, need to approach these issues delicately so that GSM individuals don't perceive judgments and, as a result, withdraw or become defensive.

Expanding the Context

In the world of social action and political advocacy, there is a marked tendency for individuals to focus on specific issues and to confine themselves within communities, organizations, and media that share their focus. While this may sometimes serve to build political power, it also reinforces some level of inflexibility via a conceptualized self. For example, a man's identity as a gay rights activist may decrease his contact with people who are working in a larger frame, and he may also be unaware of people who feel excluded by his frame. For instance, perhaps trans or gender-nonconforming individuals may perceive his "gay rights" frame as excluding rights and protections related to gender identity and expression. On the most benign level, this might lead to distrust and a missed alliance. In many cases, it might also lead to the moral judgments, blaming, and lashing out I referred to earlier. In either case, the result is that people remain isolated, which is one of the core causes of suffering for GSM individuals. Expanding the context and becoming part of something bigger than ourselves is one pathway out of that isolation and suffering.

In regard to self-actualization through prosocial action and living our values, I propose that expanding the context beyond the frame of

293

GSM issues is imperative for psychological growth and flexibility. On the most superficial level, it emphasizes interconnectedness and promotes a happier coexistence on this planet. In the language of ACT, it shakes up the conceptualized self and invites people to take greater responsibility for their values and actions. They can do this by balancing the expediency of political goals and strategies with humble attention to the suffering of others who are different from them. In grassroots and populist movements, this value is often referred to as solidarity. For a very touching depiction of solidarity in action, I refer you to the movie *Pride*, which highlights the historic, Thatcher-era alliance between a group of gays and lesbians in London and striking miners in a small, rural Welsh town. Solidarity is central to movement building (which is not necessarily the same thing as political victory), and to personal growth for everyone involved.

For the purposes of this chapter, I'll refer to that larger frame as the progressive movement—a context characterized by shared values that include the equal dignity of all people, stewardship of the planet, and an emphasis on human rights and ecological sustainability over corporate profits.

Therapeutic Interventions for Social Change

Therapists walk a fine line in this territory. On the one hand, we want to encourage clients to take risks, get outside of themselves, and engage in prosocial and values-based action. On the other hand, we don't want to impose our own values or suggest that there is some formulaic approach to resolving existential conflicts and finding fulfillment in life. As we shake off the antiquated notion that psychotherapy is apolitical, the field is calling for new and creative approaches and interventions. In that spirit, I offer some reflections on a therapy group I am currently facilitating at the time of this writing.

After six months of groundwork, I recently launched a therapeutic group for dedicated activists and professionals in social movements. They hail from a variety of movements: labor, racial justice, climate and ecological justice, and GSM rights. I carefully selected experienced activists who showed self-awareness and were prepared to form supportive relationships with others, and I screened out individuals who had higher levels of emotional dysregulation, unstable relationships, externalizing blame, and volatile anger. Most group members express some level of depression, burnout, and cynicism, and many feel a lack of meaning in "dream jobs" in the field of activism and social justice that they anticipated would be more fulfilling. I am out to the group as a gay man and as an activist, and our shared interest in building the progressive movement is part of the therapeutic frame.

In the remainder of this chapter I'll outline a model of nine two-hour sessions intended to address activist burnout, clarify values, and evoke reflection on committed action. Each session begins with a twenty-minute guided meditation to establish contact with the present moment and encourage mindful reflection on therapeutic prompts before beginning group dialogue. The first two sessions occur on the same day to create a foundation of trust, foster group cohesiveness, and introduce the practice of mindfulness and meditation.

Session 1: The opening meditation utilizes a perspective-taking exercise that involves encountering a past self—the one that first noticed that something was wrong in the world, that one could speak out or take action, and that taking action involves risk. As part of the meditation, participants are invited to contrast the experience of this earlier self with their current levels of burnout and cynicism. After discussing confidentiality and group agreements, participants are given an opportunity to introduce themselves at length and to share their experience of the exercise.

Session 2: After a break for lunch, session 2 begins with another twenty-minute meditation, this time focusing on acceptance of painful feelings. The facilitator offers prompts about current events over the last year involving social, political, and environmental issues. Participants are instructed to track their feelings and reactions to the prompts, which are expected to evoke feelings of grief, anger, guilt, and helplessness. Afterward, participants take time to process their experience of the exercise and to reflect on their experiential avoidance strategies. They are then invited to share recent experiences that give cause for hope, celebration, and inspiration.

Session 3: The opening meditation is used to identify fused thoughts related to inadequacy, despair, or shame and to cultivate self-compassion. Afterward, participants reflect on fusion and inadequacy and discuss how they might apply self-compassion when struggling with difficult thoughts and feelings.

Session 4: The opening meditation centers on a perspective-taking exercise that invites participants to witness themselves struggling with fused thoughts in a recent moment since the previous session. Afterward, participants discuss how they practiced self-compassion in these moments, or how they could have done so.

Session 5: The opening meditation involves envisioning an idealized activist figure in the form of a mentor, teacher, or hero. Afterward, participants share their experience of the exercise and discuss the values and wisdom their idealized figures represent. The facilitator introduces the ACT matrix (Polk & Schoendorff, 2014), and participants discuss moves toward and away from valued living in their activism. (For more on the matrix, see chapter 2.)

Session 6: The opening meditation utilizes a perspective-taking exercise to explore the interpersonal aspects of burnout, including challenges in personal and professional relationships and efforts to obtain external validation and support. Participants discuss their experience of the meditation, their hopes and disappointments in interpersonal relationships, and difficulties arising from engagement with social networks and other public venues. Participants are challenged to consider possible moves toward valued living prior to the next session. This is intended to generate possibilities, not action.

Session 7: The opening meditation includes a guided reflection on committed action. Participants are invited to silently consider both obstacles and resources for making moves toward valued living. Afterward, participants share their experience of the meditation, and of reflecting on committed action since the previous session. Each individual discusses specific actions, resources, and obstacles and receives feedback from the facilitator and other participants. In order to allow every individual enough time and attention, this process is extended over two sessions.

Session 8: The opening meditation deepens the reflection on committed action initiated during the previous session. Afterward, individuals who didn't present their reflections and receive feedback at the previous meeting are given an opportunity to do so.

Session 9: The opening meditation involves imagining a near future in which participants have taken a bold action toward valued living. Afterward, they discuss their experience of the meditation, along with the challenges they face and the resources they can draw on. In closing, participants share about the personal growth they experienced in the group and how their bold actions might affect both their activism and their burnout. To bring the process to a close, the facilitator leads a meditation to cultivate loving-kindness, first for the self and then for the world. Before parting ways, the group discusses the value of a meaningful and authentic good-bye.

The therapeutic integration of meditation and mindfulness exercises within an ACT framework helps focus participants, build group cohesion, and clarify values, and also promotes contemplation of committed action. In the initial trial, participants showed insight and honesty in envisioning their moves toward valued living and exploring their level of commitment to implementing these committed actions. The program also offered participants useful resources, and they were encouraged to seek ongoing individual support in moving from contemplation to action.

Conclusion

Abuse, injustice, and institutional violence still affect most GSM individuals, particularly those who are members of multiple marginalized communities. RFT provides a helpful frame for considering what future action might look like, and in this chapter we describe one possible format of an ACT group for movement builders. The RFT conceptualization we outlined at the beginning of this chapter compels us to conclude this book with the following recommendations for a more equitable future. First, we must hold on to the dream of a more equitable future that contains space for a greater range of gender and sexual identities and expressions. If all of the readers of this book were to take steps in their personal lives to create such a world, change would be eminently possible. Understanding the rules our societies use to attach values to certain types of gendered bodies, sexual behaviors, and relationships is powerful and can promote this work. Finally, history reveals that any advance in GSM rights can be reversed with an election, a religious movement, or shift in cultural perspectives. Only a diligent commitment to creating a new world can prevent this from happening.

References

Badgett, M. L. (2009). *When gay people get married: What happens when societies legalize same-sex marriage.* New York: New York University Press.

Barnes-Holmes, Y., Barnes-Holmes, D., Roche, B., Healy, O., Lyddy, F., Cullinan, V., et al. (2001). Psychological development. In S. C. Hayes, D. Barnes-Holmes, & B. Roche (Eds.), *Relational frame theory: A post-Skinnerian account of human language and cognition.* New York: Kluwer Academic.

Baumeister, R. F., Bratslavsky, E., Finkenauer, C., & Vohs, K. D. (2001). Bad is stronger than good. *Review of General Psychology, 5,* 323–370.

Beachy, R. (2014). *Gay Berlin: Birthplace of a modern identity.* New York: Knopf.

Biglan, A., & Barnes-Holmes, Y. (2015). Acting in light of the future: How do future-oriented cultural practices evolve and how can we accelerate their evolution? *Journal of Contextual Behavioral Science, 4,* 184–195.

Chateauvert, M. (2014). *Sex workers unite: A history of the movement from Stonewall to SlutWalk.* Boston: Beacon Press.

European Commission (2015). *Discrimination in the EU in 2015.* Brussels: Directorate-General for Justice and Consumers.

Faderman, L. (2015). *The gay revolution: The story and the struggle.* New York: Simon and Schuster.

Feinberg, L. (1993). *Stone butch blues.* Ithaca, NY: Firebrand Books.

Forster, E. M. (1971). *Maurice: A novel.* New York: Norton.

Hayes, S. C., Barnes-Holmes, D., & Roche, B. (Eds.). (2001). *Relational frame theory: A post-Skinnerian account of human language and cognition.* New York: Kluwer Academic.

Hayes, S. C., Strosahl, K. D., & Wilson, K. G. (1999). *Acceptance and commitment therapy: An experiential approach to behavior change.* New York: Guilford.

Hayes, S. C., Zettle, R. D., & Rosenfarb, I. (1989). Rule following. In S. C. Hayes (Ed.), *Rule-governed behavior: Cognition, contingencies, and instructional control.* New York: Plenum.

Isherwood, C. (1935). *The Berlin stories.* New York: New Directions.

Jansen, S., & Spijkerboer, T. P. (2011). *Fleeing homophobia: Asylum claims related to sexual orientation and gender identity in Europe.* Amsterdam: COC Nederlands and VU University Amsterdam.

Jordan, M. D. (1998). *The invention of sodomy in Christian theology.* University of Chicago Press.

Katz, J. (1992). *Gay American history: Lesbians and gay men in the USA: A documentary history.* New York: Meridian.

Khazan, O. (2015). The end of gay conversion therapy. *The Atlantic.* Retrieved December 15, 2015, from http://www.theatlantic.com/health/archive/2015/06/the-end-of-gay-conversion-therapy/396953.

Massad, J. A. (2008). *Desiring Arabs.* University of Chicago Press.

Meyer, I. H. (2015). Resilience in the study of minority stress and health of sexual and gender minorities. *Psychology of Sexual Orientation and Gender Diversity, 2,* 209–213.

Mock, J. (2014). *Redefining realness: My path to womanhood, identity, love, and so much more.* New York: Simon and Schuster.

Mogul, J. L., Ritchie, A. J., & Whitlock, K. (2011). *Queer (in)justice: The criminalization of LGBT people in the United States,* volume 5. Boston: Beacon Press.

Obergefell v. Hodges. 576 U.S. ____. (2015).

Polk, K. L., & Schoendorff, B. (Eds.). (2014). *The ACT matrix: A new approach to building psychological flexibility across settings and populations.* Oakland, CA: New Harbinger Publications.

Raftery-Helmer, J. N., Moore, P. S., Coyne, L., & Reed, K. P. (2015). Changing problematic parent-child interaction in child anxiety disorders: The promise of acceptance and commitment therapy (ACT). *Journal of Contextual Behavioral Science,* epub ahead of print.

Rosario, V. A., & Meyerowitz, J. (2004). Transforming sex: An interview with Joanne Meyerowitz, PhD, author of *How Sex Changed: A History of Transsexuality in the United States. Studies in Gender and Sexuality, 5,* 473–483.

Russell, G. M., & Richards, J. A. (2003). Stressor and resilience factors for lesbians, gay men, and bisexuals confronting antigay politics. *American Journal of Community Psychology, 31,* 313–328.

Shorto, R. (2013). *Amsterdam: A history of the world's most liberal city.* New York: Doubleday.

Smith, A. M. (2010). The paradoxes of popular constitutionalism: Proposition 8 and Strauss v. Horton. *University of San Francisco Law Review, 45*, 517.

Somerville, S. B. (2000). *Queering the color line: Race and the invention of homosexuality in American culture.* Durham, NC: Duke University Press.

Tan, E. S. N., & Yarhouse, M. A. (2010). Facilitating congruence between religious belief and sexual identity with mindfulness. *Psychotherapy, 47*, 500–511.

Teal, J. L. (2015). *"Black trans bodies are under attack": Gender non-conforming homicide victims in the US 1995–2014.* Unpublished doctoral dissertation, Humboldt State University.

Trappolin, L., Gasparini, A., & Wintemute, R. (Eds.). (2012). *Confronting homophobia in Europe: Social and legal perspectives.* Portland, OR: Hart Publishing.

Vilardaga, R., Heffner, J. L., Mercer, L. D., & Bricker, J. B. (2014). Do counselor techniques predict quitting during smoking cessation treatment? A component analysis of telephone-delivered acceptance and commitment therapy. *Behaviour Research and Therapy, 61*, 89–95.

Weiss, M. L., & Bosia, M. J. (Eds.). (2013). *Global homophobia: States, movements, and the politics of oppression.* Urbana: University of Illinois Press.

Werth, B. (2010). *The scarlet professor: Newton Arvin: A literary life shattered by scandal.* New York: Anchor.

Williams, A. (2005, July 17). Gay teenager stirs a storm. *New York Times.* Retrieved December 15, 2015, from http://www.nytimes.com/2005/07/17/fashion/sunday styles/gay-teenager-stirs-a-storm.html.

Wilson, K. G., & Murrell, A. R. (2004). Values work in acceptance and commitment therapy. In S. C. Hayes, V. M. Follette, & M. M. Linehan (Eds.), *Mindfulness and acceptance: Expanding the cognitive-behavioral tradition.* New York: Guilford.

Winterson, J. (1994). *Written on the body.* London: Vintage.

Editor **Matthew D. Skinta, PhD, ABPP,** is a board-certified clinical health psychologist who lives with his husband in San Francisco, CA. In addition to having a private practice, he is core clinical faculty at Palo Alto University, where he directs the Sexual and Gender Identities Clinic. Skinta's past research has focused on the impact of stigma and shame on health behaviors of sexual minority men, particularly as it relates to sexual health and HIV-related care. He is a peer-reviewed acceptance and commitment therapy (ACT) trainer, and is certified as both a compassion cultivation training (CCT) teacher, and as a trainer of functional analytic psychotherapy (FAP).

Editor **Aisling Curtin, MSc,** is a registered counseling psychologist at the Psychological Society of Ireland who lives with her partner in Dublin, Ireland. She is director of ACT Now Ireland, has a small private practice, and consults with a number of organizations to deliver acceptance and mindfulness workshops. Aisling teaches in many university training programs, and regularly gives workshops internationally on sexuality from a mindfulness and acceptance vantage point. She is a peer-reviewed ACT and FAP trainer.

Foreword writer **John Pachankis, PhD,** is associate professor of epidemiology at Yale University. He studies the mental health of lesbian, gay, bisexual, and transgender (LGBT) individuals. His research specifically seeks to identify the psychological and social contextual influences that might explain LGBT individuals' disproportionate experiences with several adverse mental health outcomes, like depression and substance abuse, and to translate the results of these studies into psychosocial interventions to improve the health of the LGBT community.

Index